In
Defence
of
Civility

In
Defence
of
Civility

*Reflections of a
Recovering Politician*

HUGH SEGAL

Stoddart

Published in 2000 by Stoddart Publishing Co. Limited
34 Lesmill Road, Toronto, Canada M3B 2T6

Distributed in Canada by:
General Distribution Services Ltd.
325 Humber College Boulevard, Toronto, Canada M9W 7C3
Tel. (416) 213-1919   Fax (416) 213-1917
Email cservice@genpub.com

04 03 02 01 00   1 2 3 4 5

Canadian Cataloguing in Publication Data

Segal, Hugh
In defence of civility: reflections of a recovering politician

Includes index.
ISBN 0-7737-3230-6

1. Segal, Hugh. 2. Canada — Politics and government — 1993– .*
3. Progressive Conservative Party of Canada. I. Title.

FC635.S43 2000   971.064'8   C00-930025-2
F1034.2.S43 2000

Articles originally published in the *Financial Post* used by permission.

"Ministerial Accountability: Confronting the Myth" is reprinted from *Crosscurrents,* 3rd edition, by M. Charlton and P. Barker © 1998 with permission of Nelson Thomson Learning. Fax 800-730-2215.

Jacket Design: Bill Douglas @ The Bang
Text Design: Joseph Gisini/Andrew Smith Graphics, Inc.

Printed and bound in Canada

THE CANADA COUNCIL   LE CONSEIL DES ARTS
FOR THE ARTS   DU CANADA
SINCE 1957   DEPUIS 1957

We acknowledge for their financial support of our publishing program the Canada Council for the Arts, the Ontario Arts Council, and the Government of Canada through the Book Publishing Industry Development Program (BPIDP).

For my daughter, Jacqueline,
in whose eyes and soul
the sun never sets

Contents

Part Three: **THE CASE FOR ECONOMIC AND SOCIAL BALANCE**

Part Four: **TOWARDS A NEW CONFEDERAL UNION**

Acknowledgements

E VEN THE ASSEMBLY AND ORGANIZATION OF PRIOR WORKS REQUIRES help from others. The support and advice from Don Bastian of Stoddart Publishing, Gerald Owen's meticulous editorial counsel, and Marilyn Banting's structural and pioneering edit all helped immensely. Vicki Ryce, my long-suffering but deeply competent administrative assistant, not only word-processed the final manuscript, but also typed all the original columns, speeches, and papers the first time around over the years. She need not read the Book of Job to understand what the word "travail" can mean.

Many of these columns and speeches would never have come into being had various newspaper editors not invited my submissions. I must especially thank George Radwanski at the *Toronto Star* and Diane Francis, aided in the day-to-day tasks by Ruth Ann MacKinnon and Natasha Hassan, at the *Financial Post*. Diane's invitation, and the patience of Ruth Ann and Natasha, made my experience at the *Financial Post* one of great and happy memories. Both newspapers had editorial policies that were either well to the left or well to the right of my approach. It is a credit to Radwanski and his boss, Beland Honderich, and to Francis that they never sought to change the content of columns with which they disagreed. That kind of civility I never took for granted.

It is by now the defining reality of my life that the opportunity to write, engage, and participate very much emerges from the encouragement, good humour, and sound counsel of Donna, who has shared her life with me for almost a quarter of a century. What I owe her for forbearance and unconditional support would dwarf the national debt — in more ways than one.

In the time since I sought and lost the Tory leadership campaign, my daughter, Jacqueline, has been an endless energy force keeping that sunlight that she alone dispenses aimed at her dad. "Let me get this straight," she said when I told her of *In Defence of Civility*. "The new book will have lots of your old columns and speeches in one place? Another page turner, eh, Dad?"

As our ageing but dignified bouvier, Angel, heard most of these columns and speeches the first time around, and as Charlotte, the slightly unfocused bouvier-sentinel, much prefers chasing squirrels to hearing my views on tax policy, they share no responsibility for this effort, its mistakes, misjudgements, or omissions. That responsibility is all mine.

H. S.
Kingston
December 1999

Introduction

MY DECISION TO SET PARTISAN POLITICS ASIDE AT THE END OF 1998 should not, on its surface, have been terribly surprising. I had been around the partisan process since I was thirteen. I had been a partisan Conservative for more than thirty-five years, both in the private sector and in government. I had been afforded the privilege of serving my country and my province in a host of interesting ways. I had been a "no surrender" Conservative, tied deeply to the ethos of partisan history and the more compelling magnet of partisan loyalty. Having served as a PC Youth Federation vice-president, a federal parliamentary candidate, an MP's research assistant, the legislative assistant to the federal leader of the opposition, the legislative secretary to a premier, the associate secretary of a provincial cabinet, and the chief of staff to the prime minister, I was living proof of the opportunities an open political party could afford a cab driver's son from Montreal. That I was allowed the privilege of seeking the party's leadership — and that, in the only ballot with five candidates, I would come second — is evidence of the generosity of spirit the party expressed towards me. The expression was more intense in ridings in Montreal, Toronto, Quebec City, Kingston, Prince George, Barrie, Corner Brook, and rural Newfoundland; somewhat less so elsewhere. But that is the way of the world. And even where the intensity was more, shall we say, restrained, the politeness and courtesy were pervasive and, as far as I could tell, sincere.

The partisan voyage had been rich and uplifting. It had been replete with ideas, battles, people, and struggles that had shaped, in some ways forever, my views in some areas. One learns more from defeats than from victories — so my own learning curve was always blessedly steep. But above all, because partisanship of any variety seems to engage only about 2 percent of the population, it was in a sense a minority experience of the most significant kind. The fact that it was incomprehensible to most of my fellow citizens did not make the experience any less textured or motivating.

Yet there is a time in everyone's life not to leave things behind — one's loyalties and passions can never truly be jettisoned — but to serve in other ways. What this book is, then, is a mix of columns and speeches from most of those partisan years and some reflections of a non-partisan nature on episodes that occurred since and during that period. Life, like most things, is a multifaceted and layered event. For half of my years since graduating from university, my service was direct to party, province, and country. For the other half, my life was spent in business or academe, while still volunteering for the partisan cause.

The perspective for many of the views reflected in this book is partisan — although the frame of reference for the whole book is more a retrospective from a position that is post-partisan. That implies no negative value judgement on the importance of partisan activity — to imply that would be to be disloyal to the democratic imperative of providing real choices between different sets of ideas, policies, and people.

These columns and speeches reflect a learning process that I was fortunate enough to share with both large and small audiences. Some reflect how I saw the world twenty years ago; some accurately reflect how I see the world today. I was delighted when my publisher thought that Canadians would benefit from seeing in one place a large representative reflection of ideas and perspectives.

Many members of various parties, and most who are members of none, will disagree with some or much of what this book contains. My hope, frankly stated, is that the reader will reflect on his or her own views on these public, partisan, policy, and people issues, and on how they have changed or evolved. That has been the wonderful part of this experience for me in this process, and I hope it inspires a similar reflection for many others.

Part of what I have learned is just how removed from everyday life the political-media process has become for so many Canadians, how self-contained that process has become. For many, it is often hard to see beyond the shrapnel from the larger and often chaotic world that invades our day-to-day activities: market instability here; political volatility there. Old alliances break down; old enemies become allies. Some people get richer and achieve status more quickly than their parents; others seem unlikely to do as well as their parents. Education is more advanced, but standards are portrayed as not as high. People have and do more, yet keep less of what they earn. Many in North America owe huge amounts. There is contradiction here, affirmation elsewhere. Confusion seems an overarching political theme.

Our access to so many competing sources of information — all of which have their inherent structural biases — does little to truly inform. If anything, it merely increases the need for us to be wary, suspicious, and cynical, adding to the confusion in so many ways.

Our prospects as a country are blocked by a profound disconnect between the political/media complex and the day-to-day reality of Canadians. The media are caught in a bubble, a complex political bubble that is a key determinant of the public agenda but fails to reach out to where people live and work. This bubble is self-contained, self-serving, and largely awash in its own bath water. While not as sinister in political import as the "military industrial complex" identified by President Eisenhower, it operates on many of the same mutual-interest rules.

- It requires significant cross-breeding and many interwoven dependencies to survive.
- It trades in shared instruments for public-agenda management, and the trade is a daily marketplace largely unrelated to real life outside the complex and its defined interests.
- No one in particular is in charge; there is no conspiracy. There is, instead, a series of discreet trade-offs and accommodations that forms the interlocking mesh of the complex and provides the momentum for its day-to-day progress and survival.

This mesh generates most of the news fragments that can be so confusing and dispiriting. It heaves and gasps under the weight of the myriad accommodations that the participants make, have made, and must make to ensure their respective and continued influence and standing. The mesh is unable to tolerate change emanating from any source outside its own comfortable structure. Whether it's Preston Manning from the West, bank presidents from the East, or progressive industrialists from the auto-parts sector — if they do not originate from within the mesh, it defensively diminishes or derails them until tribute is paid.

This screen affords a kind of permanent primacy to the federal bureaucracy, the governing party, the networks, the press gallery, and all the various satellite organisms that survive as addendums to these power centres. Some groups, like the Business Council on National Issues and others who maintain a well-organized presence within the complex, do an excellent job of discharging their mandates, as do the competent trade associations, labour organizations, and private lobby firms that honourably seek to advance a cause or a concern for legitimate outside interests.

Spending six months on the road in every large city, in small towns, and in rural communities — as I did from April 17 to October 27, 1998, while contesting the Conservative leadership — makes one understand how profoundly out of sync with street-level reality the media-political complex truly is. It is a disconnect that is both profound and worrying. There are parts of the disconnect that are truly geographical — the world inside official Ottawa, for example, is compellingly different from real life in a host of ways. This is not because official Ottawa is mean, bad, venal, or unwilling to try hard. It is simply because decisions made in office towers in Ottawa cannot adequately reflect life in Bay Roberts or Prince George, or, for that matter, Smiths Falls or Eganville. This has to do not only with geography, but also with a seriously different day-to-day reality.

There are parts of the disconnect that reflect different approaches to time and life. Inside the complex, the deadlines for twenty-four-hour news coverage, or daily newspapers, or question period, or the prime minister's Team Canada sojourns seem real and demanding. They represent a frenetic abstraction to the small business person, retiree, farmer, or high-school student. These artificial deadlines produce artificial news that simply furthers the disconnect. When the complex heads off in its own direction, as it did on President Clinton's indiscretions, or when competitive pressures merge gossip, entertainment, and news into one seamless whole, the culture of exclusion is deeply enshrined.

Now, as someone who appeared for more than a decade as a partisan pundit on "Canada AM" (CTV), and "The National" on the CBC, I have little honourable option but to attest to my own membership in that complex. As a Tory, my membership was always that of the outsider or "in transit" traveller, never to be allowed the permanence of the rooted and established. But even participation as a transitory member could distort and diminish one's real life perspective. When I worked in the Prime Minister's Office, I could feel the walls of systemic self-absorption encase and envelop. It wasn't lonely. Entire bureaucracies, the political leadership of various parties, and whole media corps were encased in there with you.

After I left Ottawa in 1993, going back to business and academe helped immensely. But my decision to seek the leadership of the Conservative Party — and not only focus on existing party members but also reach out to younger people and disaffected Canadians — did far more to chisel through the cement of dislocation before it had hardened for good. In hotels, airports, doughnut shops, community halls, kitchens, living rooms, and basements across the country, I found a Canadian reality that seemed much less complicated, dispirited, and cynical than the complex would have us believe. For those who sniff, "Average people do not understand," let me assure you that Canadians are tuned in and in touch with the larger economic and social realities, and in terms that are real and realistic. In fact, the complex would do well to take a tutorial for a few weeks to see the real face of Canada, unblemished by the pollster's questions, interest-group biases, or the media's own agenda.

Let me give you some examples:

- In Atlantic Canada, there is far less interest in government handouts and subsidies than many Canadians elsewhere believe. There is a compelling and dynamic entrepreneurial spirit that seeks nothing other than a level playing field — relative to what is offered elsewhere — in terms of taxes and opportunities.
- Even among sovereignists in Quebec, the appetite for the endless "neverendum" has passed. The hard core remains, but sovereignist and non-sovereignist Quebecers are far more concerned with taxes, health care, and jobs than constitutional projects. If we work together to find a way to help the General Motors plant stay in Ste-Therese, that will do more to promote national cohesion than will endless constitutional negotiation.
- Economic literacy is broad, and the global forces of technological innovation and capital mobility are recognized and understood.

What people from coast to coast are uncertain of is whether our democratic system can manage these forces so as to preserve equality of opportunity for honest, hard-working people.

- There is a clear division in people's minds between "the have-nots" and "the will-nots," and no lack of goodwill towards helping the have-nots.
- Ottawa may believe it has room to shilly-shally on tax reductions. It does not. There are two kinds of revolutionaries in the country: those who, because of skills, resources, or both, have the freedom to leave, or have their assets leave, the country; and those who do not have that capacity but are either avoiding or evading taxes. This situation is robbing Canada of talent and productive capacity. It does not matter whether the absolute numbers are large; what matters is the role of taxes and income in shaping the departing mindset. Only someone caught in the miasma of the political/media complex could miss the glaring clarity of where this is headed.
- The gap between urban and rural Canada, in terms of incomes, prospects, and attitudes, is broadening. If the system treats rural and small-town Canadians as irrelevant, this gap will not only destroy any hope for national cohesion, but also fragment our politics more seriously than it is fragmented today.
- The concern about failing our young people and producing a lost generation is real and pervasive. It crosses all linguistic, geographic, and ideological barriers.
- The desire for a frank and real renewal of health care — that is, dealing with what is wrong and preserving what is right — similarly crosses all party lines, all income groups, all regional barriers.
- The concern about providing older Canadians with some sense of security around retirement and the availability of health care and chronic care is pervasive. It is as much an issue for middle-aged people seeking to help their parents as it is for older people themselves.

I did not find the bigotry, regional selfishness, or lack of compassion some had said would be there. In fact, I found a deep sense of community — a deep desire for a civil society where we are prepared to match freedoms with responsibilities and where compassion and a sense of belonging truly matter.

What some of the more determined proponents of doctrinal politics so richly misunderstand is that Canadians do not live their lives by the theories or doctrines of others. We do not ask ourselves if this way of doing things is sufficiently conservative or correctly liberal. We live our lives by values that are applied in our country in practical and daily ways.

Some years ago, the economist Judith Maxwell and the Canadian Policy Research Network funded a series of quantitative and qualitative studies of our values over the years. Older data was studied alongside contemporary evidence and specially commissioned research. A continuum of consistency — undifferentiated by age, language, or region — confirmed what I also found during those twenty-nine weeks on the road:

- We abhor waste, private or public.
- We value independence and frugality but embrace generosity and support for those in need.
- We prefer local decision making but demand national standards in critical areas.
- We see success in our personal, business, family, and community lives as a result of balance, a result of working together with others.
- We abhor conflict for conflict's sake, but we do not believe in avoiding tough choices.
- We want productivity and innovation from the private sector, but we want humanity and decency too.
- We want leadership from government, especially when people cannot help themselves, but we also dislike meddlesome government that tries to control too much from afar.

The balance that is sought by so many is both expressive and cautionary. It is expressive of a genuine desire to ensure that economic growth, increased profitability, and enhanced investment co-exist with decency, civility, neighbourhood, and compassion. As a proponent of a free-enterprise society, I continue to believe that economic viability and profitability are essential to the civility we desire. But the virtues of civility and compassion are also essential to the conditions within which economic growth, expansion, and profitability can thrive.

This mutual dependency does fuel a cautionary note. Those who would break the balance or distort it for self-centred reasons — whichever side of the public-private continuum they inhabit — will face public wrath. This does not mean that the balance cannot change or evolve. In fact, if the balance between private and community interests does not evolve, it will atrophy and become disconnected from reality. But if anyone or anything renders it asunder, especially for personal economic or political gain, Canadians will be quick to discard that person, party, or corporate interest as outside the balance.

~

The chapters of this volume array ideas about people, policies, politics, the larger world, and national unity as they were reflected in speeches, columns, essays, policy papers, and monographs I published since 1984. Each puts another brick into a larger construct of nation and enterprise. These bricks reflect my views at the time of writing. Those who disagree with these essays, speeches, and columns will, I hope, engage in their own reflection on how we maintain the marriage of civility and economic opportunity. If more people reflect in their own way on how to sustain that marriage, this in itself becomes a way of strengthening the very civility of the society and economy we share.

My losing leadership campaign was overtaken by many factors — some within my capacity to control and some beyond. There is no moral victory when political realities force you to relinquish your runner-up position and withdraw before the second and last ballot. I offer no pretensions or illusions here. But the personal sense of discovering much more to be optimistic about — much more to be encouraged by, relative to the good sense, decency, and judgement of Canadians — shall remain, among other campaign experiences, one of the most inspiring and important lessons.

The columns and other pieces that follow in this book emphasize this balance with the following core ideas:

1. Free enterprise and economic growth are there to serve the citizens of a society as engines of wealth-generation and economic capacity, not the other way around.
2. The role of government is not to do what individual citizens or

communities can do for themselves — and often far more success-fully than government itself.

3. The primary role of government is to provide the infrastructure that assures genuine equality of opportunity. This will broaden the economic mainstream to include more and more citizens, who will then be able to earn their own share of the benefits.

4. There must be a baseline beneath which no law-abiding citizen should be allowed to fall in terms of basic living, housing, and income necessities.

5. The capacity of a nation to protect its legitimate international and economic interests is a direct product of its determination and will to defend those interests responsibly and firmly.

PART ONE

The Case
for Civility

JUST AS THE FORCES OF EXCESS — BOTH ON THE RIGHT AND ON THE left — seemed to dominate the evolution of our civilization during the middle of this century, a new set of movements has in recent years begun to undo the control exerted by the extremes. Winston Churchill's prescient angst over a Soviet-imposed Iron Curtain ended up sadly true, with four decades of tyranny, authoritarianism, and suffering throughout Eastern Europe. Those in America and elsewhere whose politics feasted on the fear that powerful totalitarianism breeds supped long and well. The Soviet military and political threat may be seen to have been overrated now, with 20/20 hindsight, but at the time — from Berlin in 1948, Hungary in 1956, Cuba in the 1960s, and Czechoslovakia in 1968, not to mention Soviet client states in the Middle East and Africa — the threat was seen to be global and real.

But the end of that system, brought about by resolute toe-to-toe defence spending by the West and the USSR's own disconnect from its people, is not in and of itself an indisputable basis for extolling the perfection of the economic system we call capitalism. A political system is about people and society — how we live, work, and build our lives. Because different people have different needs and strengths, a political system must be flexible enough to serve more than just the winners, or it is not much of a political system at all. The role of political parties in preserving that flexibility is often attacked by ideologues of the far right and far left as a weakness. For them, the rigidities of ideology are the bulwark against the scourge of adaptability or, worse, sensitivity to times and people.

But political parties do not need to shed their principles to defend sensitivity against the fairy-tale world-view of the extremist. Enlightened flexibility can simply expand the relevance of those principles. For example, a commitment to fiscal responsibility and economic freedom does not mean setting aside social justice or equality of opportunity. It does mean that social justice and equality of opportunity can and must be pursued within a framework that does not threaten fiscal responsibility and economic freedom.

Social justice means building safer communities where more are able to participate in the economic mainstream. Equality of opportunity, as opposed to equality of outcome — the socialist's preference — means establishing a line of income beneath which none of our fellow citizens is allowed to fall. Economic growth and free enterprise expand the economic mainstream, allowing more people to participate. These are intersecting circles of policy, not hard dividing lines. Those who preach the clarity of that line are often more interested in building a narrow political niche based on fear and division. These are not the politics of a winning society.

What is a winning society? It clearly has to be one where there is a reasonable opportunity for everyone to attempt to achieve individual, family, and community goals. It is not a society based on a "winner takes all" game that few are allowed to play. Quite apart from the injustice of keeping some people out of the game, there is the larger issue of the waste of unique skills and abilities when entire classes of people are wilfully excluded. No nation can afford simply to set these contributions aside — not without weakening its social and economic fabric in serious ways.

In my partisan years, I defended a conservatism that was a mix of faith, values, and cynicism. The faith is in the principles of parliamentary democracy; the rule of law and order; and the traditions of economic freedom and social justice that strengthen a way of life, facilitate equality of opportunity, and encourage individual achievement and social progress. The values embrace tolerance, fiscal responsibility, and the liberating balance of a truly pluralist and fair society. The cynicism is directed at those ideologies or nostrums that are absolutist and insensitive to reality — including the supremacy of the individual, the perfection of the market, or the view that all government is bad and that everything in the market is perfect. None of these impresses me as truly reflective of the reality of people, their families, and their lives.

Civility avoids nostrums that exclude other people and other ideas from having a say in the way we govern society. Civility reflects a desire to let an openness to new ideas refresh the commitment we have to the tried and the true. It embraces dissent in a free society, and questions all those on the extremes (right and left) who would impose a narrow ideology or an absolute, unidirectional public policy. As a proponent of free enterprise and an enlightened capitalism, I continue to believe that creative societies reflect both the freedom and the enlightenment, and are best able to generate the kind of growth, jobs, and wealth that make true social justice and equality of opportunity possible. In fact, that creative capacity is a key justification for capitalism and free enterprise.

A serious challenge to those who believe in a free-enterprise society is the perception among many people that they will never be the beneficiaries of that system. This perception is the most serious enemy that civility in a society must face. It tears at the fabric of community; loosens the appreciation for law and order; and weakens families, companies, communities, and even countries.

Yet while the economies of wealthy countries like Canada seem to offer more hope than most, no one should be naive about how a culture of hopelessness could spread and migrate well beyond the too numerous pockets of economic alienation we already have. In fact, containing this spread requires a vigilance that must ask whether we — as citizens, as an economy, and as a country — are doing all we can and all we should to sustain the social justice and equality of opportunity we need to thrive and grow. It is not just people in public life or the media or academe who should be asking these questions; it should not just be student leaders or union presidents. A concern for civility in society must also be a priority for the corporate directors, business leaders, entrepreneurs, investment bankers, and corporate and security lawyers. It must be a priority for all of us.

A balanced approach to economic policy cannot exclude the core issue of equality of opportunity, or it becomes neither balanced nor true economic policy. The challenge is to be consistent with the values of society, which are sustained by an intrinsic belief in fairness. Therefore, any economic policy must strive to sustain this fairness.

In Canada, fairness — however imperfect, uneven, or occasionally obscured — is, at least in part, the result of what governments will do within their range of responsibilities to encourage both economic growth and equality of opportunity. A failure of a province to create conditions that encourage reasonable levels of growth, investment, and return will harm equality of opportunity as much as any reduction in essential educational or health services. Similarly, any ideologically driven abdication of responsibility for a significant measure of social justice will have a serious impact on medium- and long-term prospects for economic growth and expansion.

But fairness is produced only in part by what governments do (as important as that role is). It is also the product of the treatment of employees by employers; of opportunities for community and volunteer activity; and of a broad range of public attitudes reflecting openness, tolerance, and a sense of opportunity.

Government can reflect the best of this spectrum. With the right policies, good people, innovation, and balance, it can have a motivating and even a leadership role. But a society that relies only on government or exclusively on public policy to sustain a real fairness will not be happy with the results. Government does not generate jobs or economic growth from its own resources. It does not make private-sector jobs interesting or productive. It is a poor replacement for economic investments prudently made by knowledgeable business people who successfully promote growth, market share, and profits.

So the challenge is clearly one of finding the balance, and that search has been at the centre of politics in the Western world for some time. There are no magic equations for producing a balance that will serve in perpetuity. In fact, imagining that a perfect policy for all times actually exists is the first folly of the ideologues of both the far left and the far right. Every generation has to find its own balance. The role of the state in wartime or in postwar reconstruction, for example, may well be quite inappropriate during times of peaceful economic expansion. The role of the government when health-care programs are being set up or universities and colleges are being built will differ when this infrastructure already exists.

Finding the right balance in a multifaceted society is not a solitary task. It involves deliberate, working partnerships with the private sector, with the scientist and the academic, with the unions and the public service. It requires innovation and commitment that are formed within the politics of consensus, sustained by the reality of economic and social necessity, and underpinned by clear conviction and purpose. Getting it right requires a mix of policy, people, and purpose that is not always found in a free and democratic society.

We can achieve more of value in how we govern ourselves and maintain our social and economic progress if we break down the walls of ritual confrontation and replace them with more open and consensual collaboration — between industry and labour; between federal and provincial governments; among regions, interest groups, and yes, even political parties.

The true strength of a country is not in the politics of division that can be easily scared up when anxiety reigns, but in the politics of common enterprise and purpose that invites people to the table of opportunity. Failure to extend that invitation — for whatever short-term political, economic, or ideological reason — is a failure we can avoid in Canada. It is a failure we must not tolerate in those we elect. It is a failure that dilutes our national potential and diminishes our reach and scope as a nation.

It is a failure for which we need not settle.

CONSERVATISM AND POPULISM

Speech to the Southshore-Bridgewater, Nova Scotia, PC Association, January 22, 1993

Sir John A. Macdonald was a builder. He was a great risk-taker, both on behalf of his party and on behalf of his country. He faced many of the unpleasant realities about our colonial situation, the linguistic challenges, and the differences in opinion that existed between Upper and Lower Canada and the Maritime provinces. He and his government sometimes faced them in a way that made him very unpopular. He began a tradition then that is very much at the root of why our party is frequently a minority party in Canada. Unlike parties that are essentially managerial, the Progressive Conservatives have been a party of ambitious national agendas — wrongs to right, new vistas to proclaim. That has a cost in politics — especially when you stray from the politics of avoidance, the leadership that is only "fellowship" in reality.

The uniquely Canadian Progressive Conservative mission is in many respects a conservatism adapted to the realities of our national psyche, geography, demography, and political structure. Our Conservative tradition, certainly from the days of Diefenbaker on, is a profoundly populist tradition tied to "small towns with big dreams" and to the particularities of a very sparse population spread in large clumps and pockets across a very broad, disparate geopolitical reality. We have a set of beliefs about the balance between individual freedom and individual responsibility, about the protection of taxpayers' interests, and about Canada in a larger community. Populism in defence of extremism is no virtue, but populism in defence of decency and fairness is no vice.

The goal for Conservatives is not to choose between populism and elitism. Rather, it is to harness the strength of populism to the national interest; to the democratic interest; and to the interest of Canadians who obey laws, pay taxes, and deserve a fair shake. Populism in the Progressive Conservative Canadian context is not a brute force to be used against compassion and caring or to narrow the Canadian mainstream — as some who use "reform" as a pretext may imply — nor is it a force to be used to divide Canadians. It is a force to be used to unite, to liberate, to share, and to build. The mix between public and private sector in this country is something that is uniquely Canadian. Our conservatism must be similarly unique. What William Buckley, Margaret Thatcher, and Ronald Reagan have done to foster the conservative cause on an international basis is of singular importance. What they know of who we are as Canadians and of what roots drive our Progressive Conservatism would not fill one page, double-spaced.

THE ENDURING TORY MISSION

Speech to PC Metro, Bathurst Heights Secondary School, Toronto, March 5, 1994

The failure to define, shape, persuade, encourage and, finally, marshal a coherent Tory coalition was the core failure of the 1993 campaign. The lack of a coalition was, and remains, the glaring cause of so many good people going to their defeat. I am not sure that a clearly defined coalition could have ensured an easy victory, but it could have preserved an official Conservative opposition.

In 1972, we were the party that would confront unemployment by reducing taxes, encouraging investment, and getting government off people's backs. When Joe Clark won a minority in 1979, we were the party to pierce the overly centralist, bureaucratic, high-spending, and high-taxing Liberal Party of Pierre Trudeau and Jean Chrétien. Under Brian Mulroney in 1984, we were the party of change, of a clear economic formula, of civil-service reform, of less government and more humanity. In 1988, we were the modern party of entrepreneurial belief in trade, open markets, our ability to compete, and our capacity to take on the world. In other words, we had a coherent thematic definition of the contemporary Conservative mission.

Peter Lougheed's first act as the new premier of Alberta was to pass the Alberta Human Rights Act. The Union Nationale in Quebec, under then premier Daniel Johnson, acted to provide per capita funding to all religious schools in the tradition of tolerance and decency that is always identified with the mainstream in the province. Bill Davis shepherded a transition from a rural and small-town economy to an urban and urbane Ontario where civility, tolerance, and minority-language education rights co-existed with provincial fiscal prudence and genuine business growth and profitability.

Historically, when we have had an agenda of conviction and growth, an agenda based firmly on individual freedom and rights on the one hand and social and fiscal responsibility on the other, then we have not only mattered but also made a profound difference.

REBUILDING THE CONSERVATIVE PARTY

Speech to the Canadian Club of Kingston, Kingston, Ontario, March 10, 1994

The neo-conservative view, which is found in many places — sometimes on editorial pages, sometimes in books that are plainly troubled at the diversity of lifestyle and population mix that now constitute our modern society — contends that a hard, ideologically pure conservative position that rejects *prima facie* the role of the state, and that is built upon the rights of the individual unfettered by social compassion or community responsibility, is the only way to rectify Canada's problems. This view is usually troubled by the historic tendency of Progressive Conservative parties, leaders, and governments to live a blend of progressivism on social and community issues and conservatism on issues of spending and taxing.

The neo-conservatives are pleased with the Free Trade Agreement because it removes many an artificial boundary to the free operation of markets in North America, and enhances efficiency, profitability, and return on investment. Progressive Conservatives are enthusiastic about free trade not only for these reasons, but also because the increase in profitability, efficiency, and economic growth would generate the resources essential to maintaining equality of opportunity in our society, an equality of opportunity that favours excellence over mediocrity and achievement over complacency.

The reason to rebuild the Progressive Conservative Party is simply to ensure that there is *a national federalist alternative to the present government* when and if Canadians choose to look for an alternative. The very moderation of the Progressive Conservative Party is what makes its reconstruction important to all Canadians who want a political structure that reflects a range of voting choices, which in turn provides for governing coalitions that are rooted in every part of this country; a structure that reflects the concerns and aspirations of more than one part of this country, and that has sufficient internal balance and sensitivity to act as an instrument of hope and opportunity.

The Progressive Conservative Party provides just that mix. In an era when Republicans in the United States were fighting Mr. Roosevelt's New Deal, R.B. Bennett Conservatives in Canada supported radical welfare and social reform to help the disadvantaged during the Great Depression. At a time when Republicans and Democrats were attacking the communist Chinese, Conservatives like George Hees and Alvin Hamilton were opening trade links that would connect China to the rest of the world, to the immediate and long-term benefit of all Canadians. At a time when conservatives in the United Kingdom were still tolerating South African apartheid governments, Canadian Tories from Diefenbaker to Mulroney were campaigning to exclude South Africa from the Commonwealth in the 1960s and to maintain sanctions until the 1980s, when a multi-racial democracy could form.

Our values are the foundation for our political structure. Our positions and coalitions have either been shaped by our courage and determination or weakened by a lack of resolve and conviction. When our resolve and conviction have faltered, the people of Canada have turned us out, sometimes for a very long time indeed. When the nature of our conviction and resolve and focus was understood and effectively communicated, the people of Canada have turned to us to change situations that clearly cried out for change. Whether one looks at Diefenbaker's nationalism and unhyphenated Canadianism on the one hand or Mulroney's strong global trading nation on the other, we have been most successful as a party when we have been the party of ideas.

The rebuilt Conservative Party must also have two-by-four supports, walls, systems, and insulation that reflect Canada today. The two-by-fours must demonstrate the principles of more freedom, less government, lower taxes, and reduced bureaucracy that make the house stronger. The weight-bearing walls must include social justice and community concern. The insulation, the only true insulation thick enough to withstand the icy blasts of the political wilderness, is the solid Tory conviction that society has a purpose — the freedom that true equality of opportunity brings and the firm and unshakeable faith we all share in the destiny of this wonderful country to remain great and united, and to become even greater.

THE WAY AHEAD

Speech to Multi-Riding Policy Conference, Kingston, Ontario, September 10, 1994

We are the party of nation. Narrow regional views have nothing to do with our history or purpose. We are the party of nation-building and reconciliation. Let others sound the call of intolerance or impatience. It sounds not for us. Our preference is to maintain a confederation where unity and purpose replace bickering and divisiveness.

We are the party of less government. In fact, as the party of Confederation, it is important to note how minimal the role of the central government was to leaders such as John A. Macdonald, George-Étienne Cartier, and another father of Confederation from Kingston, Alexander Campbell. We are a party that believes in enterprise not only as an engine of our society, but also as the only possible means of generating the capacity to promote social justice by helping those without any alternatives. We are a party that places social and community responsibility at the same priority level as rights and freedoms. As Tories, we simply do not forget that we are all part of a larger whole. Governments are no longer, in our modern age, agents of control. At best, and from the margins, governments are forces for good when they know their place and have a strong sense of limited but defined purpose.

CONSERVATISM AND PRIME MINISTERS

Speech to Ottawa-Vanier Federal PC Breakfast, Ottawa, February 9, 1995

From Sir John A. Macdonald to Jean Charest, Conservatives have often had to walk alone and tell lonely truths that many did not want to hear. When Pierre Trudeau introduced an overreaching, highly insensitive, and *dirigiste* iron-fisted federalism in the late 1960s and early 1970s, Bob Stanfield fought for less government; more sensitivity to Quebec, the West, and the Maritimes; more humanity; more co-operation; less autocracy. It was lonely, but he was right. In 1970, when Trudeau imposed the War Measures Act, which saw hundreds of Quebecers arrested without charge, it was a Conservative — David MacDonald, the MP from Egmont, PEI — who voted alone against continuing the use of the act as proposed by Justice

Minister John Turner. When the National Energy Program confiscated the natural-resource jurisdiction of all the provinces and set many in the West permanently against the central government, it was Joe Clark who fought the battle and Brian Mulroney who rectified the injustice. And when the time came to take Canada out of the centralist, protected, statist unreality, it was a Conservative prime minister who promoted free trade, producing one of the greatest export-led economic booms in our history.

WHAT KIND OF CONSERVATISM?

Speech to the National Press Club, Ottawa, June 21, 1995

The Tory tradition, its seminal context and undeniable roots, especially in British society and history, relates not to the trifling questions of left or right, but to more important ideas of order and stability on the one hand and nation and enterprise on the other. The founders of our Canadian constitution embraced the rather bucolic but sound premise of "peace, order, and good government." The American revolutionaries who tossed out the Crown, confusing a quite off-centre King George III with the larger institutions that the monarchy reflected, embraced instead "life, liberty, and the pursuit of happiness." The selfish and directionless nature of the American Revolution — which was more about self-interest, mercantile opportunity, and who collected what tax than it was about tolerance or freedom — was exposed for all time.

The Loyalists, who shunned the excesses of commercial republican populism, chose instead those British colonies where stability, monarchy, and community could co-exist with commercial and private pursuit. That immigration, those refugees from classical liberal excess (which now parades as neo-conservatism), forged a foundation for Canadian Tory reality that will forever distinguish us from the American neo-conservative and classical liberal conceit. The difference is rooted in our conflicting views about human nature. American neo-conservatives, when they began their early struggles against Democratic social and economic policies, chose to invest the rugged American individual — whether entrepreneur, wage earner, investor, or farmer — with qualities of selfless ambition, personal dignity, and human tolerance that were submerged only because the state was in the way. Tories, in a tradition that spans the Elizabethan world-view through the Georgian and Victorian eras, share no such optimism. Laws, traditions, the elements of civil society, and yes, government are essential components of a way of life where the weak are not preyed upon, where the strong are not permitted to loot or exploit, and where there is hope that some community interest can be sustained with public consensus and support.

Socialists, as Margaret Thatcher's senior mentor, Sir Keith Joseph, has so aptly argued, are often responsible for the institutionalization of envy. At the drop of a hat, they indulge in fanning the fires of class warfare — creating entire self-justifying belief systems around victims, because socialists need victims far more than victims need socialists. But that excess surely does not justify placing greed and profit at the centre of a philosophy for society as a whole. They are not, in and of themselves, values to live by. One, greed, is a human frailty of massive proportions. The other, profit, is an instrument of economic productivity, legitimate personal economic gain and betterment, a material measurement of but one aspect of a society's progress.

In the classic construct of nation and enterprise, profit — the right and opportunity to pursue profit, and the need to diminish the state's undue interference with its generation — is one of two pillars upon which the Tory world-view must stand. The other is nation — the responsibility for and to the larger whole, for and to one another. Life is more than economics. Civilization is a product of both individual and collective enterprise. Nation and enterprise sustain each other. If making money is what the neo-conservative *pro forma* life is all about, without any sense of what civilized purposes that money may serve in private, public, volunteer, or community hands, then we have a view of the world as sterile as any Marxist analysis might provide.

George Will, in *The Pursuit of Virtue and Other Tory Notions,* makes an argument about the institution of government that I take comfortably to heart. "Many conservatives," he writes, "insist that America's great problem is just government is so strong it is stifling freedom. These people call themselves 'libertarian conservatives' — a label a bit like 'promiscuous celibates.' Real conservatism requires strong government ... Real conservatism is about balancing many competing values. Striking the proper balance often requires limits on liberty, and always requires resistance to libertarianism (the doctrine of maximum freedom for private appetites), because libertarianism is a recipe for the dissolution of public authority, social and religious traditions, and other restraints needed to prevent license from replacing durable disciplined liberty."

If we are to sustain a dynamic and compelling conservatism for the future, we need to balance these competing values of nation and enterprise, not sacrifice one set for those perhaps more popular today. Our core Canadian conservative spectrum is not about rampant change for the sake of change, or about unbridled gain. It is about balance and freedom and, above all, responsibility.

CONSERVATISM ACCORDING TO JOHN DIEFENBAKER

Speech to the German Canadian Club, Regina, Saskatchewan, June 26, 1996

I entered the Conservative Party because, when I was thirteen years of age, a man came to my school during the 1962 general election and addressed our assembly. He spoke of human rights and unhyphenated Canadians — people from Eastern Europe, the Ukraine, the British Isles, and the Far East who had come and joined with the earlier French and English settlers and aboriginal citizens to build the greatest country in the world. He spoke of a Canada that cared not if you were Christian, Muslim, or Jew; of a Canada where the colour of your skin or your nation of origin was a private matter of heritage, not a public barrier to participation. He spoke of a sovereign country that went its own way. He spoke of appointing the first woman to cabinet, the first Ukrainian to cabinet, the first black and the first aboriginal to the Senate of Canada.

As he presented a copy of the 1961 Bill of Rights, passed by his government, to my school's principal, this man filled the hall with his passion, his honesty, his hope, and his optimism. He defined Progressive Conservative as the ultimate balance for free enterprise, profit-making, and economic growth on the one hand, and social justice and respect for the interests of the common man on the other.

His name was John Diefenbaker, and he was from Prince Albert, Saskatchewan.

Because of Diefenbaker, when Conservatives my age or older hear the words "Progressive Conservative," we see a fiery orator, a crusader for the common man, and a staunch defender of the monarchy and the British Commonwealth. He was a crusader against communist oppression in Eastern Europe, but a defender of the right of Canadians to be members of the Communist Party. The common-touch populism was mixed with a steely determination, as when he led the attack on an apartheid South Africa that resulted in its being removed from the Commonwealth — a measure that bore fruit when F. W. de Klerk and Nelson Mandela led South Africa to a new multiracial democracy and re-entry into the Commonwealth.

WINSTON CHURCHILL'S CONSERVATISM

Speech to the International Churchill Society Dinner at the Albany Club, Toronto, January 29, 1997

At the end of his address to the Conservative Conference at Blackpool, on October 5, 1946, after having lost the election to the Labour Party, Sir Winston Churchill summarized what the Conservative Party should reflect and undertake:

> We oppose the establishment of a Socialist State, controlling the means of production, distribution and exchange. We are asked, "What is your alternative?" Our Conservative aim is to build a property-owning democracy, both independent and interdependent. In this I include profit-sharing schemes in suitable industries and intimate consultation between employers and wage-earners. In fact we seek so far as possible to make the status of the wage-earner that of a partner rather than of an irresponsible employee. It is in the interest of the wage-earner to have many other alternatives open to him than service under one all-powerful employer called the State. He will be in a better position to bargain collectively, and production will be more abundant; there will be more for all and more freedom for all when the wage-earner is able, in the large majority of cases, to choose and change his work, and to deal with a private employer who, like himself, is subject to the ordinary pressures of life and, like himself, is dependent upon his personal thrift, ingenuity and good-housekeeping. ... Freedom of enterprise and freedom of service are

not possible without elaborate systems of safeguards against failure, accident or misfortune. We do not seek to pull down improvidently the structures of society, but to erect balustrades upon the stairway of life, which will prevent helpless or foolish people from falling into the abyss. Both the Conservative and Liberal parties have made notable contributions to secure minimum standards of life and labour. ... It is an essential principle of Conservative, Unionist and Tory policy — call it what you will — to defend the general public against abuses by monopolies and against restraints on trade and enterprise, whether these evils come from private corporations, from the mischievous plans of doctrinaire Governments, or from the incompetence and arbitrariness of departments of State.

This was Churchill's core view and decency: a profound respect for the rights of working people and the need for a fair balance between labour and capital.

Churchill left us clear and precise thoughts on how the victory over communism should prepare us for the domestic challenges faced by the great democracies. Because our generation has been spared the agony of war and the poverty of depression, we dare to assume that the hardships we allegedly face compare with what those who stood against Hitler, Japan, and Italy, both abroad and here at home, had to face daily. Because some of our generation indulge themselves in that conceit, they search for the facile and instant responses. Yet instant solutions from the right or the left are more part of the problem than the solution. "Privatize everything!" "Dilute *all* public services and programs!" It is as unseemly to institutionalize envy as it is to institutionalize greed and selfishness. A country in the end is about individuals and the common causes they are able to embrace freely in a mutual and greater interest.

Churchill's relationship with the people of the United Kingdom was terribly complex. He was not a person who defined his choices purely by partisan label. He laboured often beyond the reach of public support. At times, his views were deemed excessive or opportunistic. His compelling rhetoric worked better in times of war. His own party and many of its leading personalities doubted his suitability for high office — both before and after he attained it.

Yet in that relationship — in that complexity — clear and precise attributes emerge largely unavoidably. First, he would certainly have been dismissed by Thatcher and her people as a "dreadful wet," far too concerned with the common folk to be able to meet any rigorous ideological test. Second, he had little time for the dowdies and self-perpetuating dandies who controlled the Tory Party, for reasons utterly unrelated to the common interest in the country. They had even less regard for him, and many resented him even after he became Britain's wartime leader.

This, in the end, may well have been his strength — his pull on a people and an empire. He stood alone, often against the greatest threat to civilization in the modern era. He stood apart from the conventions of class and privilege. He surrendered peerage and title well within the reach of his inheritance. And he preserved civilization — and civility — aided only by the dominions, until help from America came.

His lessons, both in peace and in war, must not be set aside.

TWO VIEWS FROM THE CENTRE

Financial Post, *May 6, 1998*

This past weekend, the *Financial Post* published a letter to the editor from Jack Riley of North Saanich, B.C., disagreeing with my views on the excesses of ideology. His points were articulate and thoughtful, and very much appreciated. At the end of his letter, he suggested that he'd be interested in my views (if any) on the differences between Conservatives and Liberals.

Liberals in Canada are really more about management than ideas. Liberals are genuine believers in the central role of government in creating wealth and redistributing it. They see government as a means by which economic growth can be moved along. Liberals in the Canadian tradition are centralists who believe that our national government is the lead player in all matters, as if Canada were a centralized federation. Liberals are generally condescending to the provinces, which they do not see as equal partners, and Liberals use the federal spending power to invade provincial jurisdiction.

Liberals can and have spent like drunken sailors, under Pierre Trudeau in the 1960s, 1970s, and 1980s, and under David Peterson in Ontario in the late 1980s. As long as tax yields grew — whether because of inflation, bracket creep, or economic growth — spending, borrowing, and taxing made up the Liberal doctrine. (Ontario is still paying for that today.) Liberals are troubled by tax cuts. The whole notion that money should be left in people's hands or in the bank accounts of small businesses is totally foreign to them. How do you engage in munificence if the money never leaves the taxpayers to begin with?

Liberals are relentlessly naive and hopeless on issues such as defence or the administration of justice and public safety. They refuse to believe there are some quite evil people against whom decent people need to be protected. And when Liberals do act in an area, the relentless bureaucracy of their option becomes counterproductive.

Liberals use government like a giant slush fund to advance the politics of "what's happening now." Embrace free trade as if it were your idea? Why not? Impose price and wage controls after rudely condemning them? Why not? Procure helicopters you refused before, but only after wasting half a billion dollars on cancellation fees? Why not?

But the Liberals manage their public relations like pros, and they know how to avoid 90 percent of the media scrutiny directed at others.

Tories? Well, we are for decentralized government, more consultation, less arbitrary measures, cutting taxes, and addressing the debt. Tories focus more on the key principles — such as freedom, responsibility, and the balance between both. Our bias is for non-government solutions. We believe in strong government, not large or expensive government.

Tories do not believe government is at the centre of society. We view the family, the community, the small business or farm as a more important force in a civil society. Tories view national defence as a serious priority and are not naive about rogue states, terrorists, or the criminal element. We favour victims' rights and a firm approach to law and order.

Tories see central government as remote and insensitive. We trust government more at the municipal and provincial levels. Tories do not like large solutions to problems, because they can create more problems. We prefer non-government solutions whenever possible.

Tories do not see Ottawa as the dominant force in a federation, but more as a key player in a confederation where provinces have jurisdictions mandated by the constitution that founded the country. We are not impressed with a "government knows best" bias, because we believe voters and taxpayers are more to be trusted with their hard-earned dollars than any government.

The differences between Tories and Liberals are not characterized by ideological extremes. Both are parties rooted in the centre. But Tories have a vastly different and more conservative view of the role of government, the importance of order, and the role of free enterprise in wealth creation. Liberals are not burdened by their convictions — they govern best in a conviction-free zone.

PART TWO

The Difference
People Make

THE WAY IN WHICH THE RITUALS OF POLITICS, THE EXCESSES OF partisanship, and the comic-book nature of "black hat, white hat" coverage portrays individuals in business and political life is often dismissive of their significant complexities. Personality and personal morality and decency do make a real difference. Individuals do supersede party affiliation. Robert Stanfield would have been a much different prime minister from his successor as Conservative leader, Joe Clark. Party labels would not adequately have described the kinds of leadership they did or did not offer. The same is clearly true of Pierre Trudeau and Jean Chrétien. I dare say that Brian Mulroney was a very different prime minister from Joe Clark — yet they were probably not seriously divided on issues or on the left-right spectrum.

Over the years, and since I wrote my first column for the *Toronto Star* more than fifteen years ago, the personality differences of those in public life have always impressed me as at least as important, if not on occasion more so, than any detailed political or economic analysis of their period of service.

My views have changed over two decades of involvement in politics, the media, and business. This will become obvious as you read through these reflections on people and the difference they make. There are people in public life who contribute solidly, serve honestly, and have such an impact that they cannot help making a difference in the life of a country. Even if one disagrees with their policies, they stand out as a key influence on the level of civility of a society — positively *or* negatively. The following are some of these people.

LEWIS WILL REFOCUS CANADA'S ATTENTION ON UNITED NATIONS

Toronto Star, *October 11, 1984*

The appointment of a committed, moderate, and articulate social democrat to serve Canada at the United Nations will, if nothing else, make what happens at the UN of greater interest to Canadians. That, in and of itself, makes Stephen Lewis's appointment a gesture of some meaning.

Officially, the formal framework of our foreign policy still identifies the UN as a key pillar of our international stance. Simply put, the ability of a middle power such as Canada to influence other nations is not as great on a unilateral basis as it should be via multilateral agencies such as the UN.

One of Ambassador Lewis's initial frustrations is that since the Korean War, the UN has been reluctant to take defensive action against invaders when it involves choosing sides. Afghanistan, Lebanon, Central America, Africa — all have seen military aggression without UN response. Moreover, the institutional framework of the UN, the control of most matters by a Soviet Third World bloc, and the frequent intransigence of the main powers have often reduced the UN's arbitration capacity considerably.

It would have been easy for any government, especially a Conservative one, to simply accept the difficulties as too large to overcome and appoint a solid career diplomat to report back and make few waves. Instead, Prime Minister Mulroney sends a feisty, articulate, persuasive politician with a demonstrated track record on humanitarian issues and an ingrained intolerance of both injustice and inertia. Moreover, this ambassador will both attract and sustain media interest. It is as if the country that gave the UN one of its last hours of credibility — through the Middle East initiatives of Lester B. Pearson in the 1950s — has decided, thirty years later, that despite the obstacles, Canadians are prepared to give international civility at least one more genuine try. In Stephen Lewis, the Tories have chosen an emissary who, if successful, will bring credit to the government — and if not, will do the government little harm.

If progress can be made by anyone representing Canada at the UN, it is Stephen Lewis. Nations that have counted on Canada to abstain on controversial issues will now know that however the final instructions from Ottawa may determine his posture, Ambassador Lewis's advice to the government will be activist and principled, and will strengthen the Canadian presence. Canadians will be able to take genuine pride in what will undoubtedly be many opportunities for heroic stands on international human-rights and social-justice matters.

As a Tory, I have worked against Stephen Lewis and for my own party in Ontario for more than a decade. Despite what I have felt to be the inappropriateness of his domestic politics, his qualities as a human being and a democrat make him a superb choice to serve Canada at the UN. It is certainly one that Canadians of all or no affiliation can be proud of.

BOURASSA'S FEDERALISM WAS INFUSED WITH PRACTICALITY

Financial Post, *October 5, 1996*

The passing of Robert Bourassa is cause to reflect on the kind of federalism he defended and the ways in which the survival of Canada was advanced by his inimitable style. First and foremost, Bourassa was a public servant. He even put off U.S. treatment for his skin cancer because he did not want to leave Quebec during the Oka crisis. It is that cancer that finally claimed his life at the all-too-young age of sixty-three.

More than anything else, Bourassa understood, straddled, and sometimes encouraged the ambiguity that has always defined Quebec's relationship with the rest of Canada. It is an ambiguity that he did not create. It stems from the conquest in 1759 and the ensuing Quebec Act in the British House of Commons, which confirmed recognition for Quebec's language, religion, and civil laws. It also stems from 1867, when Confederation separated Upper and Lower Canada (i.e., Ontario from Quebec), so that Quebec could have its own provincial sovereignties in a province where French-speakers were not swamped. It is an ambiguity he inherited from the politics of the Union Nationale's perpetual premier, Maurice Duplessis; the quiet "*maître chez nous*" revolution of Jean Lesage; and the honourable "*égalité ou independence*" stance of Premier Daniel Johnson, Sr. It crossed party lines and generations. Bourassa's particular expression of it was *fédéralisme rentable* — a workable, flexible, and mutually beneficial federalism.

Bourassa's return to public life after being routed in the election of 1976 was masterful: a time spent teaching in Europe and the U.S.; loyal church-basement campaigning against independence in the 1980 referendum; recapturing the leadership of the Quebec Liberal Party; the defeat of the PQ; the setting aside of the PQ's twenty-one conditions for signing the 1982 constitution, and their replacement with the five conditions that became the core of the Meech Lake Accord. This accord was, with Bourassa's help, agreed to three times, and then finally done in by the premier of Newfoundland, Clyde Wells. Weathering the storm of rejection Quebecers felt after that result was perhaps Bourassa's finest hour.

I recall being in the CTV booth at the Liberal leadership convention in Calgary when Bourassa appeared on TV in Quebec to indicate how his government would respond to the collapse in Newfoundland of the Meech Lake Accord. It was precisely at that time that Clyde Wells arrived at the convention to be warmly and literally embraced on national television by one leadership candidate, Jean Chrétien. The two competing images stayed forever in my mind. For those who wonder at the perpetual lack of popularity of Prime Minister Chrétien among his fellow Quebecers, this scene is essential. It is also essential to understanding why some Paul Martin supporters left to join the Bloc during and after that convention.

Bourassa never had serious difficulty fighting off the separatists with his cool, rational assessment of other options more appropriate and less corrosive. His greatest problems came from the federal Liberals, who — whether it was through Chrétien's duplicity on Meech or Charlottetown, or the Trudeau-inspired Newfoundland destruction of Meech — were never prepared to let the more flexible Bourassa view prevail. It was as if the flexible side of Quebec nationalism, reflected by Bourassa, could prevail only by threatening the federal Liberal electoral prospects.

But Bourassa's core contribution to the politics of Canada was, through all his ambiguities and machinations, to gently, incrementally, and consistently keep Quebec within Confederation. That was the genius of his post-Meech strategy. That was the genius of his Charlottetown strategy. He had willing partners in premiers like Bob Rae, David Peterson, Bill Davis, Peter Lougheed, Bill Bennett, Don Getty, and Richard Hatfield. Clearly, his friendship with Brian Mulroney was a key element in why the country survived despite all the pressures. Bourassa's federalism was an incremental, step-by-step approach, devoid of histrionics, infused with practicality, and sustained by public acquiescence.

There are many things that could be said about Bourassa as apt political epitaphs. He was an organizer, philosopher, negotiator, intellectual, tactician supreme, and brilliant strategist. He was a Quebecer to his core. I would venture to add one final thought: He was an outstanding Canadian.

GHIZ OPENED DOORS AND FOUGHT THOSE WHO WOULD CLOSE THEM
Financial Post, *November 16, 1996*

Prince Edward Island and Canada bid farewell this week to Joe Ghiz, who died at the age of fifty-one. That he died in the same week that the last link joining both sides of the Confederation causeway across Northumberland Strait was installed underlines the kind of builder he was. He had no delusions about the influence of a province as small as Prince Edward Island. But smallness, as a state of mind, was something for which he had very little time. In fact, one could argue that he spent his all-too-short life fighting against it in every way. Yes, he was a Liberal and a liberal through and through; but the reach of his intellect and the scope of his vision made any partisan category too small to contain the voice he offered. He had little time for sophistry and less time for perfectionist extremism. He battled for the Meech Lake and Charlottetown accords, without regard to the partisan risks. The citizens of Prince Edward Island, Newfoundland, and New Brunswick were among the strongest Yes voters in the Charlottetown referendum, in large measure because of his unflagging commitment to national co-operation.

His voice in the negotiations was always resolute and focused. He talked of the costs of failure. He fought for the vision of a united and fair-minded Canada. He was as much the ally of alienated Westerners as he was the proponent of decency and fairness relative to Quebec's history, language, and culture. He had the populism of John Diefenbaker without the attendant hubris. He had the intellect of a Harvard-educated courtroom lawyer, along with the compassion of a social worker. He was the kind of person you wanted in your corner — during good times to preach humility and during bad times to ensure that surrender was never an option.

The forces of isolationism and regionalism that worked against the causeway to Canada, forces that have been part of the island's makeup since well before Confederation, were deftly managed with full freedom of expression and openness right through a difficult referendum. It may well have been the Mulroney government that delivered on a political promise made many times in the past by building the causeway, and the Chrétien government that completed the task, but the bridge would not have been started, built, or completed without Joe Ghiz. It is fitting that the causeway is called the Confederation Bridge. It would also be fitting for the Prince Edward Island start to be called the Joe Ghiz Gateway, because in many ways Ghiz devoted his public life to opening doors and opposing those who would close them for reasons of narrow ideology or partisan excess.

It was a rare privilege for me during my brief time in Ottawa to speak with him and get frank advice from him both for the government and for the prime minister. (I always wondered why he used the phone, as opening a window in the premier's office in Prince Edward Island would surely have been sufficient for his voice to carry at least as far as Ottawa.) My favourite memory came from a private session in Halifax some months after he had left politics and I had returned to Queen's University. We were both on a panel before a group of leading Maritime business people, all CEOs who were part of the Young Presidents' Organization. It was a wide-ranging discussion just after the Liberals had won the federal election and before the last Quebec referendum. There was an air of despair in the room about the deficit, about an embedded rigidity in Ottawa, about economic prospects overall. My enthusiasm and optimism, which can border on the excessive, were dwarfed by the unbridled belief in Canada, in our common opportunity and our collective and individual potential, that was expressed by Ghiz. He would brook no pessimism. He was awash in the sheer joy of an immigrant's son who had been elevated by his neighbours to the first ministers' table.

Those who contemplate the burdens in heaven may wonder whether, on occasion, as its inhabitants look down on the famine, war, hate, and despair that are still the province of too many in this world, the shadow of pessimism might sprout unheavenly wings in the ethereal councils. Well, the shadow will not fly for long. The irrepressible Ghiz spirit will see to that.

RAE DESERVES TO BE CELEBRATED

Financial Post, *November 30, 1996*

I read Bob Rae's book *From Protest to Power* with a clear disadvantage —
despite his politics, I actually like him quite a bit. His book is worth read-
ing because of what it both says and omits. It omits the "we were right, but
misunderstood" line that many in public life embrace, especially after the
people have chosen to loosen their embrace and take their affections elsewhere. It omits the "everyone I worked with was a saint" refrain that political autobiography often entails.

Not only was Bob Rae stunned to have been elected, but he also found
himself with little talent in a freshman caucus. His own experience was
exclusively in opposition, in both Ottawa and Toronto, and in socialist
opposition at that. These are not the seeds from which cedars of governmental balance and judgement can reach quickly skyward.

But the book reveals more than just the day-to-day machinations of the
Social Contract, the negotiation of the Charlottetown Accord, or the restructuring of Algoma Steel — three events in which Rae's personal role and
leadership served the public interest exceedingly well. It also uncovers the
genuine discomfort Rae felt at many of the rituals of everyday politics.
Recently, he spoke to a packed hall in Kingston of the out-of-body experience it was to go through an entire day when everything that could go
wrong did — in the legislature, in the media, in the government — only to
get home late at night, depart the next morning in a government car with
two provincial police officers, and arrive in the premier's office to be sur-
rounded by upbeat advisers telling him how well things were going! Clearly,
these rituals did not collapse Rae's grasp of reality — and the book is elo-
quent testimony to that continuing and unbitter grasp.

I disagreed with many of the measures the Rae government brought in,
especially those that seemed dictated more by debts to labour-union leadership than by the public interest. De-streaming in the education system and
raising welfare rates to levels that could not help breeding abuse spoke to a
mixture of naïveté and egalitarian excess that mixed commitment to equality
of opportunity with trying to legislate equality of outcome. It is hard to hold
any socialist to account for this kind of mistake, as it is almost a genetic fault
in their inherited world-view. That Bob Rae tried to moderate the worst of

these excesses only increased the animosity from the left. He resisted many of them, and paid the price — facing union hostility to election day. He need not feel hard done by. The capacity of public-sector union leadership to desert anyone who does not simply cave into their demands, including those in other unions or their own political parties, is now legendary.

I will always remember two events of Rae's period in office that are beyond partisanship. One relates to the final negotiations around the Charlottetown Accord in Ottawa in 1992. Joe Clark's round of consultations was over, the meetings at Harrington Lake that brought Robert Bourassa back to the table had taken place, and the penultimate week of discussions was underway. A huge roadblock around aboriginal self-government was dominating on that particular day, and there was a heavy dose of frustration and angst on all sides. Rae was working with the First Nations leaders, including Ovide Mercredi, Rosemary Kuptana of the Inuit Tapirisat, and Nellie Cournoyea, who was government leader of the Northwest Territories. He sat with them, his laptop computer working overtime, and refused to let the spirit of trust be consumed. In the end he helped achieve, along with their own leadership and judgement, an agreement they and all first ministers could embrace. Unfortunately, there would be no rewards for any of us this side of heaven.

My second memory is of his determination to ensure, in a zoning dispute that was standing in the way of an overdue French-language high school being built in Kingston, that he, his minister of education, and his staff remained steadfast in their support of the school despite the determined opposition of NDP members of the local city council.

No, his government did not deserve to be re-elected. But the honourable contribution Bob Rae made to Ontario deserves to be recognized, and even celebrated, by political ally and opponent alike.

MARTIN IS REDEFINING THE LIBERAL AGENDA

Financial Post, *March 1, 1997*

Paul Martin's 1997 budget is both less and more than meets the eye. It is less because many of the provisions shaping his fiscal program come from prior budgets. Much of the economic gain Liberals will extol in the future will come from budgets tabled in 1996 and 1995, or from Mike Wilson's budgets. But let's not quibble about who gets the credit. If things were going badly, Martin would get the blame. There is more than meets the eye in this budget because it is the pre- and post-election defining point of a new liberalism in Canadian politics, just as Bill Clinton's Democratic Leadership Council defined the new Democratic approach in the U.S. That definition has kept Republicans out of the presidency for two terms.

Paul Martin cuts a broad swath down the centre of the Liberal Party that squeezes the Copps-Goldenberg-Trudeau *dirigiste* approach to one side and the old 1960s Winters-Hellyer-Sharp "market *über alles*" approach to the other. Using fiscal prudence, he clearly is prepared to trade some Maritime, Quebec, and Ontario seats for seats in the West. If the object is to build a truly national party not totally dependent on monolithic blocks of votes in Quebec and Ontario, Martin is well on the way to a fundamental broadening of the narrow-base liberalism of the Trudeau-Chrétien school. This will be tested in the next election. If Liberals get a majority government with fewer seats from the Maritimes and Ontario, some gains in Quebec, and more seats in the West, then the transition is real. If a majority is elusive, then traditional left liberalism will be back in vogue. In a sense, the coming election will be more than a test of Jean Chrétien's popularity outside his party. It will be a test of how well Liberals can manage their new liberalism in a campaign — without being seduced by the old "promise the moon" cynicism that Martin clearly opposes.

Less government, more partnership with the community, fewer top-down social programs — this is either a real set of Liberal values or the only choice Liberals have to keep the rating agencies sweet. If Martin has his way, liberalism in Canada will have shifted to a fiscally prudent and socially less intrusive way of governing. This is the surrender some hard-line left Liberals have always feared. I suspect, though, that Martin has the pulse of the party and the traditional Liberal vote when he nudges the party more into the living, breathing centre of Canadian economic, social, and political life. With his approach to decentralization (pragmatic), to monetary policy (balanced), and to Quebec (he supported Meech Lake and Charlotte-town), one wonders where Canada would be if the Liberals had chosen Martin instead of Chrétien. It is unlikely that the 1993 Tory-Campbell collapse would have been any less dramatic. It is unlikely that Quebec would have a sovereignist government in place today. Referendums on sovereignty might have vanished from the horizon. Like his father, who was the ultimate pragmatist in the Pearson cabinet, Martin is more than an architect of the social safety net.

The challenge posed by Martin to Conservatives, Reformers, and New Democrats would be qualitatively different from the immense political opportunity provided by Chrétien. There are many photos and memories from the 1997 election campaign as far as Chrétien is concerned. The one I like the best, suggested to me by a columnist for another paper, is the photo where Chrétien has a diminutive demonstrator in a choke hold. It says a lot about the civility, balance, fairness, and spirit of the Chrétien style of leadership. In this campaign, Tories, New Democrats, and Reformers have much for which to be grateful to Chrétien. His self-effacing charm has turned into a schoolyard pout. His boyish frankness now appears more a way to brutalize friend and foe. His no-nonsense, simple approach to government appears now to be disconnected and/or mean, depending on the issue. He is the secret weapon of every sovereignist strategist.

Opposition parties have much to be thankful for in Jean Chrétien. But above all, they will be thankful he is not Paul Martin.

GROSSMAN'S LEGACY TO ACTIVIST CONSERVATISM

Financial Post, *July 5, 1997*

There are people in public life who make solid contributions, serve honestly, and move quietly to private life. There are others whose every moment in public life was so tightly focused and productive that their impact far outstrips any simple chronological record of their achievements. Larry Grossman, who served in the Ontario legislature from 1975 to 1987, was very much in the second group. His brave and ultimately losing battle against brain cancer, which ended in 1997 at the age of fifty-three, focused attention by Conservatives everywhere on the kind of public contribution he made in his short twelve years as a member of the provincial Parliament and Conservative minister.

As the minister of consumer and corporate affairs, he reduced the red tape for small business and began implementing the broadest changes in financial regulation in the province's recent history. As minister of industry and tourism, he had Ontario produce the first major initiative anywhere in Canada on reducing interprovincial trade barriers. He massively expanded tourism and industrial promotion for Ontario worldwide, while creating a new tourism marketing thrust that expanded the industry substantially. New centres for joint industry/technology development in robotics, auto parts, and food processing were established. The IDEA Corp., intended to foster technological innovation in biotechnology and information technology, was an initiative of Grossman's.

As treasurer and finance minister, he kept Ontario's credit rating in tough recessionary times and sought to reduce and lower taxes while keeping social safety nets not only in shape but also, where necessary, enhanced. As health minister, he championed the causes of disenfranchised psychiatric patients, health-systems reorganization, local district health councils, and common purchasing of supplies and services by hospital groups. In all portfolios, he pushed his public-service and political staff members relentlessly — but always treated them with respect, courtesy, and decency.

He was the kind of politician who felt that one is in public life for a short time, and that activism in defence of the taxpayer and the most vulnerable in society is the only route. As a Progressive Conservative, he was progressive socially and conservative fiscally. He was a spark plug in the Bill Davis government and a determined interprovincial activist on health-care and fiscal issues. He could debate Pierre Trudeau on constitutional issues and sit for hours chatting with a psychiatric patient or a tourist outfitter in the North. He brought an immense humanity and compassion to his task, as well as a joy with politics that was absolutely self-evident.

Both times he ran for leader of the party — the second time victoriously — his family was always with him. His caring, attractive, and insightful wife, Carol, and his children, Melissa, Jamie, and Robby, were always on the trail. Before politics came fatherhood, family, and home. This he learned from his own father, Allan, who served in both the John Robarts and Davis governments, and was a tireless crusader for penal reform and non-denominational education. Larry's devotion to his children made him a better elected politician. His family was part of every campaign, from the riding of St. Andrew–St. Patrick — which was always tough to hold — to the province-wide election campaign in 1987.

Larry might not have lost that election to as wide a Liberal landslide had he deserted the manifestly unpopular (in Ontario) free-trade platform. But having campaigned for interprovincial free trade, he truly believed in North American free trade. He stood by his federal leader, Brian Mulroney, and by Ontario federal cabinet members such as Mike Wilson and Barbara McDougall, who defended free trade. He paid a price for that loyalty — but one year later, in the election of 1988, federal PCs and free trade won a plurality of seats in Ontario and the majority that put the agreement into place. No province has benefited more from free trade than Ontario. Like so much of what Grossman fought for, the benefits will outlive him for decades to come and credit went elsewhere.

The sadness and tragedy and injustice of his untimely passing are not easily reconciled. His legacy of service, idealism, and competence will always be the gold standard for activist conservatism reflective of the best traditions of putting people first.

CHINESE NOT LIKELY TO FORGET PATTEN

Financial Post, *July 23, 1997*

Whatever misgivings Whitehall or the British foreign office may have about the ultimate reality of the handover of Hong Kong, there must be absolutely none about the choice of the final governor — Christopher Patten. As the last governor, his task — and burden — was not easy. Yet despite the "don't rock the boat" advice of old China hands, and the advice of proponents of Beijing's interests in the colony, there is no question that Patten moved democracy's yardsticks — and did so quite meaningfully. In that regard, he was paddling upstream, not only against the tough-minded Chinese, but also against a larger trend relative to politics and economics in what's left of the communist world.

The Chinese are not likely to forget or forgive his advancement of democratic institutions in Hong Kong. The People's Republic itself has precious little time for democracy as it tries to break out of the constraints and pressures of being a seriously poor country. The potential is overwhelming, but the poverty is compelling. Democracy, as we all saw in Tiananmen Square, is seen as a threat to the great march of history — a threat most communists have always fought. Whatever our affection and respect for the Chinese people, their government — backed by a People's Liberation Army that has an endless supply of conscripts and the will to use them whenever necessary — is still one of the few totalitarian regimes around. China's new theology — a rigid political control in the best Stalinist traditions mixed with expanded economic freedoms — is progress, to be sure. And when compared with the Russian experiment of ending political and economic control all at once, China's approach may well seem more orderly. (As Castro suggested to Canadians on a trade mission a few years ago, the score in Russia now seems to be Mafia 10, People 0.) But in the end, people with more economic freedom want more of a say about their own government and their own way of life. Anyone who believes that Hong Kong's free economic life can proceed undiminished, without producing pressures for a more free political life, is engaged in self-delusion.

While the communists may believe earnestly in "one country/two systems," they will face a stark choice soon enough. They must either let the virus of democracy spread unchecked along with economic liberalization or begin to dilute the economic liberalization. It's a choice between keeping your promises or keeping control.

The members of the ruling clique in Beijing, whatever their other strengths and successes, and they have had some, have not been big on succession surprises — or, for that matter, surprises generally. Strange thing about democracy — it does tend to generate the odd surprise, especially for the self-perpetuating ruling cliques.

Patten moved the yardsticks on democracy and allowed and encouraged a democratically elected assembly to come into being. What that means is that the ending by China of that assembly and the new date for elections next May holds China's feet to the fire in a most direct way. The democracy initiated is not of the "dictatorship of the proletariat" variety, but of the "evolutionary British responsible government" variety. Patten not only tweaked the dragon's nose in the interests of democracy, he also arranged for a bright light to shine on the dragon's every move in Hong Kong. For all this to have come from the work of one man during one term as governor is truly remarkable.

There are outstanding commercial reasons to treat the issue of democracy in Hong Kong as an internal Chinese matter. And the nations of the

West, Canada included, have become pretty good at looking the other way, especially when money and trade are involved. Foreign Minister Lloyd Axworthy's presence at the swearing-in of the illegitimate assembly appointees sadly underlines this point. Patten, despite the inevitability of Chinese control, did not look the other way. One can only imagine how well he might have done upon his return to the private sector, with the new masters of Hong Kong, had he chosen otherwise.

History may or may not be kind to Margaret Thatcher for agreeing to the handover, despite the conditions won to protect Hong Kong's way of life, but it will not fault the British government at all for the outstanding governor it chose.

DIANA AND THE JOYS AND STRUGGLES OF LIFE

Financial Post, *September 10, 1997*

It was about more than her celebrity and her beauty, although she had enough of both to light a thousand hearts. It was about more than being the Princess of Wales or the mother of a future king. It was even about something other than the senseless and tragic fashion of her untimely passing.

The deep and abiding nature of the loss, felt so broadly throughout the world, is about something else. It was, in the end and always, the vulnerability, the sense that this young and stunning woman, despite wealth, fame, poise, and glamour, could not, did not, and ultimately would not find happiness. It mattered little how different her life was from the day-to-day lives most of us live. She was never one of us, but the burdens that weighed her down, the emotions and pain that drove her, are experiences we all have and on occasion have seen in the people we care about. The manifestations of the pain — bulimia, depression, despair — somehow blended with her maternal determination to enjoy and nurture her boys, her charitable instinct to use her acquired fame and beauty to tilt against the scourge of AIDS, the horror of land mines, or the wretched lot of the homeless.

There was a symbolism and reality here that connected with her own and younger generations, who were less married, more divorced, more torn by the pressures of career and family, convention, and personal angst than many other generations. And even those from older generations saw much in this young woman that spoke almost too profoundly of the trouble they have seen among younger people.

It is true that the hyper-celebrity that the wired world can impart helped all that was Diana be seen and understood by so many millions. What set her apart from the normal uni-dimensional TV star, political figure, or athlete was that her impact went well beyond the single dimensions of beauty or rank or status. She was a multi-surfaced prism through which the sun always shone brightly, but the reality of pain or fear or frustration was never out of view. Grace, beauty, and royalty do not replace confidence, happiness, or love. The absence of love and happiness can rarely be compensated for by an abundance of the more apparent attributes of glamour or celebrity. We may all know this deep down, but at some level we deny it.

Princess Diana's efforts to carve out for herself some happiness beyond the artifice of jet-set travel touched many. Her ability to fight for those forgotten or avoided by so many in society, such as the terminally ill, the land-mine victim, or the AIDS patient, spoke volumes of the despair she urged all of us, including herself, to face, confront, and overcome. Her all-too-short life symbolized the determination we all make that conflicts in what we want, what we get, what we expect, and what is expected of us never fully reconcile. Facing these conflicts and finding the right balance without forgetting or forsaking those less fortunate is what much of the struggle and joy of life is about. Diana, Princess of Wales, symbolized not only the joy but also the struggle. She put a human and vulnerable face on a monarchy that has succeeded, in one measure at least, because its public face was stoic, earnest, detached, but also emblematic of a stability and nobility to which part of the human condition always aspires.

No one who dies suddenly at thirty-six years of age, whatever the reason, can be deemed to have been at peace at her passing. Diana will not get word when William and Harry graduate or marry. She will never hold her grandchild in her arms. She had so much, yet was denied so much more. She was the flag of her generation, a princess of the contradictions modern society too easily sustains. That, more than the glamour, the magazine covers, and the yachts and planes, is the true essence of her hold on us all. May God rest her soul, and protect her sons and families from all future sorrow.

CROSBIE WAS CERTAINLY ONE OF A KIND — TOO BAD

Financial Post, *October 25, 1997*

John Crosbie's colourful memoir may set the standard for frank, compelling, and important autobiography. It is a must-read for Canadians who worry that our politics have become so correct, bland, and colourless as to be somehow detached from the larger reality we all live. *No Holds Barred* not only is a unique expression of one man's will and political determination, but is also a rare glimpse for Canadians into a politics and history that may be the most intense, competitive, and focused of any English-speaking part of North America.

Newfoundland is a part of Canada that is intensely literate, somewhat apart, distinct in many ways, and given to a fierce and combative politics that speaks to the best and the worst of the human condition. Crosbie was not only a key player in that world, but also an impresario who marshalled forces against the corruption, manipulation, and Liberal arrogance of the Joey Smallwood leadership cult. His autobiography shares the intensity of that struggle, the personal commitment he brought to a politics of honesty that put the public interest first. He was courageous and about as fearless as any one human being can be.

There is, as well, a frankness about personal foibles and mistakes made that speaks to and underlines the honesty of the man, the integrity of his career in public life, and a personality that was and is among the most unique in contemporary politics. As a fellow Conservative who likes John and admires his tenacious defence of the underdog, I found his book to hold special appeal.

There is a cultural blandness to our politics today that in some respects works to deny individualism. I remember when the decent, honest, and thoughtful Robert Stanfield was viewed as being too thoughtful and too considered. He was not advised to have laser therapy, wear contact lenses, and have a hair weave or colour job. It would simply have been seen as unbecoming. That it is seen today as quite appropriate for one leader to lose weight before a campaign or for another to have a new hairstyle, laser eye surgery, and voice lessons that change his intonation is not so much a criticism of the leaders who felt so inclined, but a larger and sadder comment on a media-driven politics that makes certain kinds of presence inappropriate.

It also says something about all of us, as voters, who reward this kind of contrivance and turn away from people whose particularity may be just a bit beyond some pasteurized and homogenized norm.

To Crosbie's eternal credit, he did not ever play this game. He spoke his mind; he made his choices; he chose his policies and parties without caring a fig for how some guru of style or nice talk might respond. Some may think this slowed his political rise. I prefer to think it helped propel it.

This book also provides rare glimpses into a web of misdeeds that might help everyone under forty understand that despite present mythology, there actually was profound Liberal corruption during the 1960s and 1970s, and Newfoundland Liberals were awash in more than their share. The book leaves few questions unposed or unanswered. It also unveils, in Crosbie's own words, the strong driving forces that constituted the motivational thrust of his public life. If anything, it reveals a politician too honest, too quick to respond, too literate and glib to make it all the way to the top. In a sense, it reveals what was most important to Crosbie about life and politics. And the reader discovers that admiration for Crosbie is unavoidable.

His contempt for all those who work in public life without being elected, his frustration with the media, his frustration with statements he himself made that could have stood a bit more thought — all highlight the honesty and integrity of this chronicle and the way in which he chose to tell it. It may very well be that someone with the humour, intellect, personality, turn of phrase, and colour of John Crosbie can come only from a place with the depth, culture, history, and politics of Newfoundland. More's the pity.

ANTI-U.S. CAMPUS PROTEST AN UNBECOMING PERFORMANCE

Financial Post, *November 26, 1997*

The display of displeasure by a few members of the University of Toronto's faculty on the occasion of George Bush's honorary degree speaks far more to bad manners and arrogance than it does to academic freedom. It also reflects the rather sad pettiness and insularity of the academic anti-U.S. viewpoint.

Let us deal first with the fact that Mr. Bush's degree was approved unanimously by the honorary degree committee, on which faculty and students are represented. One can understand students not involved with that committee choosing to chant, demonstrate, and otherwise be cantankerous, which is, after all, what students should be free to do within the range of democratic dissent. But the decision of the academics involved speaks to something well beyond dissent. Their decision to display public disapproval is, in effect, a rejection of the mechanisms by which the University of Toronto considers, discusses, and approves honorary degrees in general. It is an attack on the legitimacy of that process and a clear and clarion appeal for the university to withdraw from the larger world of economic and geopolitical reality.

The singling out of this former U.S. president for attack seems quite strange. Would the apostles of left-wing analytical rigour have been happier with Bill Clinton? Or are all former and present occupants of the White House well beneath the standards of this small group of academics? The issue here is clearly the exercise of statecraft by any duly elected U.S. president — and the fact that statecraft may not have attained the ethical purity and consistency so present in these academics' lives. Surely there is a more important moral issue this small group of professors must address.

If the University of Toronto, in all its solemn councils and committees, is not performing up to their standards in the way in which degrees are awarded, perhaps, in the name of principle, the only honourable way of firmly expressing this disagreement is for those academics to tender their resignations. Now that would speak to the kind of moral courage and determination they seem to find lacking in others.

There is the possibility the professors' conspiracy theory holds true, of course. This suggests that Bush's name may have been put forward not by the classics or anthropology department, or even by the English literature department, but perhaps by a trustee or benefactor or otherwise untenured supporter of the institution. Even if this non-calamitous rumour were true, it is still the duly constituted committee of the university that approved the degree. Hence the sin of commission comes from within the workings of the university itself.

While the moral leadership of resignations would be compelling, we should not hold our breath. These protests are not the protests of the courageous. This is the self-absorbed titter from the comfortable pew — those who have views on everything, condescension for everyone, and deep personal conviction on not very much indeed.

My bias is apparent, and I gladly admit to it. Bush was in some ways an effective president, especially relative to the end of the Cold War, the commitment to stop aggression in the Persian Gulf region, the momentum developed towards a new working relationship between *de facto* allies who had united against Iraq, the extension of humanitarian aid in Somalia, and the celebration of the volunteer sector in the U.S. I expect he was less than perfect, which should not diminish his acceptability as a candidate for an honorary degree. He was engaged with Europe and Asia, and sought to assist Russia with its transition. He paid more attention to Canada than most other U.S. presidents.

The sadness of the action taken by the small group of professors is the way in which it speaks to the pettiness of that "holier than thou" bias found at the root of most anti-Americanism. I have no desire to emulate U.S. cultural, political, or policy norms, but adopting a morally superior tone is unbecoming. Showing disrespect in a petty way is, above all, rude. Unlike the parading professors, the students at least had the courage to stand out in the cold.

IT WAS SPORTING OF PARIZEAU TO GIVE CREDIT WHERE CREDIT IS DUE

Financial Post, *December 6, 1997*

I do not know if the Man of the Year awards have been given out yet by the Anti-Defamation League, the YMCA, and the Canadian Council of Christians and Jews, but I hope it is not too late to nominate Jacques Parizeau, the former prime minister (this is the correct term, I am told) of Quebec. Now, before all the neo-cons, neo-liberals, left libs, and the Gang of Thirty (UofT professors who protest almost anything from their tenured splendour) launch an all-out attack from the pages of both *Canadian Forum* and the *Alberta Report,* please allow me a word of explanation.

It strikes me as a serious outbreak from what has been, in some narrow quarters of the sovereignist movement, just a tiny touch of xenophobia for Parizeau now to be handing out credit where credit is due. He has offered badges of honour, in a spirit that shows what a jolly good sportsman he has always been, to those whose efforts seemed the most effective in defending the federalist side in the last referendum. In what strikes me as the kind of decency and fair play that surely graces the Oxbridge high table, he has singled out the Jewish, Italian, and Greek communities of Quebec, which, in his view, did so much for Canada in its hour of need.

On more than one occasion, he has made it clear that were it not for them, their ethnicity, and their money, an independent Quebec would be a reality. In fact, so determined is he to be fair and give credit that he does this by travelling the country, no doubt at immense personal cost and inconvenience. This is no longer the over-relaxed outburst of an immensely relieved premier on referendum night, a premier who could not contain his gratitude to the "ethnics with money" who assured that his arch-rival, Lucien Bouchard, would now have to carry this immense burden. We now have a man campaigning to be sure that Jews, Italians, and Greeks in Quebec are no longer marginalized by the language police or the partitionists — but that they get the status and standing they deserve. If this kind of decency on his part is not worthy of reward, then where are we as a civilized society?

The only reason I have not yet succeeded in gathering up thousands to sign the nomination forms for any of these awards is the little matter of fairness to everyone else. It's all very well for Parizeau to be the toast of every taverna, trattoria, and deli in sight, but what about all the others?

When my wife and I journeyed by train from Sir John A. Macdonald's Kingston to the Canada rally in Montreal on that cold October Friday, there were all kinds of others whom Parizeau, it would appear, has yet to acknowledge. There were the English-speaking Irish and Scottish Canadians who lined the Dorval train platform with banners that read "Thanks for Coming." Don't they deserve mention? There were the thousands of francophones from Ontario and the Maritimes who were out in great number. There were, and I know Parizeau must have overlooked this group, the 40 percent of Québécois francophones who voted No. They, in view of all the pressure they were under, surely deserve some serious credit. What about the Poles, Baptists, Moslems, B'Hai, and francophone Protestants? Is their heroism to be simply forgotten? And getting back to first principles, so to speak, do our First Nations in Quebec, who had their own sovereign referendum and voted massively to stay in Canada, get left off the list? Surely this would be the ultimate injustice.

If awards for bravery, courage, and impact are being given out by

Parizeau, we all have a duty to make sure that in the grand and inclusive spirit of Quebec, none will be left out or left by the wayside. With just a little more work, Parizeau can stride to the glass podium at a gala awards dinner soon — and, like that marvellous Aislin cartoon of Jean Marchand holding the phonebooks during the War Measures Act while affirming that, yes, he did have a full list of suspects, Parizeau, too, can have with him his full list of honourees.

BEACONS OF LIGHT IN THE GREAT BLACKOUT

Financial Post, *January 21, 1998*

Thankfully, the vast majority of those who read the *Financial Post* have never been in a disaster area or a community where a state of emergency has been declared — which is a blessing. But as an increasing number of Canadians can testify, these are the kinds of circumstances that refocus one's priorities from the day to day of academe or Bay Street or politics to the more urgent issues of keeping your family warm and safe and helping others in greater need.

Some commentators have chosen to write about what the Great Ice Storm means in relation to large issues such as sovereignty, the privatization of Ontario Hydro, and the prime minister's popularity. All of which is to belittle what folks go through in these kinds of disasters. As someone whose home was without power for almost eight days, let me share the experiences and impressions left by working through that kind of event.

- Long convoys of armed forces trailers loaded with generators and supplies moving along Highway 401 on the first Friday of the storm.
- Royal Military College and Queen's University students going door to door to check on old people and the infirm.
- The feeling of relief in Mallorytown, Ontario, without power or gasoline and cut off by trees across the roads, as a long and determined convoy of army vehicles comes down Highway 2 with help.
- The electrician who comes to your home twice on a cold Sunday night, once at ten and again near midnight, to connect a small

generator to start a furnace. His policy is no double time and no time and a half during the crisis.

- The pharmacist who drives every day from Montreal to Cowansville to dispense by candlelight even though his own home is cold and he could have closed and let people drive to the hospital for emergency prescriptions.

- The food-store owner in Mallorytown who works eighteen hours a day to keep the place open and stocked and to get food to the shelter, and then spends the nights as a volunteer fireman; whose wife helps lead troops down the back roads of the township to check on folks; and whose eight-year-old son volunteers at the sign-in desk at the shelter in the Legion.

- Police dispatched to Kingston intersections because people are being so polite we have courtesy traffic jams.

- The hundreds who turn out, many without power themselves, to a breakfast to launch fund-raising for those in uninsured difficulty.

- The *Kingston Whig-Standard,* which, despite power failure and generalized difficulty, never missed an edition, and the local private radio station, which became the centre for all communications when CBC-TV's tower on Wolfe Island collapsed.

- Radio reporters who worked around the clock giving vital information, and the *Globe and Mail, Financial Post,* and *Toronto Star* carriers who got their papers to the prescribed doors despite immense dislocation and downed trees and power lines.

- The food-store owner in Sharbot Lake who gave the key to his store to the local shelter manager with instructions to "take whatever you need," and the Kitchener-Waterloo meat packer who shipped thousands of hot dogs to shelters.

- The Kingston-based bagel shop that shipped 5,000 bagels a day from its Cornwall and Kingston locations.

- The Corrections Canada institutions that shipped food, mattresses, and generators throughout the region, and Ontario Natural Resources officials who organized catering services.

- The local restaurateur on King Street who gave discounts to linemen, soldiers, and volunteers, and the Concordia University student in Montreal who dropped everything to volunteer at a shelter.

- The newly amalgamated politicians who forgot about municipal, township, or county borders to get the job done.
- Reservists from all over Canada who volunteered to join their regular-force colleagues; the policemen and -women who worked sixteen-hour shifts.
- Companies that made donations of money and people and expertise; the Hydro linemen from Oshawa and Toronto who invaded our street with new poles and unbelievable energy in the middle of a bitter snowstorm to produce the miracle of electricity.

I have no detached analysis of what this all means. I was not very detached. And neither were the thousands who came to help, which may be the most important reflection of all.

JOHNSON FORGOES AMBITION TO ADVANCE FEDERALIST CAUSE

Financial Post, *March 4, 1998*

Daniel Johnson deserved better. The most frank and determined federalist to hold the premier's job in Quebec in a quarter of a century, Johnson, with his determined, no-nonsense, unemotional approach, should have been what modern-day politics demanded. Sadly, while he could deal with his direct foes in the sovereignist movement, dealing with his allies, especially those in the federal Liberal Party, proved in the end to be too large a burden.

It is ironic that Prime Minister Chrétien was in New York when Johnson announced that he was stepping down. Chrétien had also been at the United Nations during the first referendum campaign, when Johnson tried to confirm that, yes, Ottawa would support a measure of uniqueness within Confederation for Quebec. Chrétien knew nothing about it, or so he said when a microphone was thrust at him in New York.

In the last referendum, Quebec sovereignists had a field day. On the separatist side, there was Lucien Bouchard, still Bloc Québécois leader in Ottawa, soothing everyone about some post–Yes vote partnership and negotiation with Ottawa, with Bouchard himself as the chief negotiator for Quebec. On the federalist side, there was the stalwart and steady Johnson, backed up by the able and passionate Conservative leader, Jean Charest, and by the unfocused and complacent Chrétien.

For all the help Charest could and did give, Johnson had to carry the Chrétien dead weight. Recently, it appeared that Bouchard would have to face Johnson on Johnson's terms (economic underperformance in Quebec, collapse in social services and municipal grants, and usurious tax levels). Then along came the Supreme Court of Canada reference, which allowed Bouchard to get things back on his terms — defending the Québécois people from federal onslaught. Johnson could never trust his federal counterparts not to undercut his position or incompetently advance the sovereignist interest by sins of omission or commission. In the end, I suspect that this was the burden that forced him to say enough is enough.

A gentlemen who has always been dignified in the politics of his people, Johnson reminds me of the former Conservative leader Robert Stanfield, who considered questions before he responded and usually avoided any cheap or demeaning assault on his opponents. Johnson bears the treachery of his federal Liberal allies with a public equanimity that some confuse with disengagement. Others see it simply as dignity and good manners.

He comes from a family that has served Quebec and Canada with great distinction. As a young Conservative and Union Nationale youth, I remember going door to door in a largely English-speaking Liberal stronghold for his father, Daniel Johnson, Sr., a man who sought to bridge the solitudes with an approach to Quebec nationalism that affirmed the province's rights within Confederation. Daniel's brother, Pierre-Marc, was a moderate Quebec premier and soft sovereignist whose efforts to find a solution within Canada at first drove extremists like Jacques Parizeau from the party. The present narrow line followed by Quebec sovereignists is largely because Pierre-Marc, a distinguished lawyer and academic, is no longer active in party politics.

Daniel Johnson's decision to resign must be seen for what it is — a selfless setting aside of partisan ambition to advance the federalist cause. By stepping aside, he takes the medium-term tactical options away from the sovereignists. Further, he gives the federalist side an unequalled time for renewal and expansion. One hopes he gives proponents of the sophomoric approach of the Liberal government in Ottawa some time to cool their heels and reflect a bit on their decision to send federal ministers into Quebec to counter Bouchard. From Bouchard's view, this will allow him to make the actual opponent in the next provincial election utterly irrelevant and turn the election into a "who can best defend Quebec against federal incursion" contest. In a campaign like that, the PQ does not even need a platform.

As has been the case throughout his political career, Daniel Johnson has put the interests of the public and his province first. For the battles he has fought for Canada, and above all for his sacrifice of Monday, all Canadians owe him a debt of gratitude.

CHAREST'S RARE CHANCE TO DEFINE NEW CONFEDERAL UNION

Financial Post, *March 28, 1998*

Political courage is not a commodity in great abundance these days, what with politics by polls and media pressures. Risk-averse government has surely been the Liberals' main reason for political success at the federal level, especially when they had only that amount of courage necessary to adopt, holus bolus, all the policies of the previous government they campaigned against.

Which is what makes Jean Charest's decision to go to Quebec and join the provincial Liberals all the more remarkable. In less than three weeks, he decided to leave the leadership he sought and almost won in 1993, then accepted when the party was absolutely flat on its back after the 1993 election — and just when he was beginning to hit his stride. He was immensely popular in caucus and throughout the party. The fact that Reform targeted him as the reason their illusions of a unified ideological rump could not proceed is ample evidence of his resolve and ability to "serve and protect" the Conservative cause. At thirty-nine years of age, he had a long and compelling future ahead of him as party leader. He was at home with federal issues and concerns, and had begun to strengthen on foreign policy and defence issues.

He now enters a world filled with Quebec Liberals, who, while less doctrinaire and centralist than the present crop of federal Liberals, are nevertheless Liberals. At the same time, he has accepted the risk that a silly comment from Stéphane Dion or Marcel Masse, or even Jean Chrétien, could seriously torpedo the cause of a renewed federalism and an invigorated Quebec economy. Whatever network he will build, Charest will be in the hands of the fates in a party he does not know.

There can be little doubt that leaders in business and politics, and thousands of Canadians from all walks of life and from all regions, wanted him to go to Quebec. This is a result of the immense goodwill he earned for his outstanding support of the No side in the last referendum, as well as his performance in the TV debate in the last federal election campaign, during which he displayed a passionate determination to keep this country together. It will not be lost on him that Chrétien's response to his stellar performance in the referendum campaign was to pull the plug on his televised address to the No supporters and the nation on referendum night, while Preston Manning's response to his debate performance was to launch anti-Quebecer ads to save his own collapsing campaign. Charest will not be able to count on either of these two politicians as he sallies forth in Quebec to take on the separatist premier, Lucien Bouchard.

In fact, Charest will have an uncommon opportunity in national history to define the kind of new confederal union within Canada that Quebecers wish him to build. He will have the moral high ground and will be able to dismiss the Bouchardist view of a nineteenth-century sovereignty that is as irrelevant for Quebec as it would be for Canada itself. Charest will not be the spokesman for a tired federalism that comforts the Ottawa establishment. He is more likely to be a strong advocate of a new confederal state where all provinces have enhanced sovereignty and the central government operates more efficiently and in less dominating a fashion. This too will take courage.

Charest's caucus colleagues in Ottawa have also shown immense courage. He was their popular, vigorous, engaging, and articulate leader. They dealt with the media feeding frenzy and his difficult decision-making period with grace and dignity. He clearly felt that the country came ahead of family convenience and private political plans. His caucus gave him the space, time, support, and loyalty he needed in this difficult time. They did their ridings, party, and oath of office proud. In the end, public life in this country is about more than partisanship, one-upmanship, or even uniting the right. It is about uniting Canada. That task takes sacrifice, statesmanship, and above all, courage.

This week, Jean Charest, his wife and family, and the Conservative caucus showed that they possess all in great abundance.

NOT EVERYONE'S NOSTALGIC FOR THE DAYS OF TRUDEAUMANIA

Financial Post, *April 15, 1998*

The celebrations of late around the anniversary of the phenomenon known as Trudeaumania may have been warmly nostalgic for some. For many Canadians, however, Pierre Trudeau's period in government evokes not nostalgic warmth but a recognition that the excesses of his government defined the problems of our political landscape for decades to come.

The spendthrift nature of his government — with John Turner, as finance minister, taking Ottawa into deficit and debt — began a cycle from which we are only now emerging. The massive use of federal spending power has been both an economic and a constitutional problem. Trudeau's arbitrary use of the War Measures Act in 1970 gave fresh life to the separatist cause. His contempt for both the legitimate aspirations of Quebecers and the legitimate aspirations of Canadians living in the West divided the country further. The National Energy Program imposed on the West was a serious confiscatory attack on provincial resource revenues.

The over-regulation of investment that he ushered in with the Foreign Investment Review Agency diluted and diminished economic growth. The expansion of the state apparatus, the use of the RCMP in dirty tricks in Quebec, and the assault on the armed forces via integration all further weakened the country. Armed forces integration was not only a costly and unhelpful mistake, but also a morale depressant of serious proportions. The foreign policy made Canada unreliable and undependable. The constant anti-Americanism of his government was ill-conceived and unconstructive.

There were events that seemed to symbolize the disconnection between Ottawa and the rest of the country. High unemployment, long postal strikes, the exasperation of Western farmers all flared up in ways that exposed an administration that had replaced public sensitivity with intellectual arrogance.

Those of us who campaigned as Tory candidates against Pierre Trudeau's high-spending, high-borrowing, and over-centralized and -regulated government came close to stopping him in the 1972 general election. Under the leadership of the frugal, humane, and decent Robert Stanfield, Tories came within two seats of throwing out Trudeau's government. He was sustained in the end by the New Democratic Party under David Lewis.

The excessive use of the state continued for essentially another decade, but for the short but heroic Clark administration in 1979–80.

So while many may well wish to celebrate the Trudeau vision, some of us who fought big government door to door have a different recollection. It's one of arrogance, excessive use of the state, insensitivity, fiscal morass, and a pervasive condescension towards business, the provinces, labour, and anyone with different views. The arrogance sowed divisive seeds that sprout on a perennial basis. And they continue to remind us all that Canada's cohesiveness as a modern state requires an approach to public life that does not always impose views but consistently works with others to build consensus.

In the Trudeau government's view, the only programs that mattered were government programs, the only policies that counted were from his administration, the only answers that were correct were his answers. Dissent, broad policy development, shared consensus — all were diminished by him. His priority was dividing up the pie, not expanding it. Spending the nation's wealth on program solutions was his path. Understanding how to create wealth and standing back to liberate the forces of enterprise were not options for him.

We have all paid for that ever since, in part because the approach ushered in a period when belief in the value of an affordable safety net was replaced with a broad disregard for the effect of spending on deficits and debt. This helped produce a culture that looked to government not for what it should do, but for things it could not afford. This culture seemed to suggest that the borrowing capacity of government was essentially endless, and that the debt-bearing capacity of the Canadian taxpayer had no limit. But there are limits; frugality and fiscal discipline are not barriers to a civil society but fundamental prerequisites. That, in essence, was the area where Trudeau misled so many. That is where we must never make the same mistake again.

GENTLE GIANT DIDN'T KNOW THE MEANING OF SURRENDER

Financial Post, *May 13, 1998*

It is rare that you meet one person with the skills, heart, and integrity to combine, in one all-too-short life, the roles of outstanding journalist, crusading public servant, and inspired corporate executive to enrich the world we live in in a host of different ways. David Allen, a vice-president at Inco, died last week at fifty-five. He died as he had lived, a big person, with a large view and a big heart, who never understood the meaning of surrender.

As a *Toronto Star* bureau chief at Queen's Park, he was a journalist's journalist. Determined to find the truth, however unpleasant, he was also someone who embraced fairness and balance in all that he wrote. Unlike those who attacked governments or politicians for sport, David Allen attacked only when an attack was richly deserved. His professional commitment to the considered judgement increased immensely the power of his pen and his opinion.

In government, he served in the sensitive attorney general's department in Ontario, and was a constant source of advice, counsel, and policy on everything from violence in hockey to the war on organized crime, the patriation of the constitution, and the handling of the Mississauga rail disaster. The right of the public to know and the need to protect the public interest were not opposing principles for David Allen. They were joint pillars supporting the administration of justice and the protection of people in the community. He provided significant leadership in public-information programs that assailed drinking and driving and family violence, all of which helped save lives and avert heartache for thousands of Ontarians. During the difficult negotiations between the provinces and Ottawa on the Charter of Rights and Freedoms, David Allen was a key figure in the activities of Roy McMurtry, then Ontario's attorney general and a central player in the process, negotiations, and court challenges that saw Canada get its charter.

He left public service for the private sector and joined Inco, the venerable Canadian mining company, as a vice-president of corporate and public affairs. In that role, he led the way not only to new environmental initiatives, but also to historic wage, pension, and retirement agreements for employees that literally set the standard for mining companies everywhere. He was a trusted voice on the inside and a respected spokesperson on the outside for Inco employees, managers, and shareholders.

David Allen was a true professional as a journalist, a committed servant of the public in government, and a voice for progress, community service, and shareholder rights in the private sector. Throughout the many paths he took in his working career, he won the reputation of a gentle giant — not just for his size, but also for the kindness and loyalty he showed to his family and colleagues.

He was also blessed with an uncommon amount of intelligence, talent, and good judgement. But he was less fortunate in fighting cancer, kidney disease, and cardiac problems for many years. Here, too, he could not surrender. Though he required dialysis three times a week, Allen simply built into his travel schedule those places where such facilities were available. This meant stops in cities like Paris, London, and Jakarta en route to his various destinations.

His heart was a large as Canada itself. His patriotism was deep, gentle, and determined. His appetite for life was something to behold. The friends and confidants who knew, loved, and respected him were legion. His was not a life of self-promotion, personal ambition, or artificial celebrity. His was a life of quiet competence, pervasive loyalty, and indefatigable service to the causes he believed in. Premiers, prime ministers, CEOs, and the heavyweights of journalism all knew that he was the consummate professional always.

His wife and best friend, Jackie Boyle — also a focused and outstanding journalist and professional — will not, along with their children, Johnny, Mer, Elizabeth, and Matt, be alone in facing the sadness of his untimely passing or in celebrating the massive successes and achievements of David's life.

They will be joined by the many in Ontario, Canada, and around the world whose lives he touched so gently and in so many constructive ways.

PART THREE

The Case for
Economic and
Social Balance

THERE IS A COMPELLING "WILL TO BALANCE" IN MANY OF THESE pieces on our economic and social priorities. On occasion, I push towards the centre when the rightward pull of policies seems either disjointed or insensitive. Similarly, when taxation that is excessive or bureaucracy that is oppressive are either sustained or promoted by those who are sure they know what is best for millions of others, I will push to the right with equal determination.

The nation and enterprise balance I seek is less embracing of the wisdom of those who govern and more embracing of the wisdom of the governed. The national balance requires a mix of policies, a portfolio of ideas that err always on the side of public responsibility and personal freedom. Excess in redressing an imbalance may well produce new imbalances that are worse.

∾

It's Wrong to Assume Tax Cuts Contradict Social Responsibility

Financial Post, *September 21, 1996*

It is fascinating how the forces of orthodoxy coalesce whenever tax cuts are mentioned. It is as if the notion of giving back taxpayers' money contravenes some moral edict. The campaign launched by the Progressive Conservative Youth Federation to commit its party to tax reductions was embraced by party membership because it gave expression to the angst that Canadians have about money and government. That angst is best expressed through the adage "If you send it, they will spend it." To suggest that there is some truth to this adage is to suggest that Prime Minister Chrétien enjoys golf more than he does meeting with his parliamentary caucus.

That Finance Minister Paul Martin should attack the idea of tax cuts can mean one of two things. If Liberal opposition to free trade, privatization, and spending reductions between 1983 and 1993 was predictive, then we can expect Liberal tax-cut proposals either before the next election or right after. It could also mean that the folks at Imperial Finance have provided one of those marvellous briefings, indicating why tax cuts are unwise at this time. Their argument, for which there is both precedent and echo in every finance department around the world, is that tax cuts will slow progress towards a balanced budget. The fact that an increase in U.S. interest rates or a shift in monetary policy here, in the U.S., in Japan, or in Germany could dwarf the impact of tax cuts on our deficit is conveniently left unaddressed. These days, all economies are interdependent and held hostage by decisions made elsewhere. With only 3 percent of the world's capital normally found in Canada, this is as true of our country as it is of any other, if not more so. Saying that the greatest risk to our deficit progress is tax cuts is like suggesting that the traffic jams in Tel Aviv are the greatest risk to Mideast peace.

Joe Clark was elected prime minister of Canada in 1979 in part because his party promised mortgage-interest deductibility for homeowners in Canada. This would have been a tremendous tax cut for middle-income Canadians, yet because it had a proposed ceiling, it would not have unduly advantaged the very wealthy. But surprise, surprise, Imperial Finance was opposed. James Gillies, a professor at the Schulich School of Business at York University and a senior policy adviser to Clark at the time, often tells the story of how the Imperial Finance briefing book on mortgage-interest deduction was mostly about why it should not, or could not, be done. And it never happened.

The economist Jeff Rubin of Wood Gundy said more than a year ago that there was a lack of liquidity to fuel domestic demand, and that while inflation had been low and stable, taxes at all levels had been increasing, not to the detriment of the wealthy but to the detriment of middle-income earners who were carrying high debt loads with little disposable earnings. Discretionary savings were at an all-time low. This does not strike me as a case for avoiding tax cuts.

There are structural realities in the U.S. tax system that constitute competitive advantage. The relief that homeowners get is a key advantage, as are lower marginal tax rates. Canada is not the United States. Public health care, a staple of our economic and social stability, is but one reason we cannot simply mimic U.S. tax rates. But leaving money in the hands of working people who have earned it is never wrong. There is no contradiction between fiscal prudence, social responsibility, and tax cuts. The test is in the balance. The Reform Party has surprisingly, considering its Social Credit ancestry, chosen the bureaucratic view of Imperial Finance that tax cuts are not appropriate at this time. At present, Liberals and New Democrats are in the very same boat.

Tax cuts are not a proxy for pandering. They are a proxy for a profound redesign of how we govern ourselves. To suggest that any redesign must be mean, or driven by social irresponsibility, is insulting. Coming from Ottawa, where many millions are being spent on renewal of the Parliament Buildings (with the House of Commons about to be moved into a cafeteria), such a suggestion borders on farce. Responsible, income-tested tax cuts will help the consumer, the graduate, the middle-aged parent, and the farmer. Creatively done, they can reward work and liberate demand. They need not be unjust to anyone.

BUILDING A BASIC INCOME FLOOR FOR CANADIANS TO STAND ON
Inroads 6, June 1997

It was at a Conservative policy conference at Niagara Falls in 1969 where, based on a paper from the research office, Robert Stanfield and his party first reflected on the benefits of a more efficient and humane income-security system implied by a guaranteed annual income. The paper envisaged an eventual end to rules-based, overlapping income-security programs at the federal and provincial levels in favour of a negative tax-based universal income floor, above the poverty line, available to all Canadians in need.

I was nineteen at the time. The paper offered practical and humanitarian reasons for the collective and individual benefits of this more holistic approach to equality of opportunity that appealed to me then, and that have stayed with me in every political assignment I have accepted since. A decade after the conference, I served as principal secretary and then associate cabinet secretary at Queen's Park when the Davis government brought in the Guaranteed Annual Income (GAI) supplement for seniors: a holistic response to a compelling and measurable problem of indigent seniors, largely female, facing an unacceptable prospect of prolonged poverty.

While the GAI was more generous than Ottawa's laudable but meagre Guaranteed Income Supplement, introduced in the 1960s, it was flawed in many ways. It was one initiative in one province, limited to one age segment. It topped up existing programs for which meaningful long-term guarantees were, as we have since learned thanks to federal cutbacks and transfer "re-profiling," largely illusionary. In that regard, it simply mirrored what has been wrong with income-security policy in Canada for some time — namely, its failure to design a framework that responds to income collapse without regard to age, occupation, location, employment, or disability, and that does so non-judgmentally and without excessive bureaucracy.

It is hard to fault the motivation of those academics, civil servants, and politicians who crafted separate rationales, policy frameworks, and operative regulations for different programs designed to address income needs resulting from different circumstances and for different reasons. But in the end, whether one injures one's back at a job site or has the local steel mill or cod fishery shut down, the issue is income. The disruption to family security, the threat to a marriage's stability, and the collapse in local buying power all occur because income is gone.

Whatever the reason for the collapse in income, the local cost of living, and living respectably above the poverty line, does not change by virtue of one's eligibility for program A or ineligibility for program B. Letting the condition of people's lives filter its way through regulation-driven programs until it lands on the welfare catch-all — itself highly regulated and hypothecated on provincial and municipal particularities — is no response to the core question of individual dignity and self-respect. When companies and governments buy out senior employees, the main item in the severance package is always income. The case for the status quo in government assistance might be sustainable if it could be argued that the present spider's web of programs (which are sticky enough to entrap but not strong enough to support) had produced real progress — that is, less poverty overall, higher levels of return to the labour market, greater independence, and increased consumer confidence. Sadly, there is no such overall progress to support.

Incomes collapse for a host of reasons: illness, infirmity, a pause to re-educate or build skills, age, youth, local and massive job evaporation. It is possible, if not simple, to establish what bringing collapsed incomes above the poverty line in different Canadian communities would entail.

The principle that every citizen should have the right to bridging support at liveable levels when there is income collapse balances the principle that the state has the right to deduct tax at source from the income an individual earns. It would be the ultimate socialist excess to suggest that the state has an *a priori* right to take money from the citizen with income for its general purposes (such as hiring public servants, servicing debt, or financing tax-deferral programs for industry), but has no concurrent responsibility to respond to the citizen's income collapse.

Those who argue that any such income-insurance program would break the bank should first reflect on what we are now spending, in some cases quite wastefully. The MacDonald Royal Commission on Canada's Economic Union and Development Prospects (yes, the same one that argued for a leap of faith to free trade) reviewed income-security spending a decade ago. Highlights included unemployment insurance at $11.6 billion, old-age security at $11.4 billion, pension-related tax exemptions and deductions at $7.6 billion, social assistance at $6.6 billion, family allowance at $2.4 billion, child tax exemptions at $1.4 billion, a child tax credit of $1.1 billion, and married exemptions at $2 billion.

If you include the basic exemption — which is supposed to reflect the progressive nature of our tax system — one could add another $14 billion. This still leaves Native programs, veterans' pensions, and training allowances. In fact, when combined all together with provincial expenditures, but

excluding the personal basic tax exemption, the total reached $61 billion —
and that was a decade ago. In 1990, expenditures, excluding the personal
basic exemption and the married exemption, totalled some $67.1 billion.[1]
So this is hardly a question of new wasteful spending. There is a large, well-
intentioned spending machine now operating under a huge set of different
rule books and eligibility criteria.

Although the idea of a guaranteed annual income has been discussed
for years, no real consideration has been given to replacing all of these programs with a GAI, mainly because the federal bureaucracy has ruled out
the idea as prohibitively expensive. When I served in Ottawa in 1991, a
proposal by John Harter of the International Labour Office for a guaranteed annual income was rejected by senior mandarins, who maintained
that any new program aimed at supplementing the income of Canadians
who were among the working "poor" could not be initiated during the
fight to trim the deficit. Instead, new, modest initiatives in the same direction should be considered, they said. The bureaucracy was, in fact, following the classic incrementalist, or "Goldilocks," approach to public policy.
Policy A is too extreme or too expensive. Policy C is utterly impossible in
the present context. And the incrementalist policy in the centre (Policy B)
is just right!

The bureaucratic preference for piecemeal income supplementation by
dependency category and subgroup has been sustained by a host of different reports and commissions. These include the Castonguay Report in
Quebec in 1971, the federal "Orange Paper" under the Liberals in the
1970s, the MacDonald Royal Commission, and Ontario's Social Assistance
Review Committee. These reports have tended to take a "support and supplementation" approach to income security, assuming that the GAI is too
expensive and, in any case, that only income-tested programs for the working poor could be sold to the electorate.

Sadly, this is essentially the thinking behind the Child Tax Credit offered
by Ottawa's Pierre Pettigrew to the provinces and, at the time of writing,
largely embraced. Even more sadly, this piecemeal approach could produce
so cluttered a patchwork of expensive and poorly targeted income-security

---

[1] Michael Krashinsky, *Putting the Poor to Work vs Helping the Poor* (Toronto: C.D.
Howe, 1996), p. 99.

programs that we will see public support for this vital area of social justice and economic balance erode.

To give Pettigrew his due, there is a positive side to his approach. Having cut his teeth politically as an adviser to then Quebec Liberal leader Claude Ryan, Pettigrew has been inoculated against his government's centralist bias and thus remains sensitive to the need to ensure a strong role for the provinces in defining and delivering the program. His approach to negotiations on the Child Tax Credit was an improvement over previous top-down, "Ottawa knows best" scenarios. Any integrated basic income floor with a hope of implementation will have to be built on such a joint and collegial social-policy framework.

The twin forces of unimpeded, planet-wide capital mobility and the massive diffusion of liberating technologies mean the end of the traditional work pattern, as part of both the life cycle and the earnings-and-savings cycle. This transition will bring economic growth through higher labour and capital productivity, but with much less employment stability than was the case with an economy based on resource harvesting and labour-intensive manufacturing. This has continue to mean huge economic dislocation for millions of people in the industrialized world, including too many people in Canada. In regions with traditional and thus declining industries — fisheries, lumber, pulp and paper, mining, manufacturing, and refining — employment devastation is particularly oppressive.

Clearly, a basic income floor would be only a small part of the answer to the jobless aspects of some kinds of economic growth. Policies that encourage job sharing, improve conditions for part-time workers — by giving them broader access to benefits and pensions — assist the volunteer sector, and encourage hiring in that sector through tax-based incentives could have a significant impact. But there is no justification for leaving income security where it has always been. Continuing to approach income security by the norms of the 1960s when life, work, and income cycles are so drastically changed is utterly unrealistic.

The notion that one's eligibility for support is to be determined by some statutory or regulatory attachment to a subgroup — the handicapped, children, the aged, the narrowly defined unemployed or welfare-eligible indigents — does much for social work caseloads and program designers but very little for self-respect and personal dignity.

As a capitalist, I know that those of us who favour greater freedom to invest, and thus to expand and alter the economic framework in order to liberate the forces of excellence and growth, cannot have it both ways. One cannot radically alter the structure and nature of work, and thus the sources of economic stability for the average wage earner — as new technology and globalization are doing — without at the same time redesigning the framework for income stability to make it more supportive of the user and less biased towards the bureaucracy.

Today, applicants for income security must find a way (however contrived) to fit into programs designed on a 1960s model — when the world is a 1990s one, with far more unpredictable income and work cycles. A bias that subjects those needing income to make ends meet to 1960s rules, categories, and programs, while still allowing those with capital to invest to benefit fully from all the potential of 1990s technologies, is a recipe for social chaos. Income gaps will grow. Intergenerational pressures will build. Levels of social civility will decline as levels of criminal activity, non-violent and otherwise, increase. Unless one is in the business of private security, none of this holds any promise.

Yet despite these genuine and profound dangers, established politicians, bureaucracies, and most income-security experts refuse to consider a holistic approach to income security. It is fascinating to see how self-fulfilling assumptions and prophesies feed the holistic policy vacuum:

- As long as there is no integrated plan, there is no basis upon which to compare its effectiveness with the existing "Tower of Babel" approach.
- Using deficit constraints as a rationale for incrementalist solutions never allows for a real analysis of the cost savings that would result from replacing all group-specific income-security programs.
- The lack of a cohesive and holistic proposal around which provincial co-operation could be solicited results in the assumption of an absence of proposals for such co-operation, which in turn provides an excuse for not developing a cohesive and holistic proposal. How's that for a compelling tautology!

Not even prime ministers can break this log-jam of self-constraining half-truisms. In November 1991, as discussions that resulted in family allowances giving way to a child tax credit heavily tilted to help the working poor were proceeding, Prime Minister Mulroney wrote to his minister of health and welfare, Benoît Bouchard, encouraging his department to see this initiative as a first step in the development of what would be a sea change in income security. This reform would be set out in a White Paper that would include a guaranteed annual income as a way to radically modernize our income-security system so as to enable people to adapt to the impact of economic transformation.

As senior policy adviser in the Prime Minister's Office at the time, I had the sense that had the prime minister and the minister of health not been weighed down by the need to restart the constitutional process — which had collapsed with Newfoundland's rejection of the Meech Lake Accord — the government would have made a serious policy thrust along these lines. The minister was, in my view, genuinely interested. However, the determination of his bureaucrats, along with those in the human resources and finance departments, to kill the baby in the incubator arrested any progress on that broader front.

~

Canada's social-policy history reflects a bureaucratic bias towards a piecemeal approach to income security. Prior to the Second World War, mothers' allowances, workman's compensation, and early forms of unemployment insurance (UIC) began. Following the war came family allowances and elderly benefits (universal at seventy, and means-tested between sixty-five and sixty-nine). Special social assistance was introduced for the blind, the disabled, and the unemployed, who were not eligible for unemployment insurance. In the 1960s, the pace quickened: the Canada Pension Plan, Quebec Pension Plan, and Canada Assistance Plan were all introduced in 1966. A host of federal labour-market programs aimed at job creation and training were developed, and the age of old-age pension eligibility was lowered to sixty-five. The Guaranteed Income Supplement for seniors was introduced in 1967, and the UIC program was significantly expanded in 1971.

To be fair, those who worked on the income-security sections of the MacDonald Commission were sensitive to the limits of a piecemeal approach. The commissioners admitted that "a more complete rationalization is a worthwhile target in the reform of our income security transfer system. This will mean replacing much of the present complex range of programmes with one transfer-delivered either through the tax system adjusted to pay out benefits monthly, or through separate cheques, a method similar to that used in current Old Age Security programmes."

They expressed doubts about a GAI because, according to long-held wisdom, the guaranteed levels necessary would be prohibitively expensive. But the commissioners did at least consider different administrative and cost/variable scenarios before arriving at a more modest universal income-security program to be phased in over a long time.

The MacDonald Commission's proposal for free trade with the U.S. was taken up, but proposals on reformed income security were not. Patrick Grady summed up the observed effects of the piecemeal approach that was left us in 1995 as follows:

- The current system is ineffective and too costly.
- Child benefits were, until 1993, largely untargeted.
- Most critics find the UI program focused on passive income support rather than on improving job prospects and skills for the unemployed.
- UI prolongs higher unemployment by prolonging unproductive job search and making seasonal, rather than permanent, work more attractive.
- Ninety percent of benefits do not go to low-income families.
- Existing social-assistance benefits create a poverty trap and can foster dependency.
- Employment at low wages can result in limited to zero net benefit to current social-assistance recipients.
- People seeking to break out of low-income or income-security traps may well find any incremental earnings taxed at about 100 percent — which is twice the rate of the highest marginal tax rate on the wealthiest incomes in the country.[2]

---

[2] Patrick Grady, *Income Security Reform and the Concept of a Guaranteed Income* (Kingston, ON: Queen's University School of Policy Studies, 1994), pp. 168–72.

In order to frame a holistic guaranteed income policy (or basic income floor, as I prefer to call it), we must be frank about the philosophical divide that lies at the core of policy debates on income security in most industrialized countries. Not to do so is to be naive about the political process of design, advocacy, and implementation, and to seed any new initiative with the ingredients of failure.

The way a society poses the question of why income collapses traditionally carries with it a moral judgement about the person whose income it is. Classically, American conservatives have worried that any automatic eligibility, rather than eligibility based on infirmity, illness, or age, necessarily bestows societal approval on the non-earning citizen. Furthermore, the concentration of unemployment in a specific area or region, or among a specific group, gives rise to judgements about collective dependency attributes, judgements too often quickly embraced by policy-makers and fellow citizens who should know better.

Laurence M. Mead, an American social commentator and no supporter of entitlement programs, addressed the difference between liberals and conservatives around the issue of poverty in this way:

> Liberals tend to be pessimistic about competence, viewing people as overwhelmed by their environment. So they ask special help for them and tend to be permissive about enforcing conventional mores. Conservatives are much more optimistic, hence more demanding and less permissive. ...
>
> Liberal analysts are quick to find impediments to employment, because they view the poor as helpless victims. Conservatives see fewer barriers and call for less help, because they impute more ability to the poor. ...
>
> The poor are either innocent supplicants of whom nothing can be expected, or they are lazy exploiters who can and should shape up. These are not disagreements that any hard evidence can resolve.[3]

---

[3] Lawrence M. Mead, "The New Politics of the New Poverty," *The Public Interest* (1993): 13–16.

While this American take on the issues around poverty may well strike many Canadians as irrelevant to a Canadian debate, the truth is that similar biases have distorted Canadian income-security policy. Governments have felt comfortable only with programs that respond to income collapse for collectively defined groups ("unemployed," "aged," "handicapped," "injured in the workplace," "veteran," "child"), largely because those were seen as the collective categories for which voters would accept income support.

The fact that someone was simply short of sufficient income to live with dignity was not seen as sufficient justification for societal support. Yet interestingly enough, we seem not to care about the reasons we get tax revenue from individuals. We don't care if they were brighter, worked harder, studied more, had greater business sense, received a legal stock tip, or got outstanding tax advice. We don't care if they worked forty hours a week or ninety. We do not care if they are alcoholics or have three colour TVs.

How their income reaches a certain level is unimportant. The state simply taxes it. Yet when income collapses, the state takes a more judgemental view. I am troubled deeply by this double standard. If the state uses no moral magnifying glass as it taxes on the way up, what possible rationale — other than a meddlesome, self-important, and moralistic political and bureaucratic bias — could be used to justify the contrary view when incomes collapse?

In order to find solutions in this area today, it is imperative to understand the blurring between social and economic policy that has occurred, as well as the need to think beyond these narrow policy areas. A society that promotes free trade, capital mobility, the expansion of technology, and enhanced competitive advantage cannot ignore the resulting job dislocation and changes to the structure of the workplace and the labour market. To do so is to be mindful of the prosperity for those with capital or those who manage it, and completely disengaged from those who are not so blessed — namely, the vast majority of law-abiding taxpayers.

In this context, a basic income floor is not a new social program or an added fiscal burden. It is simply another essential investment vital to promoting productivity, competition, and economic growth. Partially jobless economic recoveries and structural employment barriers caused by rapid technological change are unavoidable elements of the current economic framework. This framework is neither reversible nor reprehensible — it is the reality of a competitive world. Failing to build a basic income floor in Canada to adapt to the vicissitudes of that new reality would be as harmful to our economic development as would be banning software development — somewhere between madness and myopia.

If it is done right, a basic income floor could diminish federal-provincial and labour-management tensions. If it is done right, it could, over time, reduce the net burden of state spending. The starting principle for a working paper exploring how to design and implement a basic income floor is clear: it should ultimately replace all non-contributory transfers to individuals from Ottawa, the provinces, and the municipalities, except for health-care and education transfers. The operating principle is also clear: transfers would be done via the income-tax filing process — which automatically includes all provinces and Ottawa.

Many of the relevant design issues were well addressed in a paper released by Human Resources Canada in 1994 as part of Lloyd Axworthy's stillborn social-policy review.[4] It stated that the goal of a universally available top-up would be to assist the working poor first; it would later be expanded to include the unemployed in a staged and realistic way. The paper then considered various formulas with which to account for special costs, such as those generated by a disability, or to account for higher costs in remote regions.

The core principles underlying a basic income floor, and the way to get there from here, are clear. The proposal should be developed by a federal-provincial working group, with input from business, labour, and the volunteer sector. It should offer meaningful incentives for provinces to participate and to pool resources.

During its implementation phase — likely no less than five years — a basic income floor program should track contributions from federal and provincial programs that it replaces. A basic income commission could be a joint federal-provincial body established to administer the year-to-year

---

[4] Canada, *Guaranteed Annual Income: A Supplementary Paper* (Ottawa: Queen's Printer, 1994).

operation in terms of rates of top-up. It would also track the impact of changing demographics. The program would be delivered through the income tax system. With the GST tax rebate system, we already have in place a mechanism that recognizes that those who may not earn enough to justify a tax return can file for tax credits and receive those credits well before the tax-filing cycle.

These are manageable working principles. The core notion that every Canadian has the right to live reasonably above the poverty line is no different from the core principle that every law-abiding investor has the right to do with his or her money whatever he or she pleases. The two principles should co-exist in our institutions and policies.

The debate about what we do with a balanced budget dividend rings rather hollow when accumulated debt is still added to by the big provinces and waste in social spending is far from fully addressed. But that debate would acquire a new significance and urgency if someone had the courage and will to put the goal of a consolidated basic income floor on the public agenda. Its benefits would be enormous. Billions of dollars now spent for group-related social programs would be spent far more efficiently as the costs of bureaucracies and caseloads in many of these programs were eliminated.

The issue of tax cuts being only for the wealthy would disappear, with all being eligible for a boost from the tax system when incomes fell. The dignity of all citizens without state judgement or meddling would be affirmed. The basic income floor would also provide clarity and purpose in a balanced economic policy for a free society.

What of the argument that such a program would produce disincentives to work? Critics who make that argument level the same charge against the current system, with its plethora of unemployment insurance, welfare, and income-supplement programs. During the fight to slash the federal and provincial deficits, eligibility criteria were tightened and rules changed to make it more difficult to collect benefits. But this has not produced any increase in employment, largely because of the structural changes discussed above, and the bureaucracy charged with designing and delivering programs piecemeal lumbers on.

A White Paper on a universal basic income floor would, of course, have to address the issue of incentives. But to simply dismiss the idea on the grounds that it would create disincentives to work ignores the massive inefficiencies in the current, tangled mess of programs. And it ignores the human and economic benefits of streamlining them into a single universal approach.

In time, the basic income floor could become as intrinsic to the Canadian identity as our universal health-care policy. And it would not amount to an expansion of the state, because large parts of the state's apparatus at the federal, provincial, and municipal levels would be shrunk to help finance it. If it was tied to the filing of tax returns, it would give a significant boost to voluntary compliance and thus enhance the government's fiscal position. It could be structured along interprovincial lines, with Ottawa providing the fully equalized tax point essential to its operation in return for agreements on portability and access. It would be flexible, sensitive, and firmly connected to local quality of life and cost of living. Those who file dishonest returns would face more serious sanctions under the tax laws than those the small percentage of welfare and unemployment insurance fiddlers now face. It would mean a society-wide commitment to the dignity and self-respect of every resident of Canada. It would respect the privacy of applicants in the same way as the privacy of those seeking investment tax credits is respected.

For some in government and academe, a basic income floor is too troublesome, too bold a stroke, insufficiently deferential to all that has come before. But we live in an age when economic, technological, and industrial policies are changing at precisely that rate and in that way. There is no reason that policies that address the dignity and self-respect of all people, regardless of age, sex, ability, health, or walk of life, should fail to keep pace.

REWARD FOR DEFICIT REDUCTION SHOULD NOT BE NEW SPENDING

Financial Post, June 21, 1997

Nothing more bone-chilling has been heard in Ottawa since the 1981 MacEachen budget. The clarion call of the newly elected Liberal caucus for turning on the taps and spending the fiscal dividend has to rank up there with Pierre Trudeau's view, expressed in 1975, that separatism was dead. The Parti Québécois was elected under René Lévesque about a year later.

The debt load in Ottawa has not declined one penny since Jean Chrétien was elected in 1993. While Finance Minister Paul Martin has cut transfers and reduced the annual deficit, he has added to the debt in all of his budgets since 1993. And the amount we all pay as interest on the cumulative debt at the federal level will not begin to reduce to 20 percent of total federal revenues until well into the next century. That number could well go up if economic growth slows or interest rates are raised to counter inflation in the United States and here at home. In other words, while present trends are encouraging, declaring victory while the debt sits there, easily convertible to larger annual interest payments, is not only premature but also irresponsible.

There is a big difference between establishing a coherent program to pay down the debt and declaring no fiscal dividend until the debt is gone. Establishing a program to pay down the debt is a serious national priority. Uncertainty about Quebec and the relative unpredictability of interest-rate policy in the U.S. are strong arguments for reducing the debt in a concerted way. There is no reason government need be afraid to walk and chew gum at the same time. But any process of tax cuts or social investment that does not run concurrent with debt reduction would be a serious abdication of fiscal responsibility to present and future generations — and to the solvency of needed social programs.

The notion that Liberal setbacks in the Atlantic region should dictate an opening of the social spending tap at the federal level is a profoundly serious misunderstanding of what election night was about. The NDP leader, Alexa McDonough, may sincerely believe Canadians voted for Ottawa to open the taps. She is entitled to that belief. She is, however, engaged in an exercise more akin to ideological wishful thinking than careful analysis.

The setback many Liberals experienced in Atlantic Canada was about arrogance, insensitivity, jobs, and promises not kept. The setbacks were about the popularity in the Atlantic region of Jean Charest and Alexa McDonough. The Liberal outcome was about the unpopularity of the harmonized sales tax, the contrived "new" GST, which is financed by Canadians all across Canada. The notion that Atlantic Canadians want a new round of fiscal uncertainty or spendthrift activity from Ottawa is a serious insult to the voters in the Atlantic region, where provincial governments have been working long and hard to balance budgets — and, it should be pointed out, not without considerable success.

It seems also fair to conclude that as Liberals, Conservatives, and Reformers campaigned for fiscal responsibility and collectively won clear majorities in all regions, including Atlantic Canada, there is no mandate anywhere for turning on the tap.

It is one of government's traditional problems that it looks at spending and redistributing money as the most central instrument of public policy. When funds are constrained, it usually moves to regulation as a tool that affords it visibility and the appearance of relevance. If all one has is a hammer, then all problems look like nails. We have the right to expect more in terms of leadership, more in terms of creativity, and more in terms of flexibility and judgement from our national government.

There is room for serious innovation and improvement without increasing spending unreasonably. There is room for new ideas that need not be expensive. One new idea would be to zero base one's approach to those functions not necessary at the federal level. If spending more is all Liberals have to offer as the reward for deficit reduction, then the work of Paul Martin and all those who have suffered through his cuts has truly been for little gain indeed.

SETTING OUR SIGHTS ON THE CHALLENGE OF POVERTY

Financial Post, *August 2, 1997*

There are many reasons for Canadians to look ahead with optimism, but they are often overlooked by those who have a professional stake in purveying as much gloom and doom as possible. Putting the reasons for optimism in perspective is as good a way as any to reflect not only on an agenda for Canada's next Parliament, but also on an agenda for the country itself.

The good news in fiscal terms is real. Ottawa is on the cusp of a balanced budget, providing Liberal spendthrift reflexes do not overtake basic common sense in some horrific Pavlovian response to a disappearing deficit. Most provinces' budgets are already balanced, in surplus, or moving rapidly in that direction. Tax increases seem not to be part of any reasonable agenda, either on the left or on the right, among those parties in power. The economy remains strong, although unemployment persists, stubbornly immune to date to job creation in the private sector.

Yet even these dynamic forces should not be allowed to obscure the need for firm and concerted action on those challenges that still threaten the economic progress for all Canadians. Simply put, economic success and genuine social progress can be snatched from the jaws of victory by complacency about the serious gaps in the national economic fabric. The fact that these gaps were not addressed in the last election campaign points to a triumph in both the Liberal and Reform campaigns of tactics over substance. Those successes notwithstanding, the problems they helped to mask are still there. Denying their existence will only see their destructive capacity increase, threatening our rationale for optimism.

Our Native population remains disproportionately overrepresented among inmates in federal and provincial penal institutions; among the poor, the indigent, the substance dependent; and among those whose children are born into poverty and at birth weights that foretell lives of meaningful disadvantage. It remains a national disgrace that there is no unified aboriginal/government/community engagement on this issue. There are programs in place, land settlements that have been negotiated, and aboriginal business organizations that are trying to be helpful. But the lack of response from all governments to the Royal Commission on Aboriginal Peoples reveals a serious effort to either deny reality or avoid Canada's responsibilities to our first citizens. It is true that in many parts of Canada, especially in areas adjacent to large aboriginal communities, political views are at best mixed about how much further commitment is appropriate or necessary. That may be a reason to consult, explain, listen, and educate. It is not justification to abdicate.

The inability of existing federal, provincial, and municipal programs to reduce the numbers of Canadians who are trapped in poverty does not imply a lack of concern or compassion. It does, however, imply a complacency that may be enhanced by the reality that poor people tend not to be active voters. Whatever the rationale for a continuing lack of creativity and determination on this issue, that lack is a reflection of our civility as a country. Strength in financial markets is of great importance to any nation's economic and fiscal health and overall prospects, but so too is the way in which a country addresses its most vulnerable, its most weak, its least powerful or affluent. This is not an issue only for social agencies, volunteer groups, or government agencies or ministers. It crosses party lines and defies any simple left or right policy framework. It requires a community-wide commitment that defies traditional class, economic, and political distinctions.

In the same way that we have as a society made commitments to overcome disease, combat illiteracy, and overtake bigotry and racism, so too must we set our sights on the broad and enduring challenge of intergenerational poverty. In too many places in Canada, both rural and urban, people are born into a poverty that denies them the message of hope and opportunity that is the soul of the Canadian dream. It is high time Canada's federal and provincial politicians, as well as Canada's business and labour leaders, embrace thoughtful, humane, and financially responsible initiatives on this front. This and no less is what any reasonable commitment to equality of opportunity for all Canadians demands.

OTTAWA JUST DOESN'T GET IT

Financial Post, *October 1, 1997*

The federal government's decision to put off tax cuts until the budget is supposed to balance in 1999 borders on the kind of public policy that can best be called delusional. It reveals a lack of real-world sensitivity that would be comical were it not so tragic. Even if one accepts the questionable argument of the left — that tax cuts help only the wealthy — there are a host of ways to reduce taxes so that lower- and middle-income people benefit first and foremost. Even the New Democratic Party, in calling for reductions in the GST, understands that. The failure of the government to embrace the seminal role of taxes in job creation, investment, public confidence, and consumer psychology speaks volumes about Ottawa. A few weeks after a near-thing election, it simply does not get it.

Instead, Ottawa has chosen to advance expectations about government spending. It is the old game of finding ways to prove that only government could possibly have solutions to national ills. The only dollars that count in this world are government dollars; the only activities with promise are government activities. This has been the central folly of Liberal public policy over the years. It is a folly that created the debt Brian Mulroney and Jean Chrétien inherited from Pierre Trudeau.

Finance Minister Paul Martin, who is guiltless in the spendthrift excesses of the Trudeau regime, seemed to understand. He seemed to want to recalibrate Liberalism in a more pragmatic and balanced fashion. Unfortunately, the Throne Speech indicates he has either given up the ghost or lost the fight. Or maybe he too dismissed the Throne Speech as little more than self-indulgence from the Prime Minister's Office, and he was waiting for later budgetary statements and budgets to actually define a more coherent and focused course. For the taxpayers' sake, I hope the third possibility is the real option. If not, it will mean the massive multi-partisan federal and provincial shift in fiscal policy during the past decade will have been for nought. International and domestic investors have responded to this positive shift through increases in investment, private-sector job growth, and stable or improving credit ratings. This has helped the broad private sector's debt markets, as well as provided the stability necessary in the sovereign debt world. But if the payoff for the period of sacrifice and constraint is a return to the status quo ante, then we are facing a hollow victory indeed.

Cumulative federal and provincial debt levels are still hovering at 100 percent of our gross domestic product. Personal debt levels among middle-income Canadians are higher than ever, and are sustainable only because of lower interest rates. Any movement in interest rates, which the governor of the Bank of Canada has cautiously indicated could well be coming, would produce genuine problems in terms of both private and public debt-servicing costs.

Ottawa has garnered its present cash-flow bonanza by slashing transfers to the provinces, which, in turn, have slashed transfers to municipalities, hospitals, and educational institutions. All of this comes to rest on the middle-income homeowner, who is facing tax hikes without any concurrent expansion in family income. Ottawa has also enhanced its cash flow by instituting intolerable increases in employment insurance premiums over the years. Paid by employees and employers directly, EI premiums amount to a tax on jobs. Put simply, Ottawa has solved its own liquidity problems at the expense of working men and women, vital social programs run by the provinces, and job creation in the private sector. Now is the time to deal directly with sovereign debt and family income. The first is too high and the second has been diminished for some time — overtaken for many years by tax increases at all levels.

Ottawa's options are clear and the opportunity immense. It can propose tax reductions that gradually replenish consumer confidence and family income. It can embrace a spirited attack on the debt. It can resist the Liberal siren call for spendthrift excess that I take, sadly, to be genetic. The government survived in the last election only because its claim on the centre of Canadian politics was uncontested. If it deserts that centre to play to a big-spending left, it deserts the mainstream of Canadian voters.

QUESTIONS NEED POSING BEFORE THE FISCAL DIVIDEND IS ALLOCATED

Financial Post, *January 7, 1998*

It is unlikely that the question of the year will be "How do we best allocate the fiscal dividend?" We can be sure it is not the central question simply by adding up all the politicians in Ottawa of all affiliations who assure us it is. The problem with the question is that, more than being in a sense irrelevant, it presupposes that a series of other questions have been answered when they in fact have yet to be posed. And these unposed questions are at the very root of what we should or should not be using government for in our society — a key foundation for tactical questions around taxes or fiscal policy overall.

Do we as a society have a view about the role of government, its relative size, and the share of gross domestic product it should occupy? Recent work done by the Canadian Policy Research Network implies rather strongly that despite the false polarity created by proponents on the far right and the far left, the vast majority of Canadians take a moderate view, wanting government to provide a firm framework for social progress and equality of opportunity without being wasteful or doing those things that communities, families, and individuals can and should do for themselves.

There is room for a broad rethinking of government's role beyond the clichés of the welfare state and the neo-con excesses that argue for hardly any government at all. For Liberals, this will require some recasting of their "cuts if necessary, but not necessarily at the federal level" approach to belt-tightening. Recent polling reveals that Canadians know precisely how much pressure federal transfer-payment cuts have put on provincial health-care services. A recent Caledon Institute paper written by Tom Kent — one of liberalism's most venerable and determined Pearson-era policy gurus, someone who was there at the birth of medicare — nails the federal government for its fiscal and transfer policies, which represent a massive withdrawal from the health-care system, itself widely supported by Canadians from all walks of life, from both major linguistic groups, and from all regions and age groups.

We must similarly address whether we are prepared to shell out what is truly necessary for a meaningful Canadian armed forces. Liberals seem unsure here, and in that state they only diminish the effectiveness of our present forces and dilute morale for the future. Canadians deserve a multi-faceted force that can be as adept at air-sea rescue as it is at the military realities of enforcing peace agreements, ceasefires, blockades, and humanitarian air and alliance activities. This requires both a larger complement and a more sustained investment in equipment. If the present government wishes not to support this, it should say this clearly to Parliament and to the people.

We must also ask whether the level of deferred income taxes for certain kinds of capital and retirement investments still reflects the values and realities of our way of life. While I believe it does, this is an issue that should be debated broadly and openly. It is time, as well, to look at basic redistributive mechanisms — equalization payments and the hodgepodge of federal, provincial, and municipal income-security programs — to see if they are achieving their purposes and whether they reflect how Canadians want to see the issues of disparity between regions and people addressed. To a great extent, part of this question will be addressed in the federal-provincial discussions that began in earnest at the first ministers' meeting in Ottawa in early December. This review of the way Ottawa and the provinces can work together is truly a positive development. It will acquire even more compelling significance if it also has the courage to ask key questions about what we hope to achieve by wealth redistribution, and whether there are other ways of enhancing equality of opportunity that should also be on the table.

Sorting out the allocation of the fiscal dividend while cumulative federal-provincial debt levels equal our total GDP and taxes are too high is one kind of disconnect from reality. Trying to do so without first sorting out national priorities is another.

WE MUST NOT FORGET THE DEBT

Financial Post, *February 21, 1998*

There will be a host of pressures on the federal minister of finance to tip his hand on long-term fiscal policy in the coming budget, and there are powerful reasons why he should resist. There are those who extrapolate budget trends in a straight line and conclude that the deficit is gone, the debt will consume itself, and the only real choice for Ottawa is how to spend the new-found excess. These people are engaging in serious self-delusion. This is no more or less serious than those who concluded at the end of the Second World War that exponential economic growth would make deficits and debt irrelevant or non-existent. We need not, in this generation, pay the price for that kind of stupidity a second time.

Many variables have yet to work themselves through. The state of federal-provincial social programs, as well as their future funding and direction, is still uncertain. Until those talks settle and a frame of reference is established, it is foolhardy to build assumptions into medium-term fiscal strategy.

While interest rates are relatively stable and moderate, in essence because the fundamentals underlying the Canadian economy are strong, it is too soon to understand the contagion effect from the meltdown in some parts of Asia. The contagion effect may require a shift in both monetary and fiscal policy, particularly as the slowdown in British Columbia becomes more pronounced. The federal government owes B.C. the flexibility to be able to respond should the downward trend not moderate, as most would hope. Regions outside central Canada have long paid for decisions taken on their behalf by Ottawa. Some attention to B.C.'s predicament is absolutely warranted.

Clearly, the need for the restructuring of the eastern Ontario and Quebec electrical grids, while not a direct federal burden, will produce some genuine costs to the economy, which, while offset by a pattern of necessary investment, may perforce involve some federal presence. It would be a mistake to reduce flexibility in face of this. There is evidence as well that productivity gains have levelled off. Investing in productivity is never wrong.

And the risk of a major conflagration in the Middle East, with impact on oil prices, military spending, and economic activity overall, should not be ignored. In the same way as logistical plans can and should be made by the defence department and the military, so too should fiscal contingencies be addressed. This does not mean that fiscal priorities such as tax relief for middle-income Canadians, support for medical research, or focusing on a planned program for debt reduction should be set aside. It merely means that small steps in the right direction, within the prudence of fiscal stability, may make more sense than grand gestures that commit our fiscal chips without truly knowing whether that commitment is sustainable economically.

We did not build our debt and deficit in a short time. They grew in real terms over almost three decades. The present point of transition should not set us off in a grand new direction when the weather and terrain in that direction are essentially unknown. If timidity in the face of a compelling challenge is no virtue, then moderation in support of careful budgeting is surely no vice.

There has been no lack of prudence on the part of Finance Minister Paul Martin in the face of cabinet pressure, interest-group representations, and Liberal caucus aspirations. Even the prime minister seems eager to start the old Liberal spending machine on its perpetual-motion journey. We have been on one of those journeys before, and have just attained that point on the climb out of the valley of debt where we can actually see the sun. This is no time for another leap of faith that will simply restrict the power of future governments to manage our economic affairs responsibly and in a balanced way.

We can achieve much as a society when the costs of excessive debt servicing are no longer mounting at an exponential rate. Not all of these achievements need be accomplished by government, and certainly not at the federal level.

TOO MUCH MASSAGING OF THE NUMBERS CAN RUIN CREDIBILITY

Financial Post, *March 7, 1998*

Finance Minister Paul Martin deserves more than modest credit for the 1998 federal budget. He not only resisted Liberal pressure to overspend, but also picked priorities like medical research in a way that will serve present and future generations extremely well. If one combines this with the eradication of the deficit and Martin's common-sense support for both free trade and the goods and services tax, despite the excessive rhetoric of Liberal campaign promises, it is hard to think of another Liberal who has so effectively anchored public policy in the real world.

That's why the emergence of a credibility problem around the present budget, fuelled more by respected analysts and economists on Bay Street than by the predictable complaints from opposition party spokesmen, is troubling. The implication is that we are seeing such a massaging of the numbers by Ottawa that normal standards of material disclosure, absolutely fundamental to decision making in financial markets, are fading out of view. Jeff Rubin, chief economist for CIBC Wood Gundy, states the problem with impeccable clarity in his company's published assessment of the 1998 budget: "Beneath the veneer of balanced budget forecasts for the next two years, the budget arithmetic conceals covert surpluses of $8 billion for the upcoming year and nearly $12 billion for the fiscal year 1990/0."

Remember that the federal government predicted a $17-billion deficit for the year we are in. That number comes in officially as a zero deficit as we speak. Were they off by $17 billion as a matter of misjudgement on revenue of $150 billion or so? Or did they mislead intentionally? Either way, Houston, we have a problem.

If there is a covert surplus of $8 billion this coming year and $12 billion in the following year, we have a $20-billion unaccounted-for rolling surplus over the next twenty-four months. The problem with not labelling a surplus as a surplus is that it has the opposite effect from that intended — namely, suppressing spending desires. As the math is easily done, Canadians will begin to suspect that the entire budget is a large manipulation of the numbers to suppress the Liberal Party's natural spending reflex. This will only feed that reflex, as it will the prime minister's desire for Millennium Fund–like monuments to his inspired service as the nation's great helmsman.

This all takes place within the context of an expanded tax gap between Canadians and Americans and a clear momentum gain for spending increases and increased tax revenue. Rubin could not be more explicit: "The fiscal choices made in this budget are a strong leading indicator that Ottawa will choose to spend the bulk of any future fiscal dividends."

That the finance minister maintain some cushions against the Asian meltdown, changes in interest rates, and the end of our own positive economic cycle is not only appropriate but also necessary. The problem with a $20-billion cushion is that if parts of it are not labelled as cushions for possible negative impacts that lie ahead, some will conclude that this is really a partisan cushion for either pre-election spending or pre-election tax cuts. Even here, our adversarial parliamentary process should cut some slack for a finance minister who is, after all, a Liberal and has every right to provide a little ballast for the Liberal Party's re-election opportunities. But even by Liberal standards, $20 billion to $30 billion over three years is a little rich.

It would be unhelpful to the country and the finance minister if the credibility he has earned in deficit reduction were to be diminished because the numbers are seen to be creative fiction, as opposed to a reasonable approximation of knowable fiscal reality. All finance ministers worldwide overestimate costs and underestimate revenue so as to maximize their flexibility and control. But to do so excessively only shortens the time between today's relative reputational high and the days when the department's numbers, in good or bad times, are simply unbelievable by friend and foe alike.

As for holding off tax cuts or real debt reduction too long, the impact of that will simply suppress economic confidence for even longer. Mortgage-interest deductibility, tax cuts for middle-income earners, and less of a tax gap with the Americans will build confidence and reduce unemployment. And nothing would help anyone's electoral or leadership prospects any more than that.

UNCOMPETITIVE INCOME TAXES ARE COSTLY IN THE LONG RUN

Financial Post, *April 8, 1998*

As we all prepare to file our income taxes, it is a good time to reflect on the disparaging effect the tax gap between Canadians and Americans has on a host of issues, from consumer confidence to the kinds of futures our young people choose. The gap, or the amount of extra tax Canadians pay at similar income levels as compared with U.S. counterparts, has begun to expand. And before we jump to conclusions that are comforting but less than true, this gap is often calculated including the extra funds Americans must pay for medical insurance. In simple terms, Canadians pay more tax in total across a host of income groups than Americans.

This is particularly true among young people. The amount of taxes a young economics graduate might pay in Canada, compared with his or her counterpart in the U.S., is a serious disincentive to starting a career in Canada. And U.S. firms in many areas are now recruiting the talented graduates of our universities not only with offers of competitive pay and benefit packages, but also with the reality of tax levels that allow young people to build their futures, start families, and begin their working lives with some incentive. Canada simply cannot afford to lose the bright young graduates of our post-secondary institutions. We all subsidize post-secondary education in Canada, in some cases by as much as 80 percent of the total cost. This investment reflects what has been the traditional postwar commitment to keep fees at a level that does not, when combined with financial assistance for students in financial need, deny a qualified young person access to post-secondary education simply because he or she cannot afford it.

Of late, Ottawa's slashing of transfer payments has forced many provinces to reduce the level of subsidy, thereby forcing up fees and con-current student borrowing. This puts immense pressure on the graduate to find work and begin to pay back debt to get ahead. The increased tax burden that he or she faces relative to counterparts in the U.S. is noticeable and meaningful. This is also true for middle-income and middle-aged Canadians trying to save for their retirement, put something away for their kids' university, and increase their own personal economic independence. Personal debt levels have increased in the past few years as discretionary savings levels have gone down. Net personal discretionary income has declined, which explains why Canadian consumer demand has been relatively weak. Real incomes have not increased since Paul Martin took over as finance minister, while tax revenue has risen across the board. Federal slashing of transfers to provinces has only meant more pressure on municipal and property taxes as provinces have tried to cope.

But at the end of the line, there is only one taxpayer. And this one taxpayer has to face the cascading tax burden on an income that has not increased meaningfully, while employment prospects have become at best more tenuous. And as the tax gap with our major trading partner and neighbour increases, this will become a compelling competitive issue. A failure to address it will, over time, make Canada a less attractive place for investment if tax levels are seen to be non-competitive. This is particularly noticeable in the way in which the homeowner is treated. In Canada, mortgage interest is seen as an after-tax expense. In the U.S., it is a before-tax expense. Making mortgage interest tax deductible frees up important amounts of income for homeowners to use for savings, investments, renovations, or other consumer purchases. It makes a significant difference in the net personal liquidity of Americans, when compared with Canadians at the same income levels. Ottawa's failure to apply its fiscal surplus to aggressive, broad-based tax reduction leaves far too much in the kitty for program expenditures made by a federal government that is sure it knows best.

What tax reductions would do is diminish the risk of Ottawa's once again starting a spending game that Canadian taxpayers can ill afford.

OTTAWA'S BOOKS LOOK BETTER, BUT MUCH REMAINS TO BE DONE

Financial Post, *April 25, 1998*

The real policy challenge that will be before Canadians very soon will be choosing the priorities that should dominate our national life in the post–Paul Martin era. Whether or not the finance minister succeeds Jean Chrétien as Liberal prime minister is beside the point. Martin as prime minister or Allan Rock as prime minister or a Tory as prime minister will all end the regime that has been ruled by fiscal matters. What are the main qualities of the Martin fiscal era? Federal spending cutbacks at the expense of the provinces; a low-interest rate, anti-inflation policy; and a modest reduction in federal government activity.

Martin's success, for which he deserves some considerable credit, was helped by an upward U.S. economic cycle and a policy on inflation based on the central bank's zero-tolerance stance, which, when pursued by the Conservative government, was energetically attacked by Martin in opposition. Negligible inflation and ensuing low interest rates combined with vigorous transfer cuts to improve federal finances. Economic expansion occurred with ensuing prosperity in financial markets and other selected sectors. But that expansion has been uneven and thousands of Canadians have been left behind, often through no fault of their own.

The lack of flexibility available to the provinces to adapt health-care services and income-security programs in response to changes in demographics and the nature of work is a direct result of unduly rigid federal legislation and serious transfer cuts. Ottawa's books look better, but hospitals, nursing homes, universities, colleges, and schools are all in some measure of crisis. If we worry about the impact of the millennium bug, we should worry more about the incapacity of our community infrastructure to adapt to social change.

Clearly, a tax overhaul that simplifies the system and reduces the tax gap between Americans and Canadians is a structural and economic priority. High taxes are oppressing middle-income Canadians and reducing Canada's competitive advantage, and the notion of letting the Canadian dollar fall far enough to compensate is, in the long run, bad economic and monetary policy.

The Liberal conversion to free trade and its benefits everywhere, all the time, and with anyone who asks seems both unfocused and ill informed. The prospect of having thirty-four countries in a trade pact that stretches from the North Pole to the South — the proposal agreed upon earlier this week in Chile — is compelling. But it is not clear that the Liberals have thought out any of the issues that will determine whether Canadians can be competitive without reducing, rather than enhancing, our standard of living.

A level playing field for financial markets to invest in is one thing, and it's a generally good thing at that. But we must address the more important issues of human capital, job creation, technology use, and the strength of our communities in Canada. A civil, free-enterprise society requires the right mix of economic growth, social justice, and equality of opportunity. If we tilt too far in one direction, we risk diluting the civility.

Safe communities, a modern population and immigration policy, skills training and upgrading, and fresh leverage for Canadians who need to build new employment or training opportunities for themselves will dominate the agenda ahead. A stronger national defence, a foreign policy of both purpose and principle, and further re-engineering of how we govern ourselves must all be engaged. The post-Martin era can be one of great opportunity. Or it can be one of drift and opportunities missed, including the main chance for Canadians — the building of a solvent, caring, productive, and achieving nation that enters the next century with confidence and purpose. A healthy debate about how we get there will be a prime feature of our nation's politics in the months to come. Labels about near right, far right, middle right, light right, or bite right couldn't matter less. Labels are for cans of soup. Politics is about people, hope, and making progress together.

Political parties will differ on the choices to be made, but this need not mean wide diversion on the goals. Political parties that can transcend simplistic notches on the spectrum and reach out to build new voter coalitions will succeed. Those that fail will simply be irrelevant.

DEBT PROBLEM WILL NOT SOLVE ITSELF

Financial Post, *April 29, 1998*

It is simply human nature to want to believe that a problem has passed, especially one that seemed as confounding and overwhelming as the national debt. But it is dangerous to dismiss a problem before it has been clearly addressed. Problems dealt with in that way are the ones that explode when you are least able to address the implications.

Our debt makes up a larger percentage of our gross domestic product than is the case with the average of the Group of Seven industrial countries — and it's not hard to see the effect this has. Ottawa's debt-servicing costs consume a significant share of the government's total revenue. While growth in the ratio of debt to gross domestic product has thankfully stopped, this trend would reverse quickly with any meaningful increase in interest rates. And for that part of our debt that is denominated in foreign currencies, any reduction in the value of the Canadian dollar can increase the amounts owing that must be rolled over. In 1997, close to 35 percent of our debt was held by non-residents of Canada.

One need not obsess on the debt to address it. But it is unrealistic to pretend it is not there or hope it will solve itself. Dealing with it must embrace a rational strategy that sees principal payments made regularly as part of the country's overall fiscal plan. Those on the left who argue this cannot happen except at the expense of stable social programs assume responsible government cannot walk and chew gum at the same time. But the risks of not doing so are very clear. While difficulty may be avoided as long as the present rate of economic growth continues, there is no guaranteeing how long that will be. Interest rates respond to international monetary and currency pressures, which can emanate from Asian economic difficulties that are not within the capacity of North American or European governments or monetary authorities to control. Debt levels that are sustainable even if interest rates increase are the best defence against these kinds of vagaries. This simply requires less debt.

The combination of a reduced debt and continuing economic growth would allow Canada and its provinces to get their debt ratio down from the current level of close to 100 percent of economic output (debt-rating agencies look at the combination of all provincial debt and federal debt) to a number that can and should be more affordable. We need both debt reduction and economic growth working with us to get the country's balance sheet back in shape. The fact that the operating costs at the federal level are now less than gross federal revenue overall is encouraging. But it does not change the balance-sheet problem. And that problem can erupt in a host of ways.

High debt-servicing costs rob the country of revenue that could be used to reduce taxes or stabilize the social safety net. The 30 percent of revenue that goes to servicing debt could be better used elsewhere, or even left in the pockets of the taxpayers who earn the money to begin with. In the event of an economic downturn, that 30 percent would become more precious and would be necessary to finance safety-net programs that are more in demand at the other end of the cycle.

Moreover, as the number of retired pensionable Canadians increases relative to the productive workforce, dealing with the debt will become more difficult because of other competitive demands for the revenue of the government. Now that revenue is up, the economy is growing, and financial markets remain buoyant, we are in the best possible position to make progress on the debt. Failure to do so is clearly burdening future generations unnecessarily.

The debt was not built in a day, nor can it be eradicated quickly. But it can be diminished, and its relative significance reduced, if we have the simple honesty to face it squarely and compare the costs of addressing it with the costs of ignoring it. Any rational analysis of that comparison keeps debt reduction a compelling priority.

PART FOUR

Towards a New Confederal Union

I HAVE BEEN PRIVILEGED TO HAVE BEEN INVOLVED IN DISCUSSIONS AND negotiations around national unity and the constitution since 1980. My perspectives from the Cabinet Office in Ontario, from the Advisory Committee on Confederation for Premier Bill Davis, as chief of staff in the Prime Minister's Office in Ottawa, from Queen's University, and from the private sector has led me to the belief that national unity is less and less about the constitution per se. In 1990–91, I helped produce, with a group of business, academic, and provincial leaders, a report titled *The Group of 22*. It became clear to us that the realities surrounding day-to-day services such as health care, social services, education, and internal trade are the real stuff of how a nation of huge geography and relatively few people manages with the things that both differentiate and unite it.

Norman Spector, as chief of staff to Prime Minister Brian Mulroney, always impressed me with his intellect, rigour, and will to encourage the resolution and closure of issues, especially issues involving the constitution. We disagreed often on how far to push for resolution, and at what cost. But his reasoning was always impeccable. My belief in the value of muddling through was equally determined.

My period with Bill Davis taught me that closure that is forced or unreflective of public sensibility could be difficult and, occasionally, unhelpful. The value of the Meech Lake and Charlottetown accords was that neither represented any terminal limit for constitutional evolution. They both would have, had they been approved, presaged ongoing work in a series of areas — social policy, aboriginal affairs, and finding the right balance between national standards and the asymmetry essential to preserving the confederal nature of our country. Neither agreement proved to be perfect, and in the end neither was ratified or approved.

We now face a new series of pressures that argue for a new confederal union — one produced not by constitutional fiat, but by genuinely pragmatic agreements that adequately reflect the past, present, and future of our confederal union.

These columns, speeches, and essays portray my bias as a modest decentralist, and my preference that there be no fundamental contradictions between nationwide standards and provincial flexibility — especially when there is a will to find the common ground.

NOT THE END FOR CANADA

Speech to the Institute of Corporate Directors, Ontario Club, Toronto, September 13, 1994

When separatist forces launched their attack on the Charlottetown Accord in 1992, they proclaimed that one could oppose the accord but not support sovereignty. With the defeat of the accord, they quickly proclaimed that now sovereignty was the only option, because Canada clearly could never reform the constitution enough to accommodate the required changes. This is sort of like someone who murders his parents asking for the mercy of the court because he is an orphan.

The collapse of the Conservative campaign in 1993, for lack of a platform on which to stand, produced regional groupings in Parliament from the West and Quebec. This, too, is not a new phenomenon. It is a classic and repeating event in Canadian history after deep recessions and when the voter coalitions sustaining a government are allowed to come apart. We have had Créditistes, Progressives, Social Credit and, in Ontario, the United Farmers of Ontario to fill the space now occupied by both the Bloc and Reform.

The September 1994 provincial election in Quebec was not a rout. In fact, the most determined and open federalist premier Quebec has had in perhaps thirty-five years made steady progress throughout the campaign, reducing the numbers for the separatist option almost daily. He is well positioned to be an articulate, able, and effective foil for the pro-independence forces. The tie in popular opinion of essentially 44 percent for both the Parti Québécois and the Liberals represents a collapse of what was a 10 percent, and often a 20 percent, lead for the PQ over the final three months of the campaign.

Daniel Johnson led the Liberals with courage and competence. That he could not translate his momentum into victory has to do only with the desire Quebecers shared — with just about every other electorate in the United States and Canada, and France, and Japan, and Italy, and Greece, and elsewhere over the past few years — to replace those governments associated with a difficult recession that reduced employment levels across the entire Western world.

The PQ faces, almost immediately, as it did in 1976, the profound contradiction between discharging its present duties to the people of Quebec within the context of its existing constitutional powers and its ideological commitment to the powers, attributes, and burdens of a separate independent state. Any time the government spends discharging its duties successfully under the present system will diminish the case for its ideological premise. Any time it steals from existing duties to advance its separatist aspirations will threaten its day-to-day legitimacy with the people who voted simply for a change in government, not a change of country.

This being said, we should all expect a measure of sustained double-speak — Quebec assuring financial markets and investors that all is well and the province is operating as per usual, while telling Quebecers and Ottawa that the federation is an endless burden on the fiscal integrity of Quebec and its programs. At some point, when the honeymoon wears off and the fiscal realities must be faced, the PQ's posture could produce a government bumping into itself coming around the corner. Let us not forget that Jacques Parizeau is the last of a more extreme portion of the Lévesque generation. He is not any more an *étapiste*, or step-by-step separatist, but is now a go-for-broke separatist of great skill, cunning, and ability. It would be a mistake to underestimate him.

For the central government in Ottawa, it is vital that the temptation to taunt or polarize be resisted. As well, Ottawa must not defer its fiscal or social policy agenda until after the referendum, especially since the PQ may well move its referendum further and further off, seeking to avoid a repeat of the 1979–80 defeat for the sovereignist cause. Furthermore, the longer the referendum is delayed, the more time it affords the Bloc in Ottawa to rationalize its role as a perpetual "Quebec first" advocate (as opposed to a "limited shelf life," pro-independence movement). It could become a problem if Ottawa puts off fundamental fiscal and social reform because of Quebec's amorphous plans. Nothing would advance the case for Quebec sovereignty and the burden on Canada more profoundly than a failure of our central government to cut the deficit and reduce the debt.

So September 12 is not the beginning of the end for Canada, but it could be the end of the beginning for the sovereignty movement. Quebecers went for the sparkle of political change, and Parizeau's semi-precious stone of sovereignty was the only gem available in the display case. Quebecers deserve more choice, and the argument that a third party will simply divide the federalist cause should be set aside. There is a lot of room on the spectrum for a truly conservative federalist and moderately nationalist option that wants less central government intrusion without wanting to fracture Canada itself.

I am optimistic. If Ottawa does not lose its resolve, if Reform does not wittingly or unwittingly provoke polarization in Quebec, if Parizeau's inevitable provocations are treated with courteous and balanced equanimity, and if we get on with reducing debt and spending, then neither economic recovery nor the return to economic health needs to be diluted or deterred by what happened on September 12.

I understand that many would like this tentativeness to end once and for all. Well, historically, when the fathers of Confederation chose evolution as the means of achieving statehood and, unlike the Americans, set aside the instruments of revolution and civil war for those of compromise, the price we paid included a continuing lack of finality, clarity, and precision. It is not, when you reflect on the American Civil War and the huge carnage it imposed, the greater of two evils — but is the lesser by far. It does mean, however, that in terms of Confederation, we will be dealing with that ambiguity as a management issue for decades to come.

The creative tension between French and English goes back almost 300 years. It has not, though, diluted our economic and social progress in Canada as a whole. Have we paid a price? Yes, but can we compare it with the price the United Kingdom has paid on the Irish issue, or that paid by other nations with more serious difficulties? Managing the problems down to a low roar is the real challenge for all our political parties.

BALANCING GOVERNMENT POWERS

Speech to the Macdonald/Cartier Luncheon, Calgary, October 3, 1994

The original British North America Act was not a strong defence of an all-powerful, all-knowing central bureaucracy or government. In fact, only a few powers, in areas such as monetary policy, defence, transportation regulation, and criminal law, were considered central by the founding colonies. For good, substantial, and historically unquestionable reasons, the provinces sought to keep as much legislative authority as possible at home, closer to the farmers, merchants, fishermen, and lumber workers who were the taxpaying and economic base of the new nation.

It is interesting to reflect on how our most epic battles as Conservatives in modern times have sought to wrench Ottawa away from the over-centralizing and excessive growth of power, spending, and taxation that has so typified post–Second World War federal public policy. Certainly our dismantling of the Foreign Investment Review Agency (FIRA) and the National Energy Program (NEP) was an attempt to reduce excessive, unconstructive, and intrusive federal power grabs from either the provinces or the private sector, or both. Privatization represented a similar effort to reduce the size and scope of the federal authority and its claim on the contingent liability of the Canadian taxpayer.

John Diefenbaker's populism and discomfort with an all-knowing, all-controlling central bureaucracy, Joe Clark's Community of Communities, and Brian Mulroney's Free Trade Agreement all sought to return the country to a confederation envisioned by the founders. This is the exact opposite of a federal government that spends too much, controls too much, interferes too much, and taxes too much. The market disciplines now imposed on governments in Canada by the need to be internationally competitive are the best long-term protections against excessive taxation, regulation, or bureaucracy that one can have.

Returning to a government that is less centralized, with more devolution to the provinces, municipalities, or private sector, is the only answer. Governments need to have the resources to do what they should and must, without depleting everyone else's resources. A federal government that sets standards and rules for programs it can no longer fund is unconstructive. A federal government competing with provinces and municipalities to give out community-centre grants when it does not have the funds to properly discharge defence responsibilities is the ultimate "ship of fools" public-policy cruise.

Attempting to redesign a social safety net is, for Ottawa, the ultimate conceit, since we know that beyond transfers to provinces and cheques to individuals, Ottawa's real role is in the area of equalization. The real client burdens, the real caseloads, the real training responsibilities, the real expenditures are faced by provinces and municipalities. It might be better if Ottawa reverted to a purely equalization role and left to the provinces the tax room and fiscal capacity to shape their own local priorities. Those provinces that are less well off could be helped through equalization.

National priorities need not be federal priorities to be real. In fact, they are often a lot less costly when the federal government is less involved. It is rather unsightly to foreign investors and holders of Canadian bonds to watch different levels of government competing for jurisdictions that none can afford. Conservatives need to make the case at a grass-roots level for a central government that does less, leaving more for the provinces and the private sector to sort out within a genuine market context.

The Canadian confederation provides a framework of social stability and order within which freedom and entrepreneurship can flourish. It is a belief that successful societies come from a balancing of powers among many participants, large and small. It is a unique message with roots that go back beyond Confederation to the British, French, and aboriginal set-tlers of our nation. Many of those who, like my grandparents, chose Canada sensed something in that balance that spelled opportunity and free-dom and, above all, a chance for individual growth and fulfilment unpar-alleled anywhere else.

Just as sir John A. Macdonald and George-Étienne Cartier sought to rebalance four colonies with a very limited central government, so must we work to rebalance a far-too-pervasive federal government with economic and political realities we can no longer afford to put off or deny.

NEXT STEPS FOR CANADA

Speech to Alberta Certified General Accountants, Edmonton, November 2, 1995

Let me offer two views of October 1995. The sovereignists may be rather bitter over the defeat of the referendum because this time all the forces were positive: the official opposition in Ottawa is under their control, the gov-ernment in Quebec City has a powerfully popular force in Lucien Bouchard, and the federal prime minister is unpopular in Quebec. It may have been the best chance to date for separation. They did not succeed.

The other view of what happened referendum night is that this was the referendum promised by Robert Bourassa when the Newfoundland legis-lature failed to vote on the Meech Lake Accord. The collapse of the ratifi-cation process around the only constitutional accord that bore the signatures of all the provinces, including Quebec, was a deep wound that forced Bourassa to promise to call a referendum, should no further proposals come forward, for October 1992 on sovereignty versus the status quo. The Charlottetown Accord constituted the proposal that allowed the premier to withdraw sovereignty from the ballot in 1992 and invite Quebecers, along with Canadians everywhere, to pronounce on Charlottetown. So this may well have been the referendum that Charlottetown allowed the country to avoid or delay.

As someone who was born in Quebec but has lived all my adult life in Ontario, I bring a particular bias to our present equation. Whatever the political costs of keeping the country together, they pale by comparison to the costs of dealing with its dismemberment. I have little optimism that deciding how the country would run without Quebec would be any easier than finding a way to keep Quebec in our federation. In fact, I believe the costs of managing the building of a new nation without Quebec would be far more onerous.

This is not because there would be any lack of will. In fact, quite the opposite would likely be the case. The departure of Quebec would unleash, apart from anger and disappointment that would poison relationships with the new Quebec for years to come, a series of very strong regional wills that would defy easy resolution. Why would Westerners want to be dominated by a federal Parliament in which Ontario's population afforded that province a majority of seats? Why would Ontario want an equal, elected Senate that would dilute the democratic authority of its superior numbers? Why would Alberta, British Columbia, and Ontario want to finance the social spending in the have-not provinces, especially during a time of fragile new national structures and pressures? And how easy would it be to accommodate our aboriginal Canadians in the context of a redefinition of the nation without Quebec?

This is not to be discouraging about Canada without Quebec, but to be encouraging about the effort necessary to keep Quebec within the family. In comparison to the "no Quebec" option, it is a lot less onerous and costly than some may have you think. The federal government is in the process of trying to rush some quick-fix solutions through Parliament and the legislatures. These solutions have already been set aside as irrelevant by the sovereignist leadership. The spectre of a federal prime minister racing about trying to garner support for provisions that were contained in both the

Meech Lake and Charlottetown accords, but that he never supported all that seriously at the time, is unbecoming and unhelpful. The best leadership from him would be to let leadership come from elsewhere.

The PQ is going through a process that will result either in Lucien Bouchard becoming premier or in having a stand-in take over the post until he is ready. A Quebec election in the spring is a real possibility, and the risk of a referendum in short proximity thereafter is also real and should not be discounted. Bouchard knows federal disarray when he sees it, and that is precisely what he now sees in Ottawa. Moreover, he can count on Preston Manning, for other reasons, to push Ottawa to decentralize the federation and oppose any resolutions on constitutional change that appear to address only Quebec's concerns. And even if such resolutions could pass the House of Commons and legislatures relatively quickly, no PQ-led Quebec National Assembly would endorse them. Before the forces of light were done, Péquistes would have turned even these new initiatives into dreaded or outmoded impositions by outsiders on Quebec jurisdiction.

The most significant voices from Quebec are no longer to be found in the federal government. Daniel Johnson, Jean Charest, and Michel Bélanger won this battle while opposing both the sovereignists and Ottawa's intransigence under the present administration. That they prevailed is a great tribute to their immense efforts, and to the dedication for which all Canadians owe them a great debt. The first sign of leadership would be for Ottawa to step back and let Johnson and Charest interact with the provinces to develop a counterforce to the status quo that could be arrayed when tactically and politically appropriate, either before or after any new Quebec referendum fight. Premiers such as Ralph Klein, Mike Harris, Roy Romanow, and others have far more credibility in Quebec than does our present prime minister. Only hubris and ego would have him or his advisers conclude otherwise.

A second sign of competent federal leadership would be a firm and unshakeable resolve to continue along the economic course established by Paul Martin in the last federal budget. Backing away from that path would imperil the economic prospects of all Canadians in all provinces and make the case that sovereignty is a better option than a federation without the integrity to deal with its own challenges straight on.

And let us remember that it is the sovereignists who advanced the case that continued social spending, high borrowing, and bottomless tax sources in order to maintain the welfare state could be ensured by voting Yes. They have not been called on this massive deception. Small business people, farmers, and pensioners in Quebec have no greater interest in high taxes, high interest rates, high unemployment, and higher debt burdens for their children than Canadians elsewhere. The best way to drive a wedge between thinking Quebecers and a separatist administration that sells magic economic elixirs available only through a costless Yes vote is to put that government on the wrong side of the "spend and tax and borrow" equation. Those are not the grounds on which the PQ and Lucien Bouchard are prepared to fight. Those are precisely the issues on which the federal government should engage. So what is the best possible leadership for Jean Chrétien to provide? Support for his minister of finance and a program of continued fiscal responsibility and spending reduction.

We are entering a challenging and difficult time, and the conduct of public affairs and the nation's interests is simply too important to leave to just one party in Ottawa. Premiers and opposition party leaders in the provinces should be working together with credible federalists from Quebec to find solutions that reflect the legitimate aspiration of Quebecers for cultural, linguistic, and jurisdictional protections that secure their role as one of Canada's founding peoples. Ottawa must stick fervently to its economic knitting. Quick constitutional fixes crafted in desperation, when combined with weakness and backsliding on fiscal and economic priorities, will push the sovereignist cause over the top.

This is a time for Ottawa to seek advice, not impose hastily concocted top-down solutions. This is a time for premiers and political leaders from across the spectrum to be in the loop. Never before has leadership been more important.

A New Confederal Union

Tabaret *46, no. 1 (University of Ottawa, Spring 1996)*

There is a measure of fresh thinking across the country that embraces a broad and moderate consensus about how a new confederal union between all the provinces can be shaped. And the federal government has a clear and stark choice — to facilitate the consensus or stand in its way. In essence, the consensus is found in terms like "rebalancing the federation," used by Premier Klein in Alberta, or "*instruments de société*," as articulated by moderate nationalists in Quebec. In the past few months, premiers such as McKenna in New Brunswick, Harris in Ontario, and Romanow in Saskatchewan have all spoken about de-layering, subsidiarity, disentanglement, and modest decentralization to strengthen and broaden the practicality of Confederation.

Most of the growth in Ottawa's dominion in areas of concurrent or specifically provincial jurisdiction has been achieved through the use of so-called spending power to advance federal programs on health, social policy, and post-secondary education. Other areas, such as tax expenditures, regional industrial development, and investment incentives, all buttress the massive billions spent by Ottawa since the 1950s — and especially since about 1974 — while in perpetual deficit.

As Ottawa recasts its fiscal policy, the spending power has begun to wilt. Moreover, in both the Meech Lake and Charlottetown accords, which were signed by all provinces and supported by all political parties except Reform, the PQ, and the Bloc Québécois, there were significant constraints on that spending power, constraints that were meant to move the day-to-day operation of the country closer to the separation of powers between Ottawa and the provinces that had been provided for in the original Constitution of 1867.

The consensus that is slowly but surely taking hold is one that sees a new confederal union that confers on Ottawa those responsibilities few disagree upon — that is, economic union, monetary policy, defence, criminal code, foreign policy and trade, and equalization. The delivery of specific services should largely be provincial. Interprovincial agreements — with enforceability in areas such as health care and social services — would ensure portability and universality by contract. This now exists, for example, in the operation of health insurance for almost all the provinces. This new balance would be pragmatic and responsive to present-day economic and social priorities and would in no way diminish the access all Canadians have to our basic health- and social-service safety net.

While the provinces are all in some measure interested in this reciprocal devolution and rebalancing, Ottawa seems tied to a minimalist and foot-dragging approach to any change. While a consensus is apparent and possible, Ottawa seems focused on partition of Quebec, or disallowance, or new referendum thresholds. The country deserves better.

As always, opportunity is within our collective national grasp. There is a real chance for women and men of goodwill to render a referendum unconstructive through a new confederal treaty or accord that reflects the best of what we have achieved since 1867 and what we know we can do far better in the future. This, plus a recognition of the legitimate cultural and linguistic requirements of one of our founding peoples, French-speaking Canadians, will move the nation ahead. If done in a contemporary way — that is, respecting all other provincial jurisdictions — it can be both a central and a complementary buttress of a new confederal union that serves Canadians for generations to come.

NO-CHANGE CENTRALIST GANG WON'T GIVE PROVINCES A CHANCE

Financial Post, *September 14, 1996*

A divide around decentralization is occupying an increasing space in our national politics. On one side we find the traditional centralists, those who fall into the Cartesian Trudeau world of federalism, where there are two orders of government — one central and one junior. On the other side are those who believe that the present federal government, like all those since the Second World War, has overstepped the provisions of the British North America Act, and done so by the use of a spending power that is really a deficit-creation engine the country can no longer afford.

The Pierre Trudeau–Andrew Coyne–Richard Gwyn–Michael Bliss federalist school, while unyielding, rhetorically muscular, and allergic to compromise, is not without merit. That it combines the "state knows best" views of the left with the "brook no moderation" insensitivity of the totalitarian new right is merit in and of itself. The mere fact that Sir John A. Macdonald tolerated any role at all for the provinces would, for some in this school, consign him forever to the slag heap of history, a place reserved for contrivers, weaklings, negotiators, and moderates. He would join all those others who let us down, including Laurier, Pearson, Robarts,

Lougheed, Davis, Allan Blakeney, Romanow, Brian Peckford, Mulroney, and Rae. These people dared to indulge in compromise. They put co-operation and practicality ahead of uniformity and rigidity. It is as if the Canada that approaches its 130th birthday next year has been a failure, especially for the millions who have come here to build their lives and futures. With our positive trade balance, our massive exports to the world, our quality of life, our civility, clearly we are awash in failure everywhere.

Would it have been better for Mike Pearson to tell Premiers Lesage or Johnson in the late 1960s that, no, we will not compromise on the pension system — go separate? Would it have been better for Bill Davis and Peter Lougheed to let Pierre Trudeau step away from compromise in 1982, and thus sustain René Lévesque's pretensions that Canada could not reform its constitution as federalists had promised it could during the 1980 referendum?

We do need a strong federal government, but only in those areas the provinces cannot handle for themselves. Social justice in Canada is the product of a lot more than Ottawa's *noblesse oblige*. Provincial programs, provincial tax dollars, and provincial economies finance the lion's share of education, health care, and welfare. Premiers like Romanow, Harris, Filmon, and McKenna have done more to modernize their systems and reduce variable costs than Ottawa has. Ottawa's courage simply extends to cutting transfer payments to the provinces.

Those in the centralist crowd are right to care about standards, right to care about even and equal application of the law, and right to care about the immutable values of citizenship throughout the land. They are wrong in being intransigent on the best ways to protect those things about which they, and all of us, should care. A recent paper by the economist Tom Courchene, which was sponsored by the Ontario government and suggests joint provincial mechanisms as the best way to protect social programs, is one positive suggestion. There should be others. This debate should widen — and become an issue in the next federal election. We should welcome innovation. One-tier medicine, for example, which is in decline, may not be better than a system where everyone has access to the best medical care without regard to income, but where the wealthier among us have to treat a portion of the service received as a taxable benefit. This idea was suggested to Premier Bourassa by a joint task force just after he defeated the PQ in

1985, but it was crushed by the no-change gang — and we have failed to improve the system as a result.

Federalism is a flexible system, which is why it is the most popular system in the world. The values we share, recently graphed superbly by the economist Judith Maxwell's Canadian Policy Research Network, shows that despite those who allege that our Canadian identity is tied only to the benefits gravy train, the opposite is true. Our common values — independence, family, responsibility, belief in community and civility — exist without exception across provincial, religious, linguistic, and geographical lines. Our identity is wed not to state handouts but to a distinctly Canadian mix of freedom and responsibility.

The desire for more local control and cost efficiency combines with our vast geographic areas and huge density differences to argue for the precise flexibility that federalism offers. Trashing that flexibility, or stonewalling its promise, serves no purpose except that of promoting unnecessary confrontation.

A FEDERALIST PERSPECTIVE

Orbis: A Journal of World Affairs *41, no. 3 (University of Pennsylvania, Summer 1997). This piece was in response to an article on the inevitability of Quebec's succession, written by Quebec's agent general in Washington, Marc Boucher.*

It is not hard to construct an elegant and moderate case for the inevitability of Quebec's secession from Canada, and to argue that such an outcome mirrors America's setting aside of the colonial yoke and move to self-determination.

But if you want to understand the issue from the point of view of most Canadians and most Quebecers, imagine that a Spanish-speaking state larger than California and Texas put together, with a population equal to just less than 70 million, remained in the American union after Spanish rule was banished. Imagine that America as a whole has sanctioned Spanish-language schools and Spanish working and official languages, and ensured equal opportunity for Spanish-speaking public servants and young people. In fact, the president of the United States is frequently elected from among the citizens of this region. Imagine, lastly, that a hard-core, nationalist minority wants this region to leave the union and become independent, provided it can retain full use of American currency and access to the North American Free Trade Agreement (NAFTA). This hard-core minority does not give up. The moderate Spanish-speaking territorial majority, despite winning two referenda on the issue of independence, cannot figure out how to make the silliness stop. That is what the secession issue would look like in an American context.

The last referendum in Quebec was a clear failure for the hard-core separatists, who, under Premier Jacques Parizeau, had taken over the Parti Québécois (PQ), driven the moderate Pierre-Marc Johnson from his leadership of the party, and polarized the nationalist cause in Quebec. Going into that 1995 referendum, those who wanted pure independence for Quebec (less than 50 percent of those who regularly vote for the PQ in provincial elections) had an enormous advantage.

Federalist forces were being led, in an absent-minded and mildly diffident way, by Jean Chrétien, the first Canadian prime minister since the Second World War to win a national majority without significant support in Quebec. His profound lack of popularity there was tied to a perception that, earlier in his government career, he had been duplicitous with respect to Quebec's interests when the Canadian provinces agreed to constitutional change under the Meech Lake Accord of 1987 and the Charlottetown Accord of 1992. Many Canadians believed that, in both instances, Chrétien put partisan interests ahead of national reconciliation, especially in Quebec.

Further opportunity for the hard-core separatists lay in the immense popularity of Lucien Bouchard, then leader of the Bloc Québécois, the official opposition in the Canadian parliament, and his fifty members from Quebec, who would campaign tirelessly in their fifty ridings — fifty out of Quebec's seventy-five.

The separatists faced no challenge from the Progressive Conservative Party, long the traditional agent of reconciliation between Quebec and the rest of Canada, because that party had collapsed and held but two seats in the House of Commons — one of which was held by the Conservative leader, Jean Charest. His seat, thankfully, was in southeastern Quebec.

Canada was also in a fiscal retrenchment mode, and all levels of government were reducing employment levels and benefit payments. Montreal had an unemployment rate well above 25 percent, and the level of poverty in Quebec was at a postwar high.

The prime minister told other Canadian political leaders — many of whom had helped defeat the 1980 Quebec referendum on independence — to stay out of the debate. Aside from Charest's passionate campaign for a unified Canada, the pro-Canada federalist campaign was a limping, colourless disaster.

Moreover, Bouchard enjoyed all the charisma and popularity one can glean from having been associated only with causes and not with the burdens of government, and he put that popularity to great use as the designated post-referendum negotiator should the referendum pass. Some months later, Bouchard had established himself as a moderating force by portraying the best context for sovereignty as a painless partnership with Canada (monetary, economic, customs, etc.), and his nomination as negotiator assured timid separatists, soft federalists, and the undecided that one could have the benefits of sovereignty with none of the hardships. Parizeau's hardline drive for independence was leavened, even constrained, by Bouchard's softer "partnership" plan. Thus voting *Oui* to the independence question simply meant sending the most popular politician in Quebec, Bouchard, to negotiate a better deal for the province with a profoundly disliked politician, Chrétien. There was no Pierre Trudeau to confront the separatists' excesses. There were no Canadian provincial premiers like William Davis of Ontario or Peter Lougheed of Alberta to make an elegant case for constitutional change within Confederation, as both had done in 1980.

Burdened with a recession and high unemployment, many economically disenfranchised Quebecers had every reason to believe they had nothing to lose. Emigration to other provinces had reduced the solidly federalist anglophone population. Anglo-rights proponents had done much, however unwittingly, to provoke francophone polarization. And even thoughtful literary greats like Mordecai Richler had vilified much of French-Canadian history, portraying it as awash in spirited and systemic anti-Semitism. (A view this author does not share, in spite of the talent of its key proponent.)

Despite all that — and despite electoral fraud in anglophone ridings that was intended to suppress the federalist vote — the Yes side was still unable to win 50 percent plus one in the referendum. Fortunately, it is highly unlikely that this depressing confluence of events will transpire in precisely the same way again. The PQ hardliners' high-water mark was October 1996.

Yet none of that diminishes the legitimate grievances that many Quebecers and a succession of Quebec governments have tried to express. To estimate the chances of any likely sorting out, one must understand the factors in the Quebec formula, in terms of both events and people.

One should first reflect on the long-standing historic division among Quebecers themselves over how best to preserve their language, identity, and unique civilization in North America. One thing Quebecers have known viscerally since the collapse of the French regime in 1759 — a collapse that owed more to France's failure to resupply than to any great British military success — is that Quebec could not count on Paris to help it sustain a francophone civilization and culture. If former British prime minister Ted Heath was justified in dismissing Pierre Trudeau's stand on NATO as offering all aid short of help, so too have Quebecers been justified in holding a healthy intergenerational disregard for France's concern or commitment. In fact, while the French head office in the eighteenth century largely ignored Quebec and showed itself to be far more interested in stirring colonial discontent in New England, the British Parliament passed the Quebec Act in 1774, establishing rights regarding the French language, Catholic schools, and French civil law — a gesture unprecedented in the British Empire. That went a long way towards ensuring Quebecers' disinterest when American revolutionaries sought to involve the colony in their initial and post-revolutionary anti-colonial struggles.

Historically, there have always been politicians like Sir Wilfrid Laurier and nationalist leaders in Quebec who have argued that the province's uniqueness is better preserved within Canada than adrift in the homogenizing, anti-bilingual melting pot of America. Separatist hardliners, on the other hand, have missed no opportunity to create mythologies, hyperventilate about alleged insults and humiliations, and blend everything into a recipe for independence. That is why it is important to separate fact from myth.

One often hears that in 1981, Canada and nine provinces concluded a constitutional agreement that limited the rights of the Quebec legislature. That assertion is without foundation in fact or practice. The Charter of Rights and Freedoms, which was as popular in Quebec as anywhere else, is the "offending intrusion" in question. It affords all Canadians the right to certain protections from undue state encroachment or legislated restrictions of expression or freedom. That affects the residents of all provinces equally. But to ensure particularity where necessary, the premier of Saskatchewan, a socialist, and the premier of Newfoundland, a conservative, introduced a clause that afforded any parliament or legislature in Canada the right to pass a law that could operate notwithstanding the charter and be renewed every five years. Quebec itself has used this provision. Hence, the notion that Quebec's legislative sovereignty is in any way diminished by the charter is sheer twaddle. But the myth is convenient for the hardliners.

The second myth about the charter is that Quebec was left out of the final night of negotiations, becoming a victim of "the night of long knives." This author was a ranking member of the Ontario delegation to those province-federal negotiations, and here is the unvarnished truth. A Quebec delegation, led by the affable and popular separatist premier René Lévesque, arrived in Ottawa in November 1981 as part of an eight-province coalition. That coalition purported to oppose Prime Minister Trudeau's proposal to produce a made-in-Canada constitution for the country. Aside from New Brunswick and Ontario, all Canadian provinces were part of this anti-Ottawa coalition, whose goal was to battle Ottawa to a compromise or a court-imposed constraint while at all costs avoiding a referendum pitting the provinces against Ottawa and the charter of rights. (The provinces would have lost badly.)

As the negotiations proceeded, it became clear that the Quebec delegation had no fall-back or compromise plan. Their strategy seemed incomplete, incompetent, or both. When, in a rhetorical flourish, Trudeau suggested the possibility of holding a referendum in Quebec on the proposed constitutional arrangement, Lévesque embraced the idea instantly as a way to polarize Quebecers once again. (His sovereignty-association option had been soundly defeated one year earlier.) The other coalition partners felt betrayed, and it became each province for itself.

Negotiations that produced the "notwithstanding clause" and language-education rights for francophones in population centres nationwide proceeded all night. The Quebecers were kept informed but decided not to participate. The profound pity is that their abdication left key issues for Quebec, such as a veto on any constitutional changes dealing with language, on the table. And why? Despite the message sent by Quebec voters one year earlier, the Parti Québécois government was prepared to advance only partisan interests. Gains for Quebec would have proved that Canada could work for the province, and would also have fulfilled promises made by the federalists in the 1980 referendum campaign to achieve change within Confederation if Quebecers voted to stay.

If there was any conspiracy to keep Quebec out of final negotiations, it was a PQ conspiracy to ensure that nothing good came from the negotiations. The elaborate canard of exclusion is pure theatre, but its resilience testifies to the hardliners' resolve. The Quebec government's decision not to be present when Queen Elizabeth II came to proclaim the new constitution in the spring of 1982 posed an interesting problem. Should Canada change its constitution when a province larger than Texas, and with a significant percentage of the country's population, objects? That issue produced an honest and important debate, led by Senator Lowell Murray, to the effect that, whatever the reason, Quebec's refusal to sign was sufficient cause not to proceed. Murray, a Conservative, was supported in the Senate by Ernest Manning, a former Social Credit premier of Alberta and the father of the present Reform Party leader, Preston Manning.

In the end, however, it would have been absurd to allow hardliners who opposed any renewal of Confederation to prevail just so they could claim that Confederation was static. Yet despite these facts, the mythology of the "purposeful exclusion" of Quebec from constitutional discussions continues to be circulated by hardliners and by others who should know better.

~

To be sure, many Quebecers may have been troubled in the past by the colonial wars of Great Britain or even the conscription issue in both world wars. But few wartime governments in history have worked as hard as the Canadian government did during the Second World War to meet wartime commitments without imposing compulsory service on elements of the population with historical and ethnic reasons for avoiding it. Canadian policy was not perfect, but it was framed as "conscription if necessary but not necessarily conscription," keeping both sides in the debate, including the anti-conscription nationalists in Quebec, essentially whole. Many Quebecers did volunteer, and many of Canada's most distinguished soldiers were

French-speaking Quebecers with deep nationalist roots. The Canadian armed forces are, in fact, among the most bilingual in the world, with recruitment in Quebec and among francophones more than competitive with recruitment elsewhere in Canada.

But more important than all of the above is the kind of sovereignty the hardline separatist leadership seeks today. At a time of greater interdependence among industrialized states, a time when the attributes of the old nation-state seem less and less relevant, the sort of nineteenth-century sovereignty sought by the Parti Québécois seems especially perverse.

If, as some proponents suggest, all that sovereignty for Quebec is about is assuring that Quebecers can move freely in the modern world while still speaking French, it would appear that independence is the least likely way to achieve that goal. One of the first results of independence would be the need to negotiate re-entry into NAFTA, which, under existing accession rules, is by no means automatic. Even assuming that what was left of Canada reconstructed and supported Quebec's entry (two very large assumptions), the United States would be free to seek new negotiations and terms. A host of non-tariff provisions that now serve to protect the French language would be opened to renegotiation. As international financial markets exerted pressure for Quebec to join NAFTA — which it would need to do in order to receive a constructive credit rating for its sovereign and debt instruments — the new government of an independent Quebec would be under immense pressure to relinquish the non-tariff barriers that the province now enjoys as part of Canada. The supreme irony here is that the erosion of protection for the French language would be an early and unavoidable price of Quebec's independence.

In fact, whatever difficulties surround the protection of the French language outside Quebec — and there have been many — Quebec's uniqueness as a French-speaking, dynamic society has always been, and will always be, best protected within Canada. One need only look at what happened to the French Canadians in Maine, Vermont, New Hampshire, Massachusetts, and Louisiana to understand the true meaning of melting-pot eradication.

Today, more French-speaking institutions, communities, schools, universities, businesses, artists, business people, and politicians exist in Quebec and Canada than ever before. French-speaking Quebecers are *maîtres chez nous* in their own majority French-speaking province to an extent not seen in Canada since 1759. The presence of huge global companies like Bombardier and SNC Lavalin, as well as leaders in animation, technology, and financial services, speaks to a strong resurgence of francophone-led, Quebec-based, Canadian-supported global business. Existing immigration arrangements allow Quebec to encourage the settlement of French speakers from around the world. The Canadian constitution ensures (as it does for all provinces) Quebec's sovereignty on matters of education and on much of social policy. That a pervasive, broad, and textured French-speaking society exists is undeniable. Independence would offer only the fiscal, monetary, and trade pressures that would make this society much harder to sustain.

No doubt many anomalies have survived over the past century as a result of a French-speaking Quebec existing within a Canadian confederated state within a British commonwealth. But when compared with the Anglo-Irish struggle, the U.S. Civil War, or the French struggle in Algeria, the measure of civility, co-operation, and practical compromise that has been obtained in Canada would strike any outside observer as quite compelling. Historical disputes, however exaggerated and mythologized they sometimes are, pale by comparison to the common benefit that a united future would bring.

But that case, while easily made in a rational way, cannot eradicate the emotional appeal of the pro-independence siren call. Understanding that side of the issue is essential to finding the necessary accommodations to keep Canada together. Ever since Quebec's secularizing revolution of the 1960s, there has existed a deeply felt desire to protect and advance, in a modern and civil context, the nationality, language, and civilization of French Canada. Various federal administrations have attempted to satisfy this desire with varying levels of success and sensitivity. Liberals have tended to develop centralist solutions, such as national bilingual rules or administrative fiats. Conservatives, who are far less often in federal office, have tended to be accommodationists seeking to renegotiate the constitution and win Quebec's confidence through a more decentralized confederation. Neither approach has succeeded fully, although pro-independence parties (such as the PQ) have historically won significant majorities during those periods when Liberals ruled at the national level. Certainly the Liberal prime ministers Trudeau and Chrétien learned that not even their own roots in

Quebec could dilute the corrosive impact of their insensitive centralism, which had the effect of fuelling the separatist cause.

To be fair, the frustration felt in moderately nationalist French Canada is to some extent paralleled in parts of English-speaking Canada, where the endless search for accommodation occasionally seems out of sync with a greater pan-Canadian nationalism. But again these strains and stresses are substantively less than might be found elsewhere. And as late as the spring of 1997, the federal government continued its centralist thrust by seeking a judgement from the Supreme Court of Canada concerning which laws would apply should Quebec's National Assembly ever vote to secede from Canada.

This obtuse initiative may actually mark the first time a country has asked its Supreme Court to describe, before the fact, the constitutional route to its own break-up. The questions submitted by the government, which are singularly shallow (e.g., does domestic or international law apply in the event of unilateral independence, and in the case of conflict between the two, which carries more weight?), reflect an intellectual bankruptcy within federal Liberal circles that must provide great comfort to separatist strategists. And one must remember that this same prime minister served in the Trudeau cabinet that, following two political kidnappings and a murder, proclaimed the War Measures Act in 1970 — an act that declared an "apprehended insurrection" and suspended the bill of rights, *habeas corpus,* and the right to be presumed innocent. Literally hundreds of Quebecers were arrested in the middle of the night, and not one of them was ever charged. No American president could have attempted such a broad curtailment of civil liberties in peacetime, but Trudeau and Chrétien did. No subsequent information has ever justified this particular travesty in Quebec.

Much of the present Liberal strategy finds its roots in the notion that the perception of a painless separation without consequences is misguided and unhelpful. That may very well be true. But daring Quebecers to cross a line, as well as arguing judicial rulings that have little chance of ever being enforced, seems to offer less hope for meaningful accommodation. That is the federal Liberals' current course, but many federalists in Quebec and elsewhere see it as a road to nowhere.

Happily, Ottawa's myopic view is balanced by a series of provincial premiers — some Liberal, some socialist, some Conservative — who take a far more sensitive and open-minded approach to resolving existing tensions. And even within the federal government, there are leading Liberals — such as the popular finance minister, Paul Martin, and the minister for human resources, Pierre Pettigrew — who seem more prepared to argue for *de facto* accommodation and decentralization. The leader of the national New Democratic Party (socialist), Alexa McDonough, and the national Progressive Conservatives' Charest share this approach, although with different nuances. As the coming federal election will not likely expand the Liberal majority in the House of Commons, quiet pressure for embracing a more confederal union will probably increase.

The genius of stressing the confederal nature of Canada as opposed to a top-down federal approach is that it responds to concerns about excessive centralization that are felt equally in the West and in Quebec, although for different reasons. A paper commissioned by the minister of intergovernmental affairs for Ontario and written by Dr. Tom Courchene of Queen's University postulated a new, more confederal approach to social policy and national standards. While some centralists in Ottawa and one or two more partisan Liberal premiers initially dismissed the report, the core idea it advanced — namely, an interprovincial approach to the social services delivered by the provinces, as opposed to a top-down approach from Ottawa — should ring a bell with Americans long concerned about the damage caused by unfunded federal mandates.

Try to imagine what would happen to state budgets if Washington imposed national medical care; mandated that universal benefits be accessible, mobile, and portable; and then cut funding substantially without reducing the statutory rule. Ottawa has essentially done that in both health care and social services (welfare), while increasing employee and employer contributions to unemployment insurance and raising various taxes.

One need not be a separatist in Quebec to feel put upon in this situation. But to be fair, Ottawa has reduced deficits and so have the provinces. Genuine fiscal progress is being made.

So the opportunity for progress on economic, devolutionary, and restructuring issues, if done in a way that will afford Quebec the *instruments de société* and help to sustain a French-speaking people within the Canadian confederation, is real and proximate. But while the ingredients for accommodation are all in place, two sorts of obstacles stand in the way. The first emerges from the Manning-Trudeau school of dismissive politics and the second places the most pressure on Premier Bouchard.

Trudeau opposed the decentralizing constitutional agreements of 1987 and 1992, and Manning's Reform Party is a Western-based, anti-accommodationist, right-wing coalition. Their dismissive school essentially views Quebec nationalists, even those who devoutly believe in a Canadian solution, as apostles of a loosening of Confederation or of a special status that could not and should not be tolerated. Although Manning is a Ross Perot–type populist with a Bible belt brand of social and fiscal conservatism and Trudeau is a leftist proponent of a munificent state, they have become almost as one regarding Quebec. Both opposed the two constitutional agreements signed by all ten provinces and Ottawa, and each provides the other with a certain unintended legitimacy.

The dismissive school seeks either to call Quebec's bluff or to establish an elaborate twelve-step approach loaded with threats to disallow Quebec independence. Some in Trudeau's entourage have already talked about imposing foreign election observers on any future Quebec referendum on sovereignty. That is a soliloquy of the deaf and could well push Quebec over a line it cannot recross.

Similarly, there is no lack of over-fuelled "flag and shield" separatists in Bouchard's government and the PQ, and these separatists will not feel fulfilled until Quebec has a network of embassies it cannot afford, its own flag at the United Nations, and its own Olympic team.

Nor is there much chance that under the pompous, self-important, and obtuse Jacques Chirac, France will pass on an opportunity to be meddlesome and mischievous. An independent Quebec could not possibly sustain sufficient Canadian-dollar deposits to ensure continued Canadian bank credits and loans, so Quebec would require its own currency. It is not beyond the delusionary foreign policy of post-Gaullist France to conjure an overseas franc zone linked to the lucrative American market. Of course, the French would promptly desert a new Quebec, just as they deserted the old Quebec in 1759. But they will dangle the prospect of support just to stir the pot.

The most serious source of pressure on Bouchard may well be the restiveness brought about by Quebec's high poverty rate and increasingly radical unions in the public sector. Since becoming premier, Bouchard has sought to increase the fiscal responsibility of Quebec's public accounts. He is nearing the crunch in that process, and depending on what provocation comes from Ottawa or elsewhere, he might seek an early election, which in turn could advance the date of a referendum on sovereignty.

But the road ahead is by no means clear. Mario Dumont, the leader of the Parti Action Démocratique and Bouchard's ally in the last sovereignty referendum, is now offering Quebecers a ten-year moratorium on any referendum and a relatively neo-liberal economic and social platform. Bouchard will not enter the next referendum as virginal and popular as he entered the last, when he was truly a white knight who wanted to save the damsel in distress but had yet to dig a moat or tax the castle. He has now done both. Taxes are high and the moat leaks.

On balance, a series of *de facto* changes in the operation of the federation will likely blunt the separatist cause. The realization that intellectual, technical, and financial relevance are the only true sovereignty will lead to an understanding that liberation for Quebec is possible only within a decentralized Canada that redefines government and the state according to principles of social justice and economic and cultural freedom.

Confederation itself was negotiated in 1867 by Sir John A. Macdonald and representatives from Upper Canada (Ontario), Lower Canada (Quebec) — which were united as simply Canada from the 1840s to 1867 — and the colonies of New Brunswick and Nova Scotia. Quebec and Ontario then split apart, permitting the formation of a confederated state between the four provinces and a new, derivative federal government. All of that took place in 1867, as Canadians made common cause against the Fenian raids launched from the United States in the aftermath of its bloody civil war. There was no revolution against Great Britain, no war, no violence, no election, and no referendum. Canada's first constitution was an act of the British House of Commons — the British North America Act — and within a year of its passage, Nova Scotians elected a majority of legislators determined to pull Nova Scotia out of Confederation. So Canadians have been through this before, and the idea of Canada has always survived — not because it is perfect, militant, imperial, or immutable, but precisely because it is none of the above.

The essence of Canada and the basis of its citizens' high quality of life, superior productivity, and relative civility is the Canadian approach to compromise. That approach embraces, when necessary, the "binding glue of ambiguity." Recently released polls indicate that 80 percent of Quebecers feel a strong affinity for, and wish to remain within, Canada. That 50 percent would vote to separate if no changes are made is not in any way a contradiction. It reflects Quebecers' desire to be part of a country that can make progressive compromises to protect the French language, culture, and civilization, which Quebec, as the only majority francophone province, has a duty to advance and promote. If and when Quebecers conclude that Canada's specific dynamism is gone, their sense of affinity will indeed dissipate.

A famous and popular Quebec comedian joked some years ago that Quebecers want a free and independent Quebec within a strong and unified Canada. After the laughter died down, this insightful apparent contradiction became an underlying theme of the debate.

Unfortunately, the present federal administration appears unwilling to make new proposals to resolve outstanding issues. But in one way or another, the federal election this year will end the stagnation, Bouchard will cease to control the agenda, and the momentum towards genuine progress will revive. At every stage of Canada's development, seemingly insurmountable problems about representative and responsible government, minority language rights and their protection, the English-speaking minority in Quebec and francophone minorities elsewhere, and war efforts overseas have given way to compromise solutions, however hard to achieve. Losing the ability to compromise in a free nation, with a federal-provincial structure and fundamental values rooted in dialogue and decency, would be an ultimate denial of what it means to be Canadian. When all is said and done, that will not happen.

DEMOCRACY IS 50 PERCENT PLUS ONE, OR IT ISN'T DEMOCRACY

Financial Post, *June 7, 1997*

The newly re-elected prime minister of Canada has one key question to address before the next Quebec referendum. It is a question that relates to the core of his government's credibility, and to the essence of his government's approach to defending and promoting the federalist option.

Since the very first Quebec referendum, in 1980, prime ministers from all parts of Canada, including Jean Chrétien, have accepted the premise that should Quebecers, or any other group of Canadians, vote democratically to secede from Canada, that vote would be valid. This all changed during the campaign, at the precise point when Jean Charest experienced a dynamic surge in Quebec.

The decision of previous Bloc Québécois voters, many of whom had never been sovereignists, along with many Quebec Liberal voters, to move to Charest's moderate and hopeful message of conciliation could have produced as many as thirty or forty seats in Quebec for the Conservatives. This could have, with appropriate resources in Ontario and elsewhere, created a Progressive Conservative official opposition and a Liberal minority government.

The Liberals reacted by having the prime minister tell Daniel Lessard of Radio-Canada that 50 percent plus one was no longer the basis upon which the Yes side could win a referendum. This, along with Preston Manning's TV ads, did two things. It told all Quebecers, including moderate federalists, that for Chrétien, democracy applies only when the good guys win. If the sovereignists had won by the same margin as the federalists last time, that result would not have been valid. When combined with the clear message of the Reform campaign, the prime minister's new take on democracy re-inflated the sovereignist vote, repolarized Quebec, and shattered the moderate coalition forming behind Charest. Liberals saved their majority, but just barely. Reform is now the official opposition. And Chrétien has a serious problem.

How can the federal government marshal arguments in support of Canada when Quebec has its next referendum if the validity of the referendum is now challenged by the prime minister? All other party leaders in Parliament believe that 50 percent plus one is a fair endorsement of either Yes or No. The government of Canada, the Liberal Party, and Chrétien now do not.

What could have been a rout for the Bloc Québécois became a first-place finish in the Quebec federal seat count. And now, any federal involvement in the next referendum will immediately raise the issue of whether the government is the anti-democratic force, seeking to deny the right of Canadians anywhere, and Quebecers in particular, to vote on their own future.

This gives the sovereignists the opportunity to make the right to decide the sub-theme overshadowing the merits of independence itself. It is unclear how this prime minister, having said what he has said, can have any moral credibility in defence of the Canadian option. And having personally acted to inflate the sovereignist vote, he will surely find that his credibility elsewhere will not be high.

Democracy is a little like truth. If you tell different lies at different times to different people, remembering what you said can be a challenge. If you simply tell the truth, it is amazing how easy it is to remember what you said.

Democracy is either 50 percent plus one or it isn't democracy. Whether the Yes side should be able in perpetuity to hold referenda until they get the right answer is a fair question. But what constitutes democratic authority is not. Besides, a prime minister with a majority government that had less than 40 percent of the vote in many parts of Canada is a little hard pressed to make the case that 50 percent plus one is not enough.

His problem is a simple digression from democracy, a simple desertion of tradition, and a surrender of credibility and relevance. He has lost the ability to lead his government during the next referendum.

The future of this country will not be sustained by denying the core principles of democracy. Leadership requires an embrace of democracy and the defence of the Canadian ideal as a matter of public choice and individual preference. That ideal is based on the pervasive value of democracy itself. Denying that core value only strengthens the case of those who suggest that Canada isn't worth defending.

WRONG TO ASSUME CANADA WILL REMAIN INTACT AFTER SEPARATION

Financial Post, *August 23, 1997*

The irony for the partition movement, and the less-than-thought-out federal support for it, is that both partitionists and sovereignists are making the very same fundamental mistake. It is a mistake that is at the root of a series of misconceptions and apparently logical conclusions that will evaporate the moment the truth becomes apparent.

What is that mistake — and why is it equally lethal to the aspirations of both sovereignists and partitionists? The mistake is the assumption that, should Quebec ever leave, there would be a successor state. Partitionists and sovereignists pin their post-independence scenarios on there being a Canada after Quebec leaves. Sovereignists want a monetary, trade, customs, debt-management, and perhaps even social-reciprocity agreement with the new Canada. Partitionists want to have their designated territories affiliated with what's left of Canada — in a sort of "Republika Srpska" strategy (upon leaving the Yugoslav federation, Bosnia was itself divided, with Srpska becoming an enclave with affiliations to Serbia). This strategy appears to be one that Intergovernmental Affairs Minister Stéphane Dion and New Brunswick Premier Frank McKenna encourage.

One can understand how partition risks fit the federal government's Plan B scenario, raising issues and questions to which there are no easy answers. The more salient point lies not in the mirage of partition or in the incomprehensible logic of a Srpska strategy on the part of Ottawa, but in the more pressing truth that the departure of any one of Quebec, Ontario, British Columbia, or Alberta would bring the country to an end. Why? Simply because if we are incapable of accommodating a constructive recon-federation when tensions are cultural and regional, how in heaven could we build a new confederation when one province had almost 60 percent of all the people and 75 percent of economic activity? Would British Columbia, Alberta, or Saskatchewan accept a parliament where Ontario has 60 per-cent of all the seats? Would they accept an economy where Ontario's min-ister of finance would control more of their economic reality than all ministers of finance across Canada combined? I see no prospect whatever of cobbling together a new confederation without Quebec, when the role of Quebec as one key counterweight to Ontario is out of the picture.

This means that there would be no Canada to which partitionists can affix their territories. And with no Canada, there would be no successor state with which a sovereign Quebec could deal or negotiate treaties. In fact, even the proposed negotiation hiatus between a sovereignist vote and a proclamation of independence — if that hiatus was ever real — would find sovereignists looking in vain for someone with whom to negotiate.

A Canadian parliament with seventy-five seats from Quebec is not an appropriate interlocutor. Premiers would justifiably want in on the process. By the time English Canada sorted out who was on first (and I recommend the Abbot and Costello video "Who's on First?" to those interested in how this process would work), Quebec would have declared independence and the disintegration would have begun. Debt-management issues with primarily U.S. lenders would dominate. The partitionists would be largely without any new place with which to affiliate.

B.C. and Alberta would likely be on their own, perhaps together. The Atlantic provinces would be seeking to cobble together a commonwealth of sorts with New England. Ontario would probably have a range of options, including becoming an independent dominion.

If a management process for the debt were found, the pressures faced by all this flotsam and jetsam to gain entry to the North American Free Trade Agreement and the Auto Pact, to ensure markets for everything from timber to fish, auto parts, and oil and gas, would be immense. And our U.S. friends, after a crocodile tear or two, would have a self-interested strategy to exact new concessions and play all parties against each other in their own interest — which is surely legitimate from their perspective.

This is the real truth that partitionists and sovereignists share a common interest in suppressing. The truth that dare not speak its name. "Disintegration" — not a pleasant word. A lot less pleasant a word than "accommodation," "compromise," "asymmetry," or even "distinctness."

It need not happen — and likely won't if the compelling common sense and fairness of Canadians is allowed to prevail. It would be truly encouraging to see the federal government appealing to this option, as opposed to tacitly supporting a hopeless and unreal Srpska approach.

OTTAWA'S POLICIES MUST REFLECT THE GENUINE CONCERNS OF B.C.

Financial Post, *October 4, 1997*

Visiting Vancouver in the fall produces in me the same impression I had during the first days of summer in Victoria. This part of Canada has developed a compelling sense of grievance with, and disconnect from, Ottawa — comparable to that experienced by Alberta in the 1970s and Quebec most of the time. That Senator Pat Carney should be the one to articulate it this round should neither upset nor surprise. Carney has never been a conventional politician, and party loyalty has never implied subservience to the conventional wisdom, even if it is from time to time the sum total of party policy.

In this circumstance, my sense is that her public reflection on a separatist option for British Columbians only gives vent to a long-established view here that Ottawa is, at best, self-absorbed and irrelevant and, at worst, focused on central Canada at the expense of places like B.C. that contribute to equalization, pay their taxes, and ask for very little.

Intergovernmental Affairs Minister Stéphane Dion's response to Carney addresses Ottawa's inability to understand how various parts of Canada are losing patience with a highly centralized, unitary federal view that denies the confederal roots of the country and seeks always to diminish or dilute the concerns expressed in provincial capitals. For better or worse, the duly elected government of B.C. is involved in a matter of compelling local concern — the salmon fishery.

It is hard, whatever one's view of Premier Glen Clark's tactics, to differ with his duty to defend the fishermen of his province. And while the federal government seems to get its policy directions from the Oxbridge high table over at the external affairs department, Canadians in B.C. are losing their livelihood, their fishing boats, and their homes. The fish are being pirated in some measure by the Americans, who are using brute politics and presidential threat to avoid any meaningful negotiation.

Whatever else one might want to say about B.C., it would be the height of folly to think it anti-American. British Columbians voted for free trade and have been meaningful beneficiaries of the trade flows that have ensued. B.C.'s general affinity with the coastal economy of the U.S. Southwest is considerably greater than that with the rest of Canada. It is well positioned to look west and south for economic opportunities and links, and has been doing so successfully for years. This is a large reason for the prosperity British Columbians have earned for themselves and the contributions they make in many ways to the rest of Canada.

The challenge here is one of both form and substance. Ottawa must not only reflect the genuine concerns of British Columbians, but also make those concerns central to its world-view. Foreign policy is not for the striped-pants set. It must be a reflection of the genuine concerns of people.

When the turbot was under foreign attack on the East Coast, a federal minister was at the United Nations and a Royal Canadian Navy frigate, the coast guard, fisheries vessels, and a submarine were dispatched to the Newfoundland coast. Canada was equally focused when Nova Scotian and American fishing fleets faced a boundary dispute off the East Coast. Even British Columbians who are unsure of the fishermen's case believe Ottawa should be more on B.C.'s side and less prone to isolating the duly elected B.C. government.

One local business leader suggested that while threatening to close a joint U.S./Canada submarine base might well have been outside B.C.'s jurisdiction and a touch over the top, no one could believe that a governor in Alaska or the state of Washington would not fail to bring the same kind of pressure to bear on the U.S. government if the State Department seemed to be playing footsie with Canada.

That is the context Ottawa should reflect upon in assessing the significance of a former federal minister of energy, former president of the Treasury Board, and former minister for foreign trade raising the independence option. The frustration she is mirroring is real and intense.

Ottawa can either engage to stop the centrifugal spiral by recalibrating its approach to B.C., or it can let the centrifugal forces spin utterly out of control. The nature of Ottawa's answer will reflect the Liberal view of what leadership in a confederation is really all about.

COURT REFERENCE A RESULT OF LIBERALS' INTELLECTUAL VACUUM

Financial Post, *February 18, 1998*

The morality play that began this week — as the federal government turned to the courts for the policy substance it lacks on national unity — reflects the intellectual bankruptcy that plagues Prime Minister Chrétien's Ottawa. While all Canadians have a right to be consulted before any part of Canada separates, history tells us that the Supreme Court of Canada is not the best way for that to happen.

This week's court reference implies that we deal best with each other by imposing interdictions, no-go zones, and legal prohibitions in place of what should be democratic debate, persuasion, innovation, and co-operation. It is a surrender on the part of official Ottawa to the forces of polarization and to the merchandisers of division, who truly believe in the use of fear and double-dare politics in the affairs of a civilized country.

If those at the extreme and largely discredited fringe of the sovereignist movement engage in xenophobic or small-minded politics, surely the federalist response should be the politics of the larger view and the innovative ideas that help renew Confederation. Instead, Ottawa's obsessive focus on Plan B — the effort at intimidation over such issues as borders, legality, and financial stability — has left the job of advancing Plan A — a creative approach to solving the problems and moving ahead in a civil and progressive way — to the provincial premiers. The Calgary Declaration, already shunned by the sovereignists and the far right in Canada, is a beginning along a Plan A path that holds promise despite Ottawa's only grudging support. The "centre knows best" dictum still controls Chrétien's Ottawa, which, in terms of the brutal absence of intellectual content, is both ironic and frightening. For example, despite the continuing efforts of premiers of all political affiliations at a true dialogue, there is no compelling evidence that Ottawa is truly committed to reforming the social-policy aspects of the federation in a way that reduces waste and expands effectiveness without sacrificing accessibility.

The court reference is neither venal nor cruel, as Quebec premier Lucien Bouchard and company contend. After all, in 1981 René Lévesque went to the Supreme Court to stop unilateral patriation of the constitution. But it is not a solution. Even if the Supreme Court rules fully in Ottawa's favour, which is unlikely, how would Ottawa actually enforce that ruling if a majority of Quebecers or Albertans or British Columbians voted democratically to leave the federation? Sadly, this is lost on the mixed and troubling alliance of hardline federalists, federal bureaucrats, partitionists, Reformers, and old-time centralizers who have joined with others who have displayed only too enthusiastic a tendency to beat up on Quebec.

The questions before the court are about far more than the law, the constitution, and international convention. They affect democratic practice, the right to self-determination, and the democratic debate that should ensue when there is honest, if fundamental, disagreement. That disagreement does have the potential of ending Canada, and therefore is everyone's business. But the consequences of failure do not justify embracing only the instruments of failure. And looking to the courts is an embrace of just such an instrument. It is an admission that the creativity necessary to resolve our national differences no longer exists at the federal level. This clearly reflects the Chrétien approach to a politics that is without vision, risk, or content. He has discovered that political longevity is sustained by standing for little, advancing less, embracing whatever seems practical, and lying low. It is the politics of no risk, no ideas, and no courage. It is from this intellectual vacuum that the reference to the Supreme Court emerged.

Anyone who dismisses past efforts to find a political solution as sheer folly because none succeeded misses the point. For thirty years of these efforts — Lester Pearson's, Pierre Trudeau's, Brian Mulroney's — minority rights have grown stronger; our economy, population, and achievements have expanded; and the greatest country in the world has stayed peacefully together. We have learned from each so-called failure. The past thirty years have extended the reach of our nation and its potential. A prime minister afraid of failure may well lack the will to hold the nation together.

Courts are about winners and losers. Confederation has always been about partners.

PART FIVE

The Political Dynamic

IT IS EASY TO VIEW POLITICS AS A STORY OF WINNERS AND LOSERS, AND of choices made that are good or bad, right or wrong. Having been associated with victories and more than my share of defeats, I can tell you that defeat and victory are perhaps the most barefaced impostors of any of the actors in the political theatre. Pierre Trudeau's election win in 1968 sowed the seeds for Robert Stanfield's near-victory in 1972; Trudeau's victory in 1974 began the process that elected Joe Clark, however briefly, in 1979. It is surely true that the nature of the pro–free trade coalition in 1988, which re-elected the government of Brian Mulroney, led inexorably to some of the defeat Kim Campbell experienced in 1993. How political parties operate, how they posture around issues, how Parliament does or does not work — all reflect both institutional and structural weaknesses and strengths.

If continued efforts to perfect our democracy, to make it more reflective, effective, and humane, are a mark of our civility, so too is understanding the dynamics of the players and the operations that are essential to that process. The idea of continuing to perfect democracy must never be set aside, since to do so means that we are complacent about the excesses and unfairnesses that still exist. That complacency is something we cannot afford.

DISCLOSURE RULES NEEDED

Toronto Star, *March 9, 1983*

Controversy surrounding former cabinet ministers often raises a key issue far larger than the specifics of the alleged wrongdoing or the ministers' protestations of innocence. The issue embraces the very nature of public service, private prerogative, and the tone and substance of politics itself in this country.

For those who have served at the ministerial or sub-ministerial level, the question this issue often boils down to is very simple: Is there life after politics? For those who have never served, the issues are patronage, propriety, and public trust. Guidelines, however well intentioned, may be inappropriate simply because they create an unreal world. For example, would a former federal minister, one who has served in, let's say, the ministries of finance, justice, trade, and energy, and has not practised law for twenty years, be a viable member of a law firm after political retirement if all matters relating to those areas of government were on the "disallowed" list for a period of years? Should a decision not to stand for election, or an election defeat, also mean reducing one's capacity to earn a living? If the answer to any of these is yes, does that imply that only those of independent wealth should seek public office?

As organizers of all three political parties will tell anyone who asks, finding competent people to stand for office is becoming very hard. And it would become even harder if the rules of the game directed that one's years in office were to be a hindrance, interdiction, and undue disability when one left to return to private life.

One means of dealing with this problem might be disclosure rules that had former politicians make public all holdings, not just during their period in government (which is the case in most jurisdictions) but for two years thereafter. The certain knowledge of public disclosure might serve as an effective balance in those grey areas where matters of "right and wrong" are by no means crystal clear. The American and British political cultures tolerate far greater levels of back-and-forth movement between private and public sectors. Walter Mondale left the vice-presidency for a key position in the American communications industry. George Shultz, a former secretary of state, went to a key international engineering and contracting firm.

It is hard to suggest that the American system was made less pure or wholesome by virtue of the career options of these men.

The public's right to be assured of limitations on undue benefit from past government associations must be balanced against the right of any citizen to seek public office without imperilling a fair career pattern after his or her departure from public life. Broader disclosure rules, if backed up by an "exit oath" upon leaving elected office, could provide this balance. The exit oath might include a simple statement about the last ministry position the officeholder occupied, with a clear listing of benefits that should not be allowable from the non-statutory areas of government funding or grant programs in that ministry.

A lifetime career in politics may be an option for some; it should never be the only option those pondering public life are forced to consider.

PARTY GOVERNMENT: THE AWFUL AND INEXORABLE TRUTH

Presentation to the School of Policy Studies MPA Policy Forum, Queen's University, Kingston, Ontario, April 28, 1995

The status of the political party as an institution capable of inspiring hope, coalescing consensus, informing and reflecting public opinion is certainly less than might be desired. Rather than being compared with an athlete at peak performance levels, the political party could more appropriately be compared with an old hockey star — more valued for the past than for the future.

The evolution, in the British tradition, from an absolute monarchy to responsible parliamentary government reflected the incapacity of monarchical forces to enforce, over time, the hegemony others sought to share. But sharing power with others, through what became an incrementally more democratic parliamentary process, was and is a far cry from the end of the monarchical role as was so heartlessly achieved by the French Revolution. The shape of the political parties in Canada comes from a system of sharing power rather than just a transfer of power. Our British roots produced an evolution of government that began with colonial governors sent out from the mother country with their absolute powers. This eventually evolved into a system of conservative councils formed from the local landed elite, and finally into responsible and elected parliamentary norms. Our confederal roots meant that the core unit was the colony or the province, which consented to the extension of confederal aspirations to the federal government. Hence, our political parties' core functions were not so much at the national level, but at the more cautious, conservative, frugal, and sceptical local county, riding, and village levels. These functions reflected not only the division of liberals and conservatives, but also the struggle between, on one side, members of the established and landed classes and their churches and, on the other, members of the merchant class, who would exercise influence over and hold business hegemony locally — either by sending one of their own to the provincial capital or Ottawa, or by determining who would be sent and to whom he would owe allegiance.

Historically, as the political columnist Jeffrey Simpson insists in his book *The Spoils of Power,* political parties were not instruments of national direction or reconciliation, but rather were partisan units for controlling and sorting out who got what from whom and when — locally, provincially, and nationally. While the broad issue of patronage may bother some in this context, it is a narrow filament in the lamp of partisan illumination. Controlling and sorting out who got what from whom is not so much about patronage as it is about public policy itself: when and where to build a railway, whether to go to war, whether to have a system of universal medical care, whether to raise taxes, whether provinces will borrow more or retire their debt. All of these issues are manifestations of who gets what from whom.

The political party, like any other institution with a purpose, roots, battles won and lost, and recruitments to pursue, has exigencies such as solid organization; financial capacity; men and women with political skill, philosophic coherence, and public appeal. But if the party cannot communicate the context of its time and place, neither the integrity of its leaders nor the competence of its policy substance will matter one bit. Sadly, the opposite may also be true. As the political party institutionalized, in response to the electoral schedule, the mass media, the broadening of suffrage, the changing political climates of post-Depression or postwar or post-television or post–Industrial Revolution, so too did it develop a framework of independent institutional needs and flaws that accompanies the embrace of those needs by both the rank and file and the party hierarchy.

The need for money requires fund-raising. The need to communicate requires competent communication of real substance. The need to be differentiated requires coherent policy, which in turn requires expert counsel and staff. However populist one's roots or pretensions, meaningful competence requires a break with unfettered and amorphous populism. It is a serious challenge faced by all movements that have even the most moderate or fleeting electoral success. As the Liberals in 1984 and the Conservatives in 1993 found out, not even the sparkle of new personalities, however compelling, can fill the gap of political competence when it is simply too wide and too deep. The competitive political marketplace now encompasses more than just other political parties. It embraces the media, a myriad of interest groups, and other forces seeking to control the agenda.

Too many players in the ideas marketplace in our democracies are simply too skilled for partisan incompetence to survive without doing great damage to our democratic institutions — including, and perhaps above all, the political party itself. When competently managed and run, a political party becomes the ultimate public instrument for resolving genuine national challenges that are unresolvable by any other institution. When incompetently run, it fails to serve the country and quickly victimizes itself.

However, when political parties are diminished — as they are in the United Kingdom, the United States, Canada, and France, for example — as too self-centred or corrupt to be of any value to our society or government, it is perhaps appropriate to ask, ever so sheepishly, "Self-centred and corrupt as compared with whom?" With which institutions could we, on matters of selflessness and morality, compare political parties unfavourably? The church? Olympic games or athletes? Corporations? The media? Benevolent or fraternal associations? Academe? The police? Union movements? Guilds? Performing or plastic arts? Construction trades? Healing arts? The military? Which have escaped the taint of corruption, self-seeking personality cult, undue influence? None has escaped because each is simply the expression of a range of human nature and character, from the most uplifting, noble, and altruistic to the most selfish, venal, and insensitive. Dismissing the political party as a source of good government is like outlawing institutional religion as a framework for faith. It will, like Topsy, re-institute and reappear. It will never disappear. Moreover, the process by which political parties have their relative salience allegedly diminished is not one for which only the practitioner or the political careerist can be blamed. There are other competitive forces at work.

If we disengage from the rather friendly myth that somehow the political party, as a holder or seeker of authority over the rest of us, is justifiably an appropriate target for more cynicism, criticism, scrutiny, and disbelief than all competing institutions, we can approximate a more reliable and realistic truth. That truth, simply stated, is that in an age when few institutions have any purchase on any kind of sustained legitimacy, political parties have become no more influential than other social institutions that are more diffused and fragmented throughout society. In fact, they have become, in many respects, somewhat less influential.

Some of this may be due to the simple reality that familiarity breeds contempt. Through the constant media coverage of state and provincial legislatures, Parliament, and Congress, politicians have been kept intensely in view at levels that are, frankly, excessive for the civilized world. Who among us can believe that events of such import transpire in our Parliament or legislatures daily as to justify nightly live reports? Yet we have them. What other institution could withstand this kind of scrutiny without devolving into something between a soap opera — with high daily values of manufactured drama — and professional sport? Surely this is where the excessive coverage has focused the political process in the minds of most North Americans. The links here between this phenomenon and the values of fiction, contrivance, irrelevance, and moral legitimacy should not be lost on any of us.

Some of the direct attacks on the legitimacy of political parties are launched by those eager for their own power. There are corporations that seek to replace duly elected political sovereignty with tax-haven head-office arrangements — all often quite legal. There are interest groups that seek to pierce any politically consensual agenda with their own no-compromise blitz for the trendy issue of the day. There are bureaucracies that can be driven by their own internal, systemic, and careerist exigencies to adopt a "father knows best" approach to restraining, diluting, or delaying a newly elected government's agenda. There is the neo-conservative bias that government has little purpose other than protecting those who are caught in the cycle of wealth from those who are not. All of the above contribute to the visceral sense of inertia that political parties emit upon gaining public office. Cynicism and despair about the process are, of course, the arch-enemies of political parties that argue from the right, left, or centre that prin-cipled, co-operative, democratic partnership is a valid instrument for social stability, enlightened public policy, and an orderly economic framework.

So the issue of party government — its prospects and challenges — is not so much a question of structure or ideology or grass roots, although all of these matter in some measure. It is instead an issue of competence in an intensely competitive environment. We must be clear that some of the more extreme on the neo-conservative right or the radical, anarchic left — aided on occasion by the paternalists in the permanent civil service who prefer political parties to be as incompetent and ineffective in matters of public policy as possible, either because they would prefer incompetent and irrelevant public policy or because they cannot bring themselves to accept that a political party is to be trusted with anything as important as public policy — dislike and deride party competence, often implying that to be competent in fundraising or communication is to be mildly corrupt! In fact, while no conspiracy exists, there is a tacit and consensual value struc-ture that works steadily against any political party that is competent.

Parties that raise money effectively or efficiently, or both, are quickly dis-missed as corruptible or sleazy. Those that debate policy or advance it coher-ently are dismissed as wonky or too ideological to be an effective political organization. Those parties that communicate effectively are attacked with the code words "slick" or "machine." Those that plan their integrated activ-ities effectively, which means not in public, are accused of being dominated by the backroom. Those that decide publicly on issues are called fragmented. Those that maintain unity are deemed to be anti-democratic and fearful of the leader's iron fist. Those that have competent and experienced activists in senior advisory roles, either elected or appointed, are said to be dominated by a small cadre to the detriment of grass-roots democracy. Finally, those that have no such centre are said, simply, to be an unfocused populist rab-ble. These views are purveyed often by editorial writers, reporters, or inter-ested members of groups working within and outside the government.

We should not, however, confuse such criticisms with some undeniable truth. In fact, if the Irish author and politician Conor Cruise O'Brien is correct in worrying that the unyielding pursuit of popularity may be democ-racy's Achilles heel, it is also true that the abdication of political competence would open democracies around the world to a more pernicious weakness: the weakness of dysfunctional and dismembered politics. As politics is the most civilized replacement we have for more violent conflict about agenda or deliberative dominance, we should think about its disappearance with some care.

Political parties need to become more aggressive if they are to be effective when in government. Margaret Thatcher, the former prime minister of Great Britain, was correct in establishing the Central Policy Unit to influence the centrist and change-resistant Whitehall establishment. A political party that gains the temporary right to govern without having the people and policy in place to begin governing has perpetuated a giant hoax on the electorate and is forced to spend the early post-election mandate months in on-the-job training. This is akin to surrendering a serious percentage of the purpose of the mandate itself. In politics, the only commodity you cannot recapture is time!

Political parties should consider owning and operating newspapers, as they once did. They should be free to compete in the marketplace of ideas — free to recruit, educate, and develop the sophisticated analytical human and leadership resources necessary to express public opinion, to contribute to the public agenda, and to convert partisan opinion and principle into public policy and direction. Just as we embrace competence in a host of areas, we should celebrate it in partisan political activity. Because, in the end, competent political parties, whether of the right, the left, or the centre, discourage social fragmentation and political disunity, and encourage coalitions that produce understanding, enlightenment, and national cohesion. Political incompetence, and hence the evaporation of partisan efficacy and legitimacy, leads to divisions and coalitions reflective of more base and troubling motivations.

In the end, the public interest can be served only when duly elected political parties have the will to execute their partisan policy preferences in a competent and cohesive way. A failure of will is a failure of the system itself. Even with governments at the margin, they must be competent.

While all groups in society have their instruments for influencing public policy, and all use them quite shamelessly, the only real instrument of public will — which is open at all levels to scrutiny and participation by the public at large — is the political party. It is the only conduit by which the public has a formal say in determining the principles of government and choosing the people who will make and carry out public policy. If we remove competent political parties, what is actually being removed is the "public" from public policy or public service. Political parties guarantee an intergenerational link with our past, our roots, our failures, and our successes. Political parties provide a framework that defines the debate, organizes the combatants, and sustains stability.

Political parties face three survival challenges. First, for those who prefer the random and often cruel, racist, sectarian, and regional debate that frequently infects the political arena, the well-organized and well-led political party is clearly the enemy. Second, unrestrained populism threatens the structure, history, collegiality, partisan loyalties, and network of the competent political party. And third, demagogues who distil racism, xenophobia, class envy, or social anxiety for their own purposes have a vested interested in joining with the media and special interests in belittling political parties.

Upon reflection, I believe these problems may be the strongest points in favour of vigorous political parties. The core issue for democratic governments throughout the world is how change is addressed in a way that reduces poverty, increases wealth, and provides a framework that has sufficient order and stability for normal people to lead reasonably safe and satisfying lives. If democratic governments fail at creating this kind of stable framework, then people will turn to other than democratic means. This anxiety is particularly real in formal totalitarian communist regimes, where the lack of a stable multi-party political culture has not only produced wild swings of instability, but also contributed to frantic economic dispossession for millions. We need only glance at democracies that emerged from right-wing dictatorships such as that in Spain to appreciate what the slide to instability would do to their fledging democratic mini-traditions.

The political party is about order. It is about freedom expressed and articulated in an orderly context. Orderly contexts, hierarchies of loyalty, structure, partisanship, and competence do not an exciting newscast make. In fact, the exciting, conflict-ridden, excessive, and unbalanced newscast is more about the network's needs than it is about the public's needs. Those who believe in democracy and prefer it to the other options had best not be too complacent about the continued need for political parties and party government. Even if you embrace, as I do, the idea that government these days is at best a limited force for good at the periphery of a society now dominated by other forms, energies, and actors, the competence of government, its cohesion, and its focus still matter. The apparatus of the modern state — however much it must be made more efficient, less costly, more privatized, and less centralized — is still the only instrument that defends, as a matter of purpose, the public interest while remaining accountable, through our laws and institutions, to the people who elected the government. And that public interest can be defined in a cohesive way only when reasoned policy and implementation options are placed on the public agenda by and for the people by political parties in government and out.

CANADIANS HAVEN'T VOTED FOR A SHIFT TO THE RIGHT

Toronto Star, *September 5, 1984*

There will be facile assessments of yesterday's election results that speak of a political realignment to the right or a total collapse of Canadian liberalism. Nothing could be further from the truth. The truth is that a premature, poorly conceived, and incompetent Liberal campaign facilitated the success of a well-conceived, competent, and carefully focused Progressive Conservative campaign. The Liberals surrendered every chance they had to stem the tide. The Tories missed no chance to put the case for change effectively to the people.

The Liberal campaign lacked focus not so much because of the party leader, John Turner, but because of the opportunity denied the prime minister by those who advised him against governing for a time before seeking a mandate. He and the liberalism he advanced went in search of a mandate without substance or direction, because we never got the chance as a nation to know how he proposed to govern. Governing for several months is a far better way to gain public appreciation for one's approach to public policy than making promises along with two other party leaders during a campaign.

The defeat for Turner is more a verdict on a Liberal past he did not take time to replace than on him personally. There is no dishonour in seeking democratic office and losing. The only dishonour is in not trying. Turner should continue to lead his party and rebuild it with the kind of liberalism

he does believe in. Compared with the important personal issues in life —
such as health, children, and marriage — losing an election is certainly no
tragedy. What would be tragic would be a legacy that portrayed Turner as a
rather naive soul who shunned good advice, took bad advice, and lost his own
sense of what being a Liberal really means. He owes himself and his reputation at least one more effort on his own terms. And frankly, the Liberal Party
would only be deepening its own malaise if it denied Turner that chance.

As for the victorious federal Tories, they are no longer hostage to the
opposition mentality, intemperance on the right, regionalist provincialism,
or outbursts of anti-French paranoia. Prime Minister Brian Mulroney has
forged a moderate coalition of nationalist and reformist elements in Quebec, moderates in Ontario, and conservatives in the Maritimes and the
West who have resented Canadian Liberal dominance for a long time. In a
sense, the Quebec portion of the victory is quite personal to Mulroney, just
as the Ontario gains respond to the essential moderation of his leadership.

The coalition of (largely non-Conservative) Canadians who elected his
government will tolerate little, if any, partisan ideological self-indulgence.
What is called for is a broad outreach to all Canadians with a socially progressive and fiscally moderate program tied to clear and precise reform of
the entire process of government. Anything less will begin the Liberal
comeback. In simple terms, the coalition built carefully by Mulroney must
be nurtured or it will not survive. All in all, Canadians have turned the page
on a new era with some considerable style and a genuinely broad consensus. For the nation, the opportunity this presents is also encouraging.

SEPARATING JOURNALISTS AND POLITICIANS

Speech to the Canadian Association of Journalists, Belleville, Ontario,
September 14, 1993

Elections, it is often said, bring out the worst in everyone — politicians,
journalists, and voters. The politicians are allegedly desperate for election, journalists are eager for the career-advancing "gotcha," and voters are
advancing selfish, local, or regional interests. I have never fully believed that
analysis, but I know that the weight of evidence is not necessarily on the side
of my disbelief. In fact, my idealism has likely been marginalized by events.

A cardinal threshold was crossed when it was decided that journalists and party campaigners should be thrown together on campaign buses, planes, and trains. A symbiotic relationship was welded together, producing two types of chemistry, neither of which has much to do with truth. The journalist is there to advance his or her career with a "front-page story," if possible. The party organizer is there to present the candidate in the best possible way at all times. Often, the marginal story becomes mainstream, the mainstream becomes contrived, and the people whom journalists are supposed to serve are no closer to the truth. And we wonder why people are cynical at election time?

Those who are elected have their jobs to do, and those who report on them have their jobs to do as well. But the press has *no* particular role to play in helping to shape the truth or the essence of a government's or a party's programs, policies, performance, or people. In fact, all that was *ever* possible was the specific, collective, individual, or passing interpretation of the facts. These facts may be biased by journalists' intense opinions, which skew reality, or by predispositions that portray reality in a less distorted way. But truth has nothing to do with it.

The press has its own career issues, market forces, competitive pressures, and dwindling resources to address. Furthermore, it is not the role of the government to help spoon-feed, influence, cajole, beg, importune, or complain about the press. The government should have its own information process, and the press should have fair and equal access with all other interest groups. With freedom-of-information laws, that framework seems most appropriate.

Which brings me to the importance of the local media. The intrigues, by-plays, and incestuous relationships of Ottawa are part of the reason that the city — and whoever serves there for any length of time — gets so cut off from the national reality. This supports the argument for limits to be applied to the terms of office of members of the House of Commons, the Senate, and the senior bureaucracy, as well as to parliamentary press gallery assignments.

Good local newspapers and broadcasters avoid wire copy, and instead spend their time gathering news on local agricultural, social, educational, medical, business, sports, and government issues. These are the issues that are relevant to communities and to readers, listeners, and viewers. Reporters should not become victims of contrivance, thereby consigning readers and viewers to being similarly victimized. If a hall is half full, what does that mean? If the hall is half full on the same night as a World Series ball game, what does that mean? If a leader's event is flawless, should that individual be prime minister? If a heckler is wittier than the leader, should the heckler become prime minister? Surely policies and issues are more important than the size of a leader's entourage.

> [People] believe that the media do not report the country's problems, but instead are part of them. Increasingly, people perceive no difference between the narcissistic self-serving reporters who ask the questions and the self-serving politicians who evade them. (Michael Crichton, *Sunday Star,* 1992)

We are still somewhat better than that in Canada — both those in public life and those covering public life. But the virus has spread, and the national travelling leaders' parade is a veritable welcoming host for viral infestation of the symbiotic and disengaged from reality.

Keep your distance. Keep your principles. Keep your local priorities and focus. Assess through local eyes and perspectives. Don't help the virus of contrived irrelevance spread.

THE CASE FOR POLITICS OF CONVICTION AND OPTIMISM

Speech to the Don Valley Progressive Conservatives, Toronto, October 3, 1995

The great moments for Conservatives in the Tory tradition — whether that Conservative was Margaret Thatcher, John Diefenbaker, or Brian Mulroney — had their success generated by the simple and compelling inspiration of a deeply held conviction. Conviction can be neither contrived nor created. It cannot be manufactured or prefabricated. It must be real, intense, and genuinely and deeply rooted.

Each of us must share our Conservative conviction with one another, as our leader shares his with us and with all Canadians. The modalities of the program we shape upon that base of conviction are important, but they will not hold up if the conviction itself is seen to be flagging or unclear. The Conservative mission should be about liberation, freedom, and responsibility.

We need liberation from excessive taxation, excessive government, and undue centralization. These often hold back economic growth, overregulate and dilute innovation, and massively overburden honestly earned incomes and prudently made investments. We need to support the kind of liberation that promotes growth, individual achievement, and risk.

The freedom that we have as Conservatives is not only the state-mandated, politically correct version of that word. It must be a new and robust sense of freedom that precludes undue state interest in our private lives and undue state involvement in decisions about education or culture or work. It must be a freedom that pushes the boundaries of the state out of our homes, our church basements, our private lives. I offer as an example the proposed registration of all firearms. It will not work. It will not advance gun control. It will not slow down violent crime. We should be opposed when the state defines a procedure that will not achieve its stated purpose, but will only increase revenue, bureaucracy, and the intrusion of the state into the lives of honest and law-abiding people.

Responsibility, the most Tory of Conservative values, must be part of our vision and conviction. This is about protecting those who cannot protect themselves; it is about law and order, a strong national defence, and fiscally responsible support for equality of opportunity in education and health care — not equality of outcome by government fiat. Keeping this nation together is important, and involves opening our doors to the kind of immigration that builds up a country, its markets, and its economy.

These three convictions — liberation, freedom, and responsibility — will mean growth, opportunity, prosperity and, above all, hope. A growing economy is the best guarantor of our capacity to sustain those who, because of handicap or infirmity, require support and encouragement. The fact that we want to bring this liberation about by a radical de-layering of what Ottawa no longer does well and can no longer afford does not mean that we are wobbly on the need for strong national government. But that strength should be defined not by what it does most or by the size of its reach, but by what it needs to do and does well.

In order to achieve a reasonable policy process in economics, defence, foreign policy and trade, equalization, health protection, and criminal justice, only five strong departments are necessary: defence and foreign affairs; finance and equalization; justice; trade and immigration; and transport and communications.

We must have the courage to make these kinds of changes. These could herald the implementation of a reinvigorated equalization program that focused on people's needs and taxpayers' capacities, as opposed to government's per capita spending aspirations. The present formula is not really about genuine social infrastructure needs. It is about averaging out the wealthiest provinces' per capita revenues so poorer provinces' revenue numbers are roughly comparable. That is no way to finance equality of opportunity. It is, in effect, a guaranteed annual income for governments! If we are going to ensure a basic income floor, one based on real cost factors, then it should be for families and the working poor — not for governments and their bureaucracies.

LIBERALS' ELECTORAL REFORMS ARE ANTI-DEMOCRATIC IN NATURE

Financial Post, *February 8, 1997*

There can be little doubt that with the CBC's gesture to consolidate and share election coverage, the Liberals have a masterful opportunity to avoid a TV debate. While this may not be the intent of the CBC proposal, the presence of a fixed daily time slot when leaders may appear will be a useful tool should Prime Minister Chrétien's handlers decide, as they surely will, that avoiding direct comparisons with Jean Charest and Alexa McDonough is in their interest.

Also helping the Liberals here is the shorter election period they passed through the House of Commons and the Senate. By shortening the election writ period to thirty-seven days, they have created a key advantage for themselves as powerful incumbents. A shorter writ period provides less time for challengers to change perceptions of the governing party. In 1972, Liberal numbers held for a month before any movement transpired. In 1984, Liberals stayed in the lead until the TV debate some weeks into the campaign. In 1995 in Ontario, the Liberal favourites held their lead for almost three weeks until the debate and the impact of the Conservative message moved the numbers.

In other words, a smaller window is to the advantage of the incumbent. While it is pretty tough for negotiators for any party whose real purpose is to avoid a debate to rag the puck and delay for eight weeks, it is a lot easier to rag the puck over a five-week election period in order to bypass the debate window. For a televised debate to be meaningful, it must happen after some issues have taken hold, yet with sufficient time remaining for the viewers to assess what they have seen and heard and reflect upon their voting intentions. Clearly the shorter writ makes this tougher.

The new permanent voters list, also an anti-democratic imposition, is another benefit for the Liberals from the new electoral changes that are slated to come into effect in April. It will favour people who do not move, who live in the same place for a long time. This tends to disenfranchise young people, lower-income people, and new arrivals in any community. Incumbent governments tend often to do better with established, home-owning populations.

There may be some benefit to the networks in pooling coverage or having, as the CBC has proposed, a daily, all-party drop-in at their offices across the country. However, this would, if accepted, represent the total hijacking of the campaign by the media. Naively, I still think the role of the media is to cover what politicians say or do not say. To have politicians showing up daily at the local CBC studio would be a serious surrender by the parties of their legitimate right to say what they want, when they want, and where they want. It is equally the media's right to cover or not cover what the politicians say. This is not a joint enterprise or a friendly co-operative. Canada's political leaders should collectively resist this CBC proposal, however well intentioned. Print journalists should also resist the CBC's effort to take control here. They have as much right to cover stories and politicians in ways not dictated by the CBC's convenience. No one network should be setting the rules and norms. The print journalists and other networks have every right to establish their own approaches to coverage.

What the CBC should consider is reducing the capacity of any party or parties to dither with a TV debate. The network can do this simply by agreeing with other networks on a time, place, rules, and dates for that debate, and issuing the traditional invitations. Leaders can decide to accept or decline. Voters will judge however they wish.

Democracy is a fragile form of government because it is tied to the twin pressures of legitimacy and voluntary compliance. The new Election Act imposes constraints that can be, whatever the drafters' intent, used to distort the process. What is most startling is that opposition parties did not dig in and fight this bill to the end.

The CBC proposal for daily drop-in media sessions, while no doubt positively intended, serves only to regularize further what should be a free and open democratic fight about the future. The less media regularity and confinement, the better.

PAST WILL RETURN TO HAUNT BLOC, REFORM, TORIES, AND LIBERALS

Financial Post, *March 15, 1997*

I have always argued that election campaigns are about the future. Success in the coming election, however, may well come to the party best able to deal with the past.

Let's start with Reform. Since the "Fresh Start" departure of a few months ago, no policy has come forward to handicap the party and Preston Manning in the coming campaign. There will be debates over elements of the platform, especially the part that finds more money for health care by collapsing equalization for some provinces. But that will be a legitimate political debate, and an option Reform has every right to advance.

If anything cripples Reform, it will be voter apprehensions about the party's past — its roots, its membership structure, the initial appeal to some anti-Quebec or anti-immigration folks. Preston Manning's response that bright lights attract flies is just a little disingenuous. Rancid meat also attracts flies. I do not doubt that Manning, his colleagues in Parliament, and the overwhelming majority of Reformers are committed to a modern, pluralist, and utterly non-discriminatory Canada. The country will benefit, and has already benefited, from some of the causes Reform has championed. But to avoid an unfair ambush about the past, Reform would do well to come clean about the challenges and mistakes that come when starting a new party. Manning & Co. could only gain in stature and momentum by being frank before the election on the yesterday they have left behind and the brighter tomorrow they champion today.

Our NDP friends face a similar challenge about the past. Whatever issues of fairness Alexa McDonough and her colleagues advance in 1997, she will be hobbled by the perception that the NDP past is doctrinaire, socialist, and utterly tied to class conflict and an inflated bureaucratic state. If New Democrats now claim they are market-sensitive social democrats looking for the right balance between social justice and economic incentive, then breaking with the more rigid past is certainly called for. A failure to address that past will only provide opponents with an instrument to compress the NDP and its chances for meaningful progress.

The Bloc Québécois is not immune either. Its past includes a solemn commitment to advance sovereignty and leave Parliament if the referendum on sovereignty was lost. It was. They stayed. Why? Shuffling one's feet nervously and hoping it doesn't come up is tantamount to whistling through the political graveyard. Liberals and Tories will hammer them in Quebec unless they come clean on their past.

The Liberals also have a similar problem with their past. They opposed free trade and now support it. They opposed the North American Free Trade Agreement and now support it. They opposed the goods and services tax and now embrace it. They opposed pharmaceutical patent protection and now defend it. They blew the 1995 referendum and have yet to admit it. They cancelled development of Pearson International Airport because the alleged profits for the private sector would have been too high; now they allege in court that the profits are too low to justify damages.

Unless they come clean, at least once, they will be vulnerable on any commitment they advance in 1997. There is no dishonour in changing a policy for good and substantial reasons, or even in admitting a mistake. The dishonour comes in not levelling with the electorate. It would be the irony of ironies if the Chrétien crowd was tripped up for not telling the truth.

The Progressive Conservatives are not immune to the need to reconcile with the past. To pretend that 1984–93 never happened is to negate a reality of courage and leadership that was important and exceptional. Free trade, privatization, reducing the deficit by 50 percent as a percentage of the gross domestic product, three constitutional agreements, sustaining Hibernia, building the fixed link to PEI — this may not be the best governmental record in the world, but apologizing for it or pretending it did not happen only increases one's vulnerability. Mulroney, like prime ministers such as Sir John A. Macdonald or William Lyon Mackenzie King, will always be controversial, with both supporters and detractors. But it would be naive for Tory strategists to pretend he didn't exist. That would deny Tories the benefit of his many successes, and subject them only to their opponents' views of his weaknesses.

EXPLODING A FEW MYTHS SURROUNDING ELECTION '97

Financial Post, *June 14, 1997*

It is impressive how quickly mythologies have developed about the election of 1997, mythologies based not on fact but on private and pre-existing agendas. The first such distortion is the "country has become more regionalized than ever" myth. It is advanced by Liberals seeking to appeal to people's fears, Reformers desperate for credibility in any urban or eastern setting, the Cassandra School of Journalism (ageing CBC types, usually Ottawa- or Toronto-based), and those columnists and magazine publishers based in the West who have made a living out of touting or manufacturing regionalism.

Many people in Ontario and the Atlantic provinces voted for the same Reform Party chosen by voters in many parts of Alberta and B.C. Many people in the West voted the same way as those Ontarians and Maritimers who voted Liberal. Believe it or not, just as Canadians voted for and elected Conservatives across six provinces, so too did many Canadians in the West vote Tory. New Democrats were supported and elected across five provinces from coast to coast.

Were it not for our distorted first-past-the-post pure constituency system, Reformers, Tories, Liberals, and New Democrats would have had support — and seats — right across the country. Only the Bloc would have been shut out in the provinces where it did not run candidates, just as Reform would have been shut out in Quebec, where its total vote was less than one percent. The notion of a more regional result is pure fiction. The problem here is not any alleged prejudice on the part of Canadians or some deep-rooted new regional animus, but the sheer mathematical perversity of a five-party system flowing through a first-past-the-post electoral process. Imagine how much better we might feel about the outcome of this last election, my partisan preferences aside, if the party of the opposition had seats from right across Canada, as did the Conservative, NDP, and Liberal parties.

Another pervasive and seductive myth is that had the parties of the right been united, somehow they would have fared better. It is wonderful to see columnists of the far right bumping into themselves coming around the corner on this one. Some (with whom I disagree) argue that small "c" conservatives in the West will never vote for Charest because he is too focused on Quebec or, worse, because he is from Quebec, which apparently, as part of a larger conspiracy, has found a way to be in the deep dark East. Then these same myth-taken people argue that a merger would advance the right end of the spectrum. If we look at this last go-around — accepting the point of view of those who argue that Quebecers, along with Ontarians, will never vote for a Reform leader who appears to fan regional animosities to earn the rights to an official, if more modest, residence and chauffeured car — this grand union would have been singularly unproductive. Tories, had they been associated with Manning in any way, would have had zero seats in the six provinces that span the centre and east of the country. And Reform numbers, having allegedly been contaminated by Charest's presence, would have tumbled in the West.

The theologians of the new right contend that this would have been progress. If 225 Liberal seats is progress, they may have a point. Besides, the fact that Progressive Conservatives and Reformers disagree on foreign policy, defence policy, human-rights policy, social policy, tax policy, constitutional policy, and Quebec is surely no reason to quibble. I am always struck by the degree to which some columnists on the far right see conservatism as a narrow, one-dimensional political world, without any room for diversity, pluralism, or differences of opinion.

That a maturing democratic society with a broadening multi-ethnic population and global outlook should want more than one shade of conservative is quite normal. That theologians of the far right should want to deny this pluralism and compress the vitality into one narrow framework is truly confusing. If this kind of narrowness came from the far left, guess who would be the first to call it totalitarian?

A LIBERAL REFORM PARTY MAY BE A MATCH MADE IN HEAVEN

Financial Post, *February 28, 1998*

In a recent column, Jeffrey Simpson, the distinguished Ottawa columnist, advanced the idea of how, using the same principles employed by the Bank of Montreal and the Royal Bank of Canada, two political parties might merge. To keep his tongue firmly in cheek, he suggested that the two merging parties of his metaphor be Reform and the Liberals. As I enjoyed his rich and humorous treatment, it struck me that sometimes, perhaps this time, the joke may well have within it the kernels of a truly great and serious idea.

A Liberal Reform Party (sounds pretty good) could indeed build on some of those points of heritage and history they share. In politics, the greatest challenges often relate to dealing with hypocrisy, maintaining policy clarity, and ensuring the quality of leadership. Surely, if Reformers and Liberals were to merge, we would have a truly heaven-made national marriage.

Let's address the hypocrisy issue. If there were ever two parties that could offer each other expert resources and comfort on this question, Reform and the Liberals are they. A party that opposed wage and price controls, only to bring them in once in power, that opposed free trade and the goods and services tax, only to maintain both after the election, surely has much to offer a party that began as a Western populist expression of anger and frustration and now campaigns for Bay Street approval from the taxpayer-financed official residence zone in Ottawa.

Reformers have, in the past, sought to profit politically by turning west against centre and throwing a pinch of anti-Quebec rhetoric into speeches or advertisements when the going got rough. In this, they were not alone. Pierre Trudeau and Jean Chrétien have both done well by posing as the kinds of leaders English Canada could count upon to keep Quebec in its place, and then, when in power, using "French power" to try to keep Quebecers' votes soundly in the Liberal camp.

All of which suggests that despite the Liberal Party's long tradition of hypocrisy and turning region against region, Reform deserves not to be diminished just by reason of its short history. It has achieved immense progress and made huge conceptual strides in the hypocrisy category, and deserves almost parallel standing with the long and established Liberal tradition.

Moreover, in today's policy reality, as Preston Manning's praise for Intergovernmental Affairs Minister Stéphane Dion clearly indicates, Liberal get-tough, Plan B tactics on Quebec are music to Manning's ears. The two parties have a *de facto* merger on the critical issue of national unity. Both want the courts to tell Quebec what its voters cannot do democratically. Both seem happy with a long list of pre-separation conditions that are to be imposed on Quebec. Both seem to feel their future is dependent on Ontario's voter trends.

All of which is to say that a Liberal-Reform coalition or merger, producing well over 200 seats out of 300 in the House of Commons, might finally achieve what both parties want — a narrowing of the political spectrum and a permanent domination of that spectrum by both parties.

Now I know there will be quibbling about who is really on top. One idea would be to do a reverse takeover, where the smaller party becomes the owner but the brand name of the bigger party becomes dominant. This is, I think, preferable to the Reform Party operating as a subsidiary of the Liberal Party. Liberals bring Reform almost every seat in Ontario while Reformers brings large chunks of Western Canada.

Before the terminally ambitious begin to worry about the leadership thing, I would suggest a universal suffrage convention, with only Liberal patronage appointees and retired RCMP officers added as *ex officio* voting delegates to the two membership lists, which, while redundant, is only fair. Before Paul Martin and Stephen Harper become too anxious about their respective main chances slipping away, they can both take comfort. Paul Hellyer will certainly be a candidate, surely not something to sneeze at.

CANADIAN VOTERS FROWN ON PARTIES SEIZED BY IDEOLOGY

Financial Post, *April 4, 1998*

The Liberal victory in the by-election in British Columbia points directly to the core fallacy in Preston Manning's personal obsession with a so-called unified right. Here we have the federal Liberals in their second term, fighting in a province on the verge of recession, actually taking a seat from the opposition Reform in a by-election. Normally, by-elections are times for local voters to express their opposition to a government at little, if any, cost. Instead, the seat was lost by Reform, indicating clearly that the push by Manning for uniting with the Tories results from the hard fact that he is running on fumes. There is, as several published polls have said, no room left for Reformers to grow. They need an acquisition to keep from collapsing. Hence the unseemly ambulance-chasing of Reform leadership on the unite-the-right front.

What many thoughtful Reform voters may begin to notice is that the official opposition is actually declining in popularity and voter support at the precise point when the opposite should be the case. A cynical and tired Liberal government, showing callous disregard for people like the hepatitis-C sufferers, among others, should be an easy target for the official opposition. Instead, Manning seems caught up in parliamentary flag antics and all the precise shenanigans he sought office to change. If there are any voters who have a right to feel left behind as Manning chases goals like uniting the right, it is the Reform voters who in good faith supported the party for solid reasons, such as fiscal prudence and lower taxes. Who can remember the last major initiative taken by Reform to get national attention for those goals? In a move that is worse than accepting the perks of office he campaigned against, Manning has simply deserted voters he should respect by getting tied up in ideological sandal straps rather than attending to the nation's business.

Whatever hours Manning, or one or two other MPs in his caucus, spends on the obsession of uniting the right are hours he is not spending on attacking government policy, unearthing misuse of taxpayers' money, or, horror of horrors, actually making positive suggestions about how government can be improved. And it is highly unlikely that the folks any of us share the checkout line with at Canadian Tire actually give a fig about this kind of incestuous self-indulgence.

More than thirty years ago, Manning's father, Ernest C. Manning, the distinguished and capable former premier of Alberta and senator, wrote a small book calling for a realignment on the right involving his party, the Social Credit Party of Alberta, and the Progressive Conservatives. It was a well-reasoned and thoughtful book that made the case for a Social Conservative Party. Since that book was written, Peter Lougheed's Progressive Conservatives replaced Social Credit in Alberta, Joe Clark and Brian Mulroney's Progressive Conservative governments were elected, and the world of Canadian politics has moved, thankfully, to a more right-of-centre fiscal position. The centre of Canadian politics has moved to the right, and not a moment too soon. But the centre of Canadian politics has not become narrowly ideological. And Canadian voters frown on parties, of the left or the right, that obsess on ideology rather than on the pragmatic mix of conservative fiscal policies and humane social policies that produce genuine economic growth and opportunity.

There is a lot of room on the thoughtful right for serious disagreement with present Liberal policies on fiscal, economic, defence, social-policy, and foreign-affairs matters. There is ample room to build a robust alternative that is about broad and enriching new ideas, not narrow and limited ideology.

Ideology is for students of history, self-absorbed think-tanks, and the intemperate. Modern conservative politics is about practical issues that matter to people, such as tax cuts, the state of health care, lowering the debt, restraining government, and enhancing equality of opportunity. If those on the right in Canadian politics look inwards only, voters will look elsewhere. Conservatives win when they reach out. The voters of Port Moody–Coquitlam have just sent Manning that message. They may have been the first to do so. They will not be the last.

LEADERS MAY WANT TO UNITE THE RIGHT, BUT VOTERS DON'T

Financial Post, *April 18, 1998*

The politics of accommodation are not always popular. Some see accommodation and compromise as the symbols of a constructive, consensual approach that sets Canada apart. Others see accommodation and compromise as weakness — a form of unprincipled politics that should be beneath honourable people. In Canada and elsewhere, it has largely been proponents of the far left and the far right who have been for the anti-compromise view. Hard-core union leaders have often embraced rhetoric not unfamiliar to the extreme right in opposing conciliation.

Which brings us to the issue of uniting the right. This debate takes place at two levels. The first level is made up of members of the party elite — spin masters, columnists, and the like, including riding presidents, members of Parliament, former candidates, and local volunteers — the backbone of any party. The other level, the more important one, takes place where the vast majority of citizens, who are not holders of any party card, decide: at the ballot box.

Whatever might be positively said about Reform, it is clear that the politics of compromise was not its initial theme. Its positions were about yes and no, bad and good. Those who argued that some issues were more complex were dismissed or attacked as flawed defenders of the status quo.

Reform's early days saw the most vitriolic attacks on Conservatives, their leaders, policies, and priorities. All of Ottawa was dismissed as awash in perks and corruption. Its early days saw the divisive politics of language and anti-Quebec sorties used to build a coalition of anger.

In a democracy, this is fair enough. Reform voters in 1993 felt deserted by a Conservative Party that did not in that election offer a fiscal plan or a coherent social policy. The ascendancy of the Bloc Québécois encouraged many Canadians to vote for countervailing forces — largely Liberals in Ontario and the Atlantic provinces and Reformers in the West.

But Reform's leadership now seems to have discovered conciliation in the search for common ground on the right. Compromise, so distasteful before, has a new appeal. In part this is because the writing on the wall is clear: Reformers have no more room to grow in Quebec, Ontario, the West, and the Atlantic. The party leadership wants desperately to merge now with the Tories they once maligned, attacked, diminished, and sought to destroy. Any wonder there seems no enthusiastic response?

There may also be no response because the math, in electoral terms, does not work. All across Canada, Tory voters, according to reputable pollsters, choose the Liberal Party as their second choice. There is no evidence that a merger of party head offices will bring Tory voters with it. In fact, the evidence points to increased Liberal seats in Quebec, the Atlantic provinces, and the West. The merged entity would have a public following of 21 to 24 percent — not enough to emerge beyond third place. Ultimately, it is the voters, not the elites, who shape our democracy. Voters had ample opportunity to produce one right-wing party after the election of 1993. They chose in 1997 to do just the opposite by increasing Tory seats tenfold and walling up Reform in the West.

The Conservative Party must always believe in the nation-building benefits of compromise and conciliation. Despite the anger and resentment Reform tactics may engender, a spirit of openness and respect for Reform voters is more than appropriate. When my fellow *Financial Post* columnist David Frum walked out of the Conservative meeting in Winnipeg in 1996 (a meeting, incidentally, which proposed tax cuts) and joined the Reform Party, I wrote that we in the Conservative Party should always keep a candle in the window for thoughtful Canadians who might return. The same is true for people like Stephen Harper, if they are prepared to buy a Tory membership and leave Reform.

For Conservatives — whoever seeks the leadership — the task of building a large tent and a representative platform that attracts voters from both Reform and the Liberals must be a key priority. This platform must not be about leaders or tribal wars on the right. It must be about the realities of Canadian life — law and order, economic growth, job creation, a secure and affordable safety net, lower taxes, and the preservation of a civil society.

The future for Conservatives and Reformers will not be determined by contrived alliances between party elites. It is the voters who will decide.

PART SIX

Advancing
and Defending
Our Interests Abroad

THERE IS A MYTH THAT FORMS THE BASIS OF A CONTRIVED BIPARTISAN consensus on foreign policy in Canada. That myth, as with many myths, is not completely without some factual basis.

Lester Pearson's success in the Suez crisis, the creation of the UN peacekeepers, Canada's role as a leader among peacekeeping nations — all of this, when combined with Pearson's Nobel Prize and chronic Liberal underfunding of national defence, has produced a doctrine of questionable value.

Simply stated, today's version of the Pearson doctrine is that Canada's best interests are secured through multilateral action within the parameters of the United Nations, other alliances, and international security agreements. This doctrine holds that Canada is an "honest broker," and as such is able to make a contribution to the world, on issues from international famine relief to a treaty banning land mines, through a consistent and principled presence. This doctrine holds that our active membership in NATO, NORAD, the UN and its agencies, the Commonwealth, la Francophonie, APEC, NAFTA, and the Organization of American States increases our influence well beyond our relative size and military capacity. Being part of the G7 affords us a seat at the table of the economic superpowers — a further enhancement of our international role and impact.

None of this is bad — it is only modestly naive, is certainly constructive, and is perhaps even well intentioned. But this doctrine alone — without a Canadian military to protect our sovereignty, citizens, and interests abroad, along with discharging our duty to our allies effectively and competently — is at best wishful thinking and at worst a hollowed-out pretence. Our armed forces are being placed in an untenable position, and our national interests are truly at risk.

Exploding this myth is not about building a military presence beyond what we can afford. It is about ensuring that we have the complement, training, equipment, and strategic base essential for Canada to be able to act if necessary. A well-equipped, positive, well-paid regular and reserve force will better protect interests at home and abroad. From disaster relief to aid to the civil power, from protecting the environment and the fisheries to protecting our sovereignty, Canada has a duty to build and train its military to match our own growth and the complexities of Canadian and global society.

Canadian forces today are smaller and less well equipped than they were at the end of the Second World War, despite the growth in the economy, the population, the use of technology, and in the complexity of our foreign and domestic interests.

We must do better.

Boosting Conventional Forces Could Strengthen Our Influence

Toronto Star, *June 22, 1983*

The sad thing about the recommendations contained in the National Defence Sub-Committee report on Canada's Maritime Command is that they would not have had to be made if the national government were focusing thoughtfully and peacefully on the importance of Canada's regular and reserve naval forces. Defence policy is the extension of a country's domestic policy, and hopefully an expression of the values and principles that guide the way a country and society operate.

Internationally, the prime minister has already indicated some genuine uneasiness towards any ongoing nuclear activity. There is obviously some concern in this country about the degree to which Canada will become involved in nuclear military activity. At the same time, Canada is unhappy about the level of consultation within the Western Alliance. We must ask ourselves to what extent we could earn the right to be consulted more and to help provide the Western Alliance with non-nuclear options if we were prepared to strengthen our conventional-force commitment to Western security. Our responsibility to protect our own sovereignty, as well as the responsibility Canadians and Americans share to resupply any European theatre in the event of a conventional engagement, underlines the importance and significance of our naval forces.

The Senate sub-committee calls for an extra $500 million per year to be dedicated to the acquisition of capital equipment for Canada's Maritime Command. This would represent a 7 percent real increase in the defence budget, a 0.64 percent increase in the national budget, and an increase in defence expenditures as a percentage of the gross national product of 0.2 percent. To be fair, some of the technology will have to be purchased from abroad, but much of the hardware can be produced in Canada, in Canadian shipyards, using Canadian technology. Here, then, is the opportunity a Canadian government, either Liberal or Conservative, would have if it understood and pursued the recommendations put forward by the sub-committee.

Canada would develop the potential to make a stronger contribution to NATO's conventional capacity, as well as more efficiently and effectively protecting its own sovereignty, through an area of military excellence and endeavour that has always been one of the nation's proudest — its navy. By so doing, Canada would gain the right to greater consultation within the alliance, and would also strengthen the alliance's overall conventional-response capacity. Canada would begin a capital works project in this country that would mean literally thousands of new jobs — not make-work jobs, but opportunities of a capital-investment nature that would add to this country's balance sheets genuine, measurable assets of both an economic and a tactical nature.

The senators have afforded the country an opportunity to do the right thing. If one accepts that the use of nuclear weapons will most likely be occasioned by a sense that one does not have the conventional forces to withstand a Soviet attack, the wisdom of strengthening one's conventional-force capacity — and keeping it modernized and effective — is overwhelming. The question we must ask is simple and straightforward: Does anyone in the present government of Canada care?

FOREIGN AND DEFENCE ISSUES: PERSPECTIVE FROM THE PMO

Speech to the Royal Military College, Kingston, Ontario, October 29, 1993

When Canadian forces are overseas, as part of an undertaking such as the Gulf War or UN policing, peacekeeping, or peacemaking, their exposure to any measure of danger is taken seriously. There are no turf wars at the top — especially when decisions about committing individuals to life-threatening risks are concerned.

The chief of the defence staff, the deputy minister of defence, the under-secretary of state, and senior defence and foreign policy advisers are all in the cabinet room during presentations of strategic briefings, mission outlines, terms of engagement, or in-theatre fundamentals. Careful and direct questions are asked about conditions, measures of risk, contingency plans, and logistical issues. The cabinet wants to understand what is required and what it means for the troops, so attention is paid to the range of action, as well as to strategic and tactical considerations.

It is important to understand that unlike in some other countries, there is in Canada no competition between the services at the political level relative to assignments, procurement, or policy matters. The cabinet is not presented with competing procurement lists by the different services. The chief of the defence staff works with his colleagues on the general staff, as well as those within the department, on the priorities for military procurement, with those lists of priorities then going to the cabinet via the minister. The cabinet has no "pick and choose" option; if there is to be a procurement within the annual defence budget, it is recommended jointly by the defence department and military staff. The cabinet either approves or declines, fiscal realities permitting.

The amount of material that the prime minister reviews relative to foreign and defence policy rarely constitutes less than 35 to 40 percent of the five legal-size suitcases that are prepared and sent home with him every night. This material might include briefing notes on emerging international situations, dispatches from our embassies and legations abroad, or situational analyses from National Defence Headquarters (NDHQ). Added to that are the myriad of telephone discussions and letters from foreign heads of state, international institutions, and our own external and related affairs reports. Specific and detailed briefing documents relative to the UN, NATO, G7, and other meetings are also reviewed in great detail. At one point, we had forces in Croatia, Bosnia, Cambodia, Namibia, Cyprus, Central America, and throughout the Middle East. This meant more exposure for Canadian forces in differentially dangerous assignments and theatres than we had seen since the Second World War.

If there was any serious and compelling regret that was broadly shared among ministers, it was the effect of the recession and the ensuing fiscal squeeze on funding levels for the Canadian forces. I believe that the relative dominance of the finance department in these matters was unfortunate and unhelpful. Opportunities to substantially increase funding, to hold levels constant, and to move up procurement dates rather than spread them out would have been very much in the national interest, especially when the real gains in employment, training, trade, and foreign policy were tabulated and put in true dollar value. The Cabinet Committee on Foreign and Defence Policy played a very important role in working out, in considerable detail, many of the more complex foreign and defence questions, such as those involving an appropriate stance on Yugoslavia, the status of nuclear arsenals in countries with rapidly declining infrastructures, or the levels of appropriate aid to the emerging Russian federation (next to Germany, Canada had the highest per capita assistance numbers of any country in the world). This means that both cabinet and policy and priority meetings were able to be more efficient in dealing with the main points of policy choice.

In order to ensure a common frame of reference, the prime minister reports weekly to cabinet on discussions or correspondence with foreign leaders. This ensures that there is a broad context within which the government can understand why Canada is taking one side or another on an international issue, or providing certain types of assistance. Often advice comes directly from a minister, an ambassador, or the field. The suggestion that a Canadian ship and its crew stop in south Florida to assist in the clean-up after Hurricane Andrew, and to help rebuild a community school, came from Derek Burney, Canada's ambassador to the United States. Canada was the only country to send material aid. This was an important signpost in our long-term relationship with the United States.

The prime minister sees everything dealing with foreign embassy assessments and/or foreign heads of state immediately upon its arrival. He gets, as well, advice from senior Privy Council officers with specific military and foreign-service experience. These individuals, acting as senior advisers to the prime minister, come from the defence and external affairs departments. They assure that he has expert, experienced advice to use when assessing departmental recommendations or information from abroad. Once a decision has been taken, however, I see it as our role to ensure that the decision is implemented.

Despite the normative issues of political will, I was impressed with the professionalism and focus displayed by armed forces senior personnel who had contact with the Prime Minister's Office. They represent what Canadians have the right to expect from those who serve without regard to partisan interest or bias. Those whose full-time career is national security act with professionalism, competence, and loyalty to Canada. They perform these tasks despite increasing cuts to their resources and equipment. If an elected government is to maintain national security, the capacity to carry this out is essential.

A NEW MILITARY AND SOVEREIGN REALITY

Speech to the Royal Military College, Kingston, Ontario, January 20, 1994

Our traditional multilateral foreign-policy stance — which is tied to UN decisions and inefficiency, and to alliances that seem more able to negotiate the past than prepare for the future — must be seriously reappraised. The idea is not to be critical of past alliances or UN initiatives, but to evaluate whether structures from the past are appropriate for the future.

As we assess the new Parliament and the new players, we must be aware that the tide of isolationist disengagement is rising. Comments made by the new insiders — the Reform Party, the Liberals, the Bloc, and the NDP — on our activities in Bosnia, on defence spending, and on defence procurement seem to imply a wide consensus that Canadian forces should be called upon to do less, with less, for fewer reasons. In fact, unless a new strategic focus is developed and sold, it is clear that the present Parliament and government want to ensure that there are fewer Canadian forces overall, less equipment, less logistical and strategic capacity. Nothing could be more injurious to Canada's strategic and geopolitical interests. Nothing would weaken us more at home, diminish our drug interdiction, fishery patrol, and coastal sovereignty capacity more seriously than the kind of withdrawal and disengagement clearly contemplated by many of the newly elected.

In our parliamentary system, these issues are the purview of parliamentarians, bureaucrats, and the media. A myriad of unilateral disarmament groups, often funded by government, advocate a complete withdrawal from arms, while those who believe in the importance of a strong, well-equipped force must rely on retired officers' associations and strategic think-tanks to advance a more balanced case. They do their best, but they are hopelessly outnumbered; and the media are rarely responsive or interested.

We have reached the point that all nations reach when their own defence and military costs seem to exceed the conventional wisdom about what, in fact, is needed in the contemporary world. That consensus, hastily forged by liberals and optimists, reflects three conclusions: the Cold War is over and the long night of mighty nuclear arsenals pointed at each other has passed; there is a new peace between East and West, allowing for the winding-down of serious defence costs; and the new world order and a renewed internationalism are making traditional national defence forces less relevant, especially for middle powers. These conclusions are intriguing, inviting, and for some, even compelling. They are also quite wrong.

While the Cold War, as we know it, has changed with the reorientation of the old members of the Soviet Union, no one can seriously look at the present disarray in Russia, the ascendancy of nationalist and imperialist forces, or the growing commitment of Mother Russia to protect ethnic Russians throughout the Commonwealth of Independent States (CIS) without seeing the real risks we face. Huge nuclear and conventional arsenals still exist, and the apparent political will to set aside military options looks anything but durable and dependable, however meritorious the intent of the present Russian administration of Boris Yeltsin. The Cold War of old has passed. The threat of a terrible thermonuclear war has not.

The so-called durable peace is neither durable nor very peaceful. In fact, Russia's self-absorption has simply freed many former client states to pursue territorial or nationalist aspirations without meaningful constraint. The availability of arms and technology from the countries of the CIS is troubling and alarming. Proliferation is real and dangerous. New corrosive regional conflicts are killing thousands of innocent civilians, and there is a potential for a worldwide problem. The Yugoslavian conflict alone has explosive links through Croatia, Serbia, and Bosnia to Germany, the CIS, and the Muslim world that would make the outbreak of the First World War look like a local skirmish. China's emerging military might and economic capacity are further reasons for avoiding strategic complacency. As for the new international order and its capacity to render national defence forces largely irrelevant, that too requires a willing suspension of disbelief.

The United Nations is overcommitted, understaffed, and unable to effectively coordinate its military activities. A permanent UN general staff plus a permanent brigade staffed by joint rotation and co-operation are absolute basic minimums that Canadians should be demanding before making any further commitments. Sadly, we are a long way from the UN having the resources or the political will to meet just these two minimum commitments. Pulling out of existing commitments is not the answer. Establishing future terms in advance most decidedly is.

As our new prime minister and his foreign minister found out in Brussels, Canada must work harder and be smarter than he and his delegation were able or prepared to do if Canadian concerns are to be more than a footnote to a broader consensus in which our views actually did not matter at all. All of us who believe in the importance of our defence forces to Canada's self-interest, strategic reach, and domestic and national security must also work harder if something other than the present defence force wind-down is to prevail. The wind-down vision foresees a smaller, almost token force with diminished combat-trained personnel performing essentially ceremonial and training duties at home. Even more insubstantial tokenism abroad would involve fewer Canadian forces than ever before.

Now is the time to be prepared for the genuine risks that face this country from global instability, UN impotence, and alliance fatigue. It is time to increase our part-time reserves to 250,000 people — a number that will maximize training and service opportunities for younger Canadians everywhere. It may take us five or ten years to get there, but the journey will be one of building commitment, military capacity, and experience as we add to our strategic strengths and abilities. Next, we must revisit the capacity of Canada's forces to assist Canadians who may find themselves under attack outside our borders. We must be certain that our capacity to aid the civil power through the military is sustained while we ensure that the armed forces' real growth rate parallels the growth of the population, not the growth of peace groups opposed to any armed force. Completing present procurement remains vital. Patrol frigates without an operating range to patrol effectively are not acceptable.

The new mission is as strategic as it is simple: (i) to advance, where the use of force or its threat is unavoidable, Canada's geopolitical interests and to protect the national security and sovereignty of Canadians and Canada with all resources at our disposal; (ii) to protect Canadians at home and abroad from genuine risks to our national security by foreign powers, nationalities, or those who would subvert the country by force and threaten our own democracy; (iii) to sustain Canada's natural sphere of influence and security wherever our trade, economic, and development links are most vital to our national and strategic interest; (iv) to maintain the capacity to move meaningful troop strength quickly — within days, not weeks — to trouble spots where Canadian interests may very well be at risk; (v) to provide aid to the civil power; (vi) to partner with alliances whose initiatives have a higher prospect for success and are not just security council bluster without logistical support.

We are better off forming partnering efforts with the United States, Britain, France, and others under a UN mandate than submitting collective efforts to the UN bureaucracy. Strategically, I would call this new posture a selective multilateralism and defined intervention approach, rather than an automatic multilateralism approach, which is often executed at the expense of our national interest. To do this properly, we must sustain a regular-force level of 100,000 people and move to the larger reserve. To do this, we must broaden the reach of military-training opportunities to our high schools and colleges on a voluntary basis. The youth corps proposed by the new government should also have a military-training option, again on a voluntary basis. The armed forces and the reserve units need to be integrated more fully into society, and vice versa. The addition of the citizen soldier to the solid professionalism and training of our permanent and regular forces must be seen in the context of making national defence and Canada's geopolitical interests everyone's business. As we expand our trading horizons, as our trade surpluses grow and more jobs become dependent on a world with stable economic regions and peaceful realities, we must have the capacity to assert our interest, protect it and, where necessary, reach out and define it with a measured use of force.

None of this requires a lessening of our role in alliances that have mattered in the past. But there needs to be a sharper definition of what Canadians consider to be important — freedom, national security, economic interests, and above all, safety — and of the role of the military in protecting these.

NOW IS THE TIME FOR CHRÉTIEN TO MOVE ON DEFENCE PRIORITIES

Financial Post, *November 23, 1996*

The Somalia inquiry continues while Canadian forces are called upon to respond to challenges in Africa. It is likely the Zaire mission would have benefited from Somalia-based recommendations. We will never know.

One hopes the inquiry will recommend against a parallel civilian and military structure throughout the reaches of the defence department. The military chain of command and accountability should not be diluted, circumvented, or otherwise fudged by the presence of civil-service agendas.

The military's chief of the defence staff should be the deputy minister of national defence. He or she should be answerable directly to the minister, who is accountable, with his or her government, to Parliament. A civilian deputy minister with a career outside the military in the past and aspirations to one in the future adds no public-policy benefit. It is not the military's job to decide on deployments or their purposes. It is the government's job to decide to deploy under the provisions of the National Defence Act and whatever guidelines are in place, and the military's job to advise whether it has the resources necessary to respond. Adding civil-service mandarins to this process cannot be helpful. There is always a risk that a government will get the advice that senior civil servants believe governments want, as opposed to the clear, unvarnished truth. The unstable nature of the world in which we live cannot be responded to effectively on that basis. Whatever government is in power, it has the right to get the truth from its military leadership, without regard to where the chips may fall.

I have been critical in the past of Defence Minister Doug Young. In the transport and human resources departments, he was unconstructively and excessively partisan and pugnacious. But he deserves genuine credit for securing approval for the Somali Medal to be struck for the more than 99 percent of our troops who served in the Somali theatre with great distinction, in difficult circumstances, including escorting food convoys that saved hundreds of thousands of lives. They brought order and medical care to a region that was lawless and heavily armed. Clearly, Young has shown courage on this issue, and a level of clout at the cabinet table that was lacking in his predecessor, David Collenette.

The challenge now is to continue doing what is right relative to national defence, to make some progress against the forces of Imperial Finance, and to get the submarines that are leaseable from the British. Ensuring that we have proper equipment for our men and women under arms should clearly extend to off-the-shelf purchases and leases if they provide the quality required. The time to move on defence priorities is now, before the pre-election policy freeze takes effect, as it always does. Instability in Russia, chronic non-payment of Russian nuclear scientists and members of the military, unavoidable difficulties in the handover of Hong Kong that will likely produce a migration problem (which, it is to be hoped, will see many more Hong Kong Chinese welcomed to Canada), tensions with Taiwan, continuing tensions about the delayed expansion of NATO to embrace those Eastern European democracies that should be welcomed into an alliance their democracy has vindicated — all point to a world of greater instability rather than less. Add that to the continuing humanitarian problems in Africa and the instability in the Middle East, and the notion of Canada winding down its military capacity seems more and more ludicrous. This is the time to expand the reserves that leverage the reach of our regular force.

It is a time to beef up military intelligence and anti-terrorist capacity. It is a time to put our forces on notice that, whatever emerges from the Somalia inquiry, if and when it ever ends, they are a valuable part of our national infrastructure, our sovereignty, our discharge of Canada's global and strategic responsibilities. Reaching this conclusion may well have taken having, as our ambassador to Washington, Jean Chrétien's nephew, a man who as envoy to Zaire was able to pry the prime minister out of the sand trap of isolationism. We should rejoice at the apparent awakening of those in the Liberal clubhouse to the existence of a world beyond Team Canada cheerleading and junketeering. The challenge now is to ensure our forces' capacity to assist Canadians in dealing with that world as effectively as possible.

WE MUSTN'T FORGET THOSE WHO HAVE SACRIFICED FOR CANADA

Financial Post, *April 26, 1997*

The eightieth anniversary of the Canadian victory at Vimy gave me cause to reflect for a moment on the question of sacrifice for one's country. The thought that really hit home is how little my generation has been asked to sacrifice in defence of the things we take for granted, such as freedom and democracy. It is one thing to work tirelessly to spare several generations the pain of war, and quite another to take for granted the things we cherish simply because the sacrifices made for them were made by others in other times.

It's hard on the eve of an election, when most everyone dreads the political ads, speeches, and media noise, to reflect on the value of democracy and freedom, and how little of it there is. Throughout large parts of Africa, Asia, South America, and the Middle East, there are democratic pretences but few real democracies. Had Canadians not stood shoulder to shoulder with our allies in two great wars and in Korea, it is unclear whether there would be as much democracy around as there is. I think of good friends like Col. E.A. (Eddie) Goodman, who lead a tank unit across Normandy in the Second World War as part of the Fort Garry Horse. He was seriously wounded when his tank was shot from under him. He was hospitalized, but stole out of the hospital without permission to return to the front lines and fight on with his men. Goodman continues to serve today as an active and leading counsel in a prestigious law firm, and he is a prodigious volunteer for charities, the community, and public service. I think also of Max Dankner, my mother's youngest brother, who lied about his age to enter the war effort and saw action in Italy as part of the Princess Louise Dragoon Guards. After taking a serious shrapnel wound at Hill 253, near Monte Cassino, and being hospitalized for some time, he was first reported alive and well to my grandparents through the kindness of a Canadian forces chaplain who found him in a hospital and wrote to report on his recovery. Upon that recovery, he went back into the fray, joining his unit at Remeni and fighting through to Holland. In house-to-house fighting, he put himself at great risk to save a comrade in the line of fire from a German machine-gun nest.

Many Canadian families have stories as compelling and important as these. They can be told in English and in French, in every Canadian city and every one of our regional accents. Aboriginal homes have heard these stories about their parents and uncles and aunts, as have non-aboriginal homes. The acts of sacrifice and courage occurred at sea, on land, and in the air.

That second war was the defining moment of this century. It was a battle that saw 50 million human beings — civilian, military, urban, and rural — perish in a six-year period. While our landmass was spared this war, our per capita human sacrifice was well in excess of what the U.S. experienced. At the end of that war, Canada ranked fourth in the Western world in military might, after the U.S., Britain, and Russia.

As an unpaid constitutional adviser to Premier Mike Harris, I was asked recently about the nuances that may distinguish the views on the constitution of Bill Davis from those of Brian Mulroney or Mike Harris or Jean Charest or Ralph Klein. It is hard to take these passing nuances terribly seriously, or to believe that they would matter much in the event the nation was truly at risk. The will to survive and go the extra mile to resolve difficulties is said by pundits and pollsters not to exist in various parts of the country. Some would have us believe that the children and grandchildren of the men and women who defended Canada overseas care not one whit about the country and freedoms and nationhood defended in those faraway places. Whatever sacrifices or modest concessions the future may ask us to make to preserve Canada, they will pale, massively, when compared with those already made by others. That is something we must never forget.

OUR MILITARY DESERVES BETTER THAN THE MEDIA HAVE GIVEN

Financial Post, *July 12, 1997*

It was once suggested that the role of the media in modern society is to wait in the hills till the battles are over, then descend quickly to machine-gun the wounded. Canada has hundreds of honourably defeated politicians who can attest to that compelling reality. If there are any Canadians who have been the recent victims of this phenomenon, it is surely the men and women who serve in our nation's military. While some may take comfort from the fact that the U.S., Italian, and Belgian militaries are being subjected to the same joy, I do not. Our military deserves better.

It is hard to think of one circumstance where we have asked the military to take on nearly impossible tasks without receiving outstanding performance in return. Yet the ability of our society to forget all that, and quickly, when a media feeding frenzy begins seems, sadly, equally dependable. Performance in countless difficult United Nations peacekeeping and peacemaking theatres has been outstanding. These fields of action usually are less stable than the diplomats and politicians who committed the troops to begin with had hoped. The rules of engagement often create an unfair advantage for the sniper, the local militias, or armed local combatants. Yet time and time again, Canadian forces have performed well, achieving humanitarian or stabilizing goals with minimum casualties and immense restraint. Time and time again, in naval or air exercises or joint land activities with NATO allies, Canadians perform to a superior or superlative standard.

Recently, whether it was fighting the floods in Saguenay or in the Red

River flatlands in Manitoba, the forces, both regular and reserve, have been there, making a crucial and compelling difference to safety of life and limb and the common community effort. It is interesting to contrast the two realities that seem to exist in the media and in society as a whole in this context. On the streets of Winnipeg, when members of the forces would leave their bases in uniform, people would stop them to say thank you; local residents would drop off cakes, pies, and perogies; and corner-store owners would refuse to let them pay for a cup of coffee or a chocolate bar. The troops were cheered by the local population as they left Manitoba to return to their bases, some of which they had left on a few hours' notice to aid in the flood effort. Locally throughout Canada, regular-force and reserve units are popular and integral parts of their communities, serving in countless ways.

Many Canadians remember that when the politicians and local and provincial police had failed miserably in resolving the tragic Oka standoff, the stability, discipline, and focus of the armed forces produced a peaceful resolution. Who can forget the discipline of the young soldier in the face of the profane and menacing provocation of one masked thug, who used legitimate aboriginal grievance as a pretext for the kind of behaviour that would embarrass a motorcycle gang? Who can forget the speed with which our navy and air force re-equipped and deployed to sustain the allied effort during the Gulf War, when Canadian naval forces took command of the entire allied fleet in the logistics and blockade operation and the air force flew countless sorties in support of the overall anti-Iraq effort? Who can forget the many risks and frustrations of the successful activities to date in the former Yugoslavia, the different and successful deployments in the Middle East, or the compelling humanitarian efforts in central America?

In the end, when a society asks people to put themselves in harm's way on a regular basis in the defence of their country's interests, those citizens, all volunteers, have the right to expect more than fair-weather support in return. They have the right to know that they will be paid fairly, equipped to the best of the nation's capacity, and given the benefit of the doubt when individuals or units make difficult or mistaken judgement calls in good faith. One gets the sense from the military justice system and the media that all soldiers, airmen, and sailors are guilty unless proven innocent within the Kafkaesque circus that has unwittingly been created. Reprehensible individual conduct is not condoned by anyone. Losing perspective on its rarity doesn't help.

In the Middle East, Peace and Security Are Interdependent

Financial Post, *September 17, 1997*

Canadians who took heart at the Oslo agreement between the Palestinian Authority and the state of Israel have had cause lately to despair. The steady erosion of trust on either side has looked and sounded too much like the old Middle East, where the hatred, anger, and distrust overwhelmed the forces of rationality. Any search for cause and effect seems as fruitless as the search for peace itself. Palestinians blame the harder line of Prime Minister Benjamin Netanyahu, whose supporters in turn blame the lack of Palestinian good faith on the anti-terrorist provisions of the Oslo Accords, signed in 1993. Every suicide bomber who kills an innocent civilian advances the cause of mutual distrust and hatred. More than 200 Israelis have died this way since Oslo, and many more have been wounded or maimed. The irony that Yasser Arafat's capacity to control terrorism depends upon Israeli adherence to Oslo, as well as the return of land, taxes, and royalties, gives new meaning to not rejoicing in the fall of your enemy. Economic opportunities for Palestinians have not increased and seem largely under the control of the Israelis.

All of which produces the overwhelming conclusion for many Palestinians that the wages of peace for them are meagre to non-existent. For Israelis, meanwhile, the Palestinian uprising known as the intifada has been replaced with the risk of random terror. One need not be an extremist on either side to wonder about the durability of Oslo over the long haul, or its relevance to the day to day.

In a recent piece published in Canada, Norman Spector, formerly Canada's ambassador to Israel and high commissioner to Cyprus and now publisher of the *Jerusalem Post,* made the case that when animosities have been endemic to a region and its inhabitants for centuries, it may be naive to hope one agreement signed a few years ago in Oslo will undo those animosities in any significant way. His newspaper recently published a hard-hitting editorial attacking the U.S. for continuing to try to revive the peace process in a way that appears insensitive to the impact of terrorism. But Canadian interests in the region depend upon stability. Counselling despair, as Spector appears to do on occasion, advances no cause. Israel must, as a

Canadian prime minister once courageously advanced, do what it must to protect the security of its people, cities, and neighbourhoods. There is nothing about Israel's past that should cause any of its enemies to doubt its will or determination to do so. But that security cannot be sustained only by the use of military, intelligence, and police capacity, as the disastrous raid against an alleged terrorist location in Lebanon sadly illustrated.

Without a political framework for regional security, no real peace or safety is possible. One cannot wage war against all one's neighbours at all times in perpetuity and sustain a society where industry, education, culture, democracy, and freedom are dominant forces, as is the case in Israel. The forces of terrorism are not driven only by local factionalism, extremism, or fundamentalist political and religious views. They also feed on success and money. Every terrorist attack that puts off progress on peace, be it in the Middle East or Northern Ireland, benefits someone who is prepared to finance more of the same. Links between terrorist groups around the world have been documented and made public. Those who gain from their success are nations that sell arms for foreign currency. In today's Middle East, Iraq, Syria, and Iran, which sadly benefit most from deteriorating regional security, join the communist Chinese, who seem only too prepared to sell missiles to share the benefits of this sort of terrorism.

Sustained instability in this part of the world cannot be contained. A contagion effect in the countries of northern Africa, already evident, will spread. Canadians are not without a vital interest in the rebuff of terrorism in the Middle East. Netanyahu was elected on the promise of peace with security. His slogan says it all. One cannot have one without the other. Anywhere.

GIVE THE LIBERALS CREDIT FOR CHOOSING THE RIGHT HELICOPTER

Financial Post, *January 24, 1998*

I am not among those who are happy to pile on the Liberal government for its final acquiescence to the technical recommendation for the best helicopter. It is a little discouraging to hear many of those who criticized the government for not proceeding to choose the clear technical recommendation now criticizing the same government for having done the right thing.

Having been critical of the government for delaying the ratification of the military's recommendation, it seems hypocritical to criticize it now for ending the delay.

This decision is about more than just choosing the best helicopter as determined by the people who must take responsibility for its deployment and use. It is also a vote of confidence in the minister of defence, the senior command of the armed forces, and the new chief of the defence staff. And confidence in its leadership is essential if our relatively small and over-tasked military is to have any chance of executing the many jobs it is called upon to do.

Clearly, the Prime Minister's Office decided that as it would face criticism whichever way it went, it might as well make the right decision, however painful in partisan terms, about the effectiveness and safety of air-sea rescue.

Some have said that the criticism the Liberals now face means their partisan luck has run out. I think that is a little overdramatic. The partisanship that caused them to cancel the original contract was simply about appearing to be different from the prior Conservative government and more decisive than Kim Campbell, who tried to cut the size of the order in response to the unfair criticism of the procurement. Once the Liberals chose this tactic, the $500 million they paid to cancel the contract was not only excessive but also a massive waste of government and taxpayer dollars. But to be fair, this act was part of the Liberal record when the party was re-elected with a majority just last year. The public already passed judgement on that episode.

What the Liberals had to decide was whether to face criticism for continuing the partisan charade and rebuff the right helicopter for face-saving reasons, or to do the right thing by the forces. They chose to do the right thing and face the music. If nothing else, they deserve credit on this narrow issue for displaying guts and public morality, however belatedly. I believe history will say that this decision was the one where the Department of National Defence turned the corner; the pendulum that swung so excessively and unfairly against it on Somalia is now poised to swing back towards the centre.

I offer only two of the smallest quibbles. What other country would make a virtue of sending its armed forces out in a Chevrolet when others in the field may have Cadillacs? Our military units are undermanned and overburdened. They should at least have the very best equipment this nation can afford. And as the economies of scale, transferability of parts, and ease of maintenance would be immeasurably more manageable if the shipboard helicopters were the same as the air-sea rescue ones, the government could save millions of dollars and precious time by simply completing the procurement for the Eh101 for the Royal Canadian Navy. Otherwise, the run-up to the next election will be dominated by the same histrionics we had during the past few months.

Moreover, precious time, time when our helicopter pilots are either grounded because of the Sea King review or at unacceptable risk flying them, need not be lost. Acting with dispatch on this issue would not only move the military's sharp end and its readiness meaningfully ahead, but also signal that the people and the government of Canada are serious about standing by our men and women in the armed forces and supplying them with the tools to do the job. They certainly have the right to expect no less from a country that maintains an international peacekeeping profile, patrols thousands of miles of coastline, shares serious alliance commitments, and performs more peacekeeping and humanitarian work abroad than almost any other nation of similar size. As Canadians in the Saguenay region, the Red River valley, and Kingston can attest, the armed forces never fail to stand by us.

WORLD CAN'T AFFORD ANY MORE DIPLOMATIC DITHERING WITH IRAQ

Financial Post, *February 4, 1998*

The need to deal resolutely with Iraq, and to do so in a way that is not attenuated by Saddam Hussein's diplomatic dithering, has never been more compelling. With its oppression of its own people of Iraq, imposition of a reign of terror throughout the region, and continuing efforts, by all accounts, to build chemical and biological weapons in clear violation of international law, Iraq's undemocratic leadership is a blight upon a proud people and a worried world.

The fact that the French and Russians continue to advance their own diplomatic aspirations in the region is interesting but should not deter military action. It is essentially shallow to look at the broad expanse of either

Russian or French history in terms of any left-right, communist-capitalist analysis. The critical factor in the history of Russia is expansionist imperialism. It was true under the czarist regimes, it was true under the Bolsheviks, and while diminished by other pressures, it is no less true today. While Russian president Boris Yeltsin and other moderate forces have done well to suppress this tendency in Russian politics, the echoes and siren call of imperialism are never far from the surface. Meanwhile, the core reality of French history in modern times is colonialism and the maintenance of a sphere of influence.

For both these countries, the Middle East was a critical area of colonial and imperialist history and aspiration. And quite frankly, their record in the areas of exploitation, setting up client states for strategic reasons, and deploying those clients often in the cause of instability is not terribly noble. During the Gulf War, President François Mitterrand deployed French forces as part of the allied multilateral effort, much to his credit. The Russians simply stayed out of everyone's way. The decision of the French to meddle so as to advance their commercial interests now, or of Russia to expand its influence, must not deter the resolve of the democracies to force Iraq to comply with United Nations transparency requirements relative to chemical and other weapons of mass destruction.

The notion that Iraq would use its presidential palaces — whose splendours stand in sharp contrast to the suffering of the average Iraqi — to hide illegal weapons speaks volumes of the kind of leadership we must confront. The British are lending support, and the Kuwaiti government is offering its territory as a strategic launch site if Iraq fails to comply with UN resolutions. The Palestinians are making a clear distinction between the Iraqi people, with whom they have a great deal of solidarity, and their leaders, about whom they are deeply concerned. There is now precious little reason for the military effort to stand down.

What the world cannot afford is another bait-and-switch cycle, where Saddam goes to the wire, then appears to relent, having used the hiatus in UN inspections to move the weapons to other secure sites. We have been through this once before, and the price of this cycle is an increase in Saddam's manoeuvrability and a further reduction in global security. Every time this cycle repeats itself, nations like Libya and Iran, which continue to advance international terrorism, have further reason to feel both secure and encouraged. While Iraqi compliance is to be hoped for and pursued, being ready for the alternative is the only option.

Canada should not wait to determine its own role in any alliance against Iraq. Ships can be dispatched now and contingency arrangements for an air presence can be executed. The cabinet and Parliament should debate the issue. Failing to participate would be a mistake. Failing to take logistical decisions now so Canadian armed forces can engage within acceptable boundaries of risk would also be a serious mistake in judgement. Ottawa owes the country and the forces both foresight and resolve.

And we should show no timidity in terms of the core question of alliance solidarity. The end of the bipolar world that defined the Cold War also means the start of a world where individual regional conflicts can get out of control. This has meant less stability in some regions and an even greater need for all civilized countries to ensure a multilateral and binding commitment to act with determination when there is no other option.

CIVILITY ON BOTH SIDES WOULD END CUBA-U.S. STAND-OFF
Financial Post, *February 14, 1998*

The papal visit to Cuba, all but lost in the sea of speculation about what did or did not transpire between President Bill Clinton and a young aide, should not be lost on anyone looking for some progress in hemispheric affairs. The pope used his visit not only to revive and encourage the Roman Catholic Church in Cuba, but also to push for a general embrace of civility by both sides in the larger debate about Cuba. On one side are the U.S. government and Congress, which wish to continue the embargo, largely in response to the U.S.-based, anti-Castro Cuban lobby. On the other side is the Cuban government, which has not yet embraced any consistent pattern of liberalization or democracy.

On humanitarian terms alone, the pope's criticism of the U.S. embargo is inspired by the genuine hardship imposed by it on average Cubans, a hardship that includes lack of medicine, even for children and seniors. Unlike Iraq, Cuba represents no strategic threat to anyone, especially the U.S. Canada's Commonwealth allies in the region, the Caribbean democracies with whom we share a common parliamentary and colonial history, have all tried to normalize relationships with Cuba, while continuing to press for further democratization.

The papal message to Castro was clear. The sooner repression and anti-democratic constraints are shelved, the sooner Cuba can attain a greater global acceptance. The Holy Father did not take sides, but instead advocated a greater measure of civility for both parties. In that context, he did a service to all those who believe the excesses by the Cubans and the U.S. are not only unnecessary, but also wildly counterproductive. It is perverse but true that the excesses on both sides serve the opposite interests. And as often happens with political perversity, it is the innocent, broadly apolitical civilians who suffer the most.

The continuation by the U.S. of its embargo allows Castro and the communists to portray U.S. policy and capitalism as the source of all evil. Castro's failure to move the yardstick on democracy and a more open society, meanwhile, sustains the U.S. view that the evil of oppressive and confiscatory communism can be addressed only with a hardline embargo policy and laws — including the Helms-Burton bill, which punishes foreign firms doing business in Cuba.

Nothing is more likely to produce Cuban democratization than a lifting of the embargo. The ensuing rush of investment and growth of a genuine market economy would increase pressure towards embracing pluralism and democracy. It would likely produce more diffuse sources of economic influence in Cuban society and help strengthen a middle class, absolutely vital to any sustained democracy. Similarly, a more intense pursuit of political pluralism and openness on the part of Castro would increase Cuba's capacity to negotiate away the embargo and increase contacts with the U.S. on a host of fronts.

This would allow the highly literate people of Cuba to broaden and modernize industries — such as pharmaceuticals, tourism, and mining — that already show great promise. As the standard of living rises, the capacity to arrange a peaceful succession from the present regime to one that is younger, more open, and more democratic would be seriously enhanced. Flooding investment into Cuba may appear to aid Castro, but in the end it will facilitate a more democratic society. Embracing democracy with some enthusiasm, along with developing a program to implement it, may appear to advance the U.S. agenda. In fact, it would strengthen those seeking to end the U.S. embargo while diluting the impact of the rabid anti-Cuban lobby.

It is as if "turning the other cheek" was more than just a Christian invocation. For Cuba, it appears to be the best possible strategy for freedom, prosperity, and growth. The Holy Father's determined articulation of this message underlines the value of his under-reported trip. It also suggests an opportunity for those allies of Cuba, like Canada, that have remained steadfast for decades to launch a democratic initiative in our own hemisphere.

PEACE AGREEMENT A STRATEGIC VICTORY FOR SADDAM HUSSEIN

Financial Post, *March 14, 1998*

Praising Kofi Annan seems, on the basis of his skills, energy level, and dedication, quite natural. The secretary-general of the United Nations has, after all, produced a break in the drumbeat of war over Iraq and seems sincerely determined to find diplomatic solutions. It is hard to fault his efforts or intentions — or, on the face of it, his results.

Yet an analysis of the interim peace brokered by him with Iraq indicates the extent to which the UN Security Council, on whose behalf he went to Baghdad, is held hostage by its five permanent, veto-wielding members. Britain and the U.S. clearly wanted a more comprehensive compliance with UN resolutions on chemical and biological weapons. France, Russia, and China were much more focused on advancing their interests in the region. France has oil companies that wish to broaden their business with Iraq and Iran in defiance of existing embargoes. Russia, as it returns to its imperialist tendencies — tendencies that transcend any change from communism to free markets — seeks to rebuild its Middle Eastern power base. China sells missiles and military technology to Iraq and Iran.

As all three of these less-than-disinterested powers hold Annan hostage, the victory for peace he achieved is really a simple agreement to abide by the prior agreement Iraq had signed at the end of the Gulf War. As there can be little doubt that the multi-week pause in inspections allowed Iraq to move its chemical and other facilities to places not soon to be inspected, we have both a tactical and strategic victory for Iraq — especially when the possibility of lifting existing sanctions is added to the new understanding.

The fault here is not Annan's. He had a job to do, and he did it exceedingly well. His job is to keep wars from happening and to prevent innocent loss of life. Those who have likened his effort to the pre-war peace treaty between British prime minister Neville Chamberlain and the Third Reich are overstating the present context and, by comparison, trivializing Chamberlain's folly.

But the hard truth is that Iraqi president Saddam Hussein emerges with the undiscovered sites of his chemical weapons largely unexplored; his Republican Guard and intelligence units intact; his standing among the anti-peace, anti-Israeli extremes in the Middle East enhanced; and new diplomatic options very much at hand. His quiet allies, Russia, France, and China, are victorious. Countries that sought to confront the clear and present danger of his weapons of mass destruction, limited essentially to Australia, Canada, the U.S., and Britain, are unable to break through the diplomatic fog of an apparent "peace agreement."

There is, of course, no peace for the Kurds, whom Saddam mercilessly oppresses, or for his neighbours, who share the vulnerability faced by Kuwait. Nor is there peace for various moderate regimes — from Egypt and Jordan to the Gulf States to Saudi Arabia — whose fundamentalist minorities now see Saddam as the modern-day reflection of the anti-American and anti-Israeli hero. Saddam emerges as someone Annan now says he "can do business with." Not terribly encouraging.

Today's so-called peace only makes more certain an even worse conflict down the road. It allows Iraq more time to build delivery systems that will threaten the entire region and beyond. Yet in the present political context, military action is clearly to be delayed. If the military response has been stalled, then it is high time that Western intelligence and diplomatic forces be seriously deployed to support the opposition to Saddam in every constructive way. They should begin an all-out assault in the world of public opinion against those, like France and China, that actively seek commercial gain with Iraq at the price of global security.

Not only should Britain, Canada, and the U.S. keep their forces in the region in a state of moderate alert, but Canada should send another frigate and a CF-18 squadron to the area. This will help make it clear to Russia, China, and France that any further failure of Iraq to comply will result in something more than an agreement that enhances Saddam and betrays, rather than serves, international security — Kofi Annan's good faith notwithstanding.

Soldiers at the "Sharp End" Are Woefully Underpaid

Financial Post, *March 18, 1998*

I am not one of those who begrudge senior public servants for being paid competitively with employees in other areas of the public sector or even some parts of the private sector. But I deeply resent any adjustment going through while our rank-and-file soldiers and reservists are woefully underpaid or, as is the case with reservists, not paid at all for weeks and months at a time.

In our society, we ask police officers, firemen, and members of the military to put their lives on the line in the interests of others or in the interests of us all. These people should be paid in a way that reflects that fundamental difference from the responsibilities of other public servants. This should be particularly true at the lower ranks, the "sharp end" of our operations. I can think of no reasonable Canadian who would argue with this basic premise. As a recent series of Commons' committee hearings have been told, too many of our enlisted men and women, especially those with families, rely on food banks or welfare or need to moonlight to make ends meet.

That the high command of our forces should tolerate this at all is a serious betrayal of our enlisted men and women. While I am opposed to the unionization of our armed forces, it is not hard to see how, for many on the edge of poverty, such a suggestion might not be dismissed out of hand. And if the situation of the regular-force member in the lower ranks is desperate, the situation we put our reservists in is tragic to the point of comedy. Reservists, because they are not part of the regular-pay system, can often go for weeks, even months, with no pay, even when they volunteer for full-time service periods, as happened in the Manitoba flood or the recent ice storm in eastern Ontario and Quebec. I would not be at all surprised to learn that there are still members of the reserve who, as volunteers for days and weeks during the ice storm, have yet to be paid fully for their service.

The Department of National Defence is alleged to have been fixing this pay problem for literally years. A determined minister of defence might try putting the entire high command on the reserve pay system until the matter is fixed. If that happened, my bet is it would be fixed straight away.

In the same way as I believe the minister of defence should be flying around in Sea King helicopters until the new ones arrive, it would be helpful for him to spend a weekend a month living in the permanent married quarters on bases across Canada with the men and women of our armed forces. He is, after all, the only spokesperson the forces have who is free to speak out. He would do well to live the No Life Like It slogan for himself. Of course, the minister, Art Eggleton, is not an insensitive or evil person. Quite the contrary. But he would enhance his credibility further if he engaged at the level of the reservist and lower ranks of the regular forces.

To date, with the helicopter procurement partially done, with the prospects of a lend-lease, no-cash deal on modern conventional submarines at hand, this minister has begun to win his share of important battles for the material and technological needs of the forces. It would be truly an outstanding story if he began to address the compensation requirements of the lower ranks and the regular-pay requirements of the reserve. The naval, air, and army reserves seriously extend the reach and capacity of our regular forces. They are also the key link between day-to-day society and the nation's military. In a country with a military as small as ours, real links with the general population and the careful use of capacity-enhancing technologies are absolutely essential.

In exercises on land, sea, and air with our NATO allies, including our U.S. and British friends, Canadian flyers and seamen excel. In difficult civil challenges, such as the floods and ice storms that have ravaged large parts of Canada, members of the regular forces and reserves have defined the meaning of service beyond the call. It is high time they got the respect and pay they deserve.

RUSSIAN IMPERIALISM IS ONCE AGAIN REARING ITS UGLY HEAD

Financial Post, *April 11, 1998*

Last month's decision by the Russians to once again use their Security Council veto to stop a United Nations–sanctioned embargo on Belgrade speaks eloquently to the renewed imperialism of Russian foreign policy. While Russophiles at foreign affairs in Ottawa and in Western diplomatic circles may deny the obvious, the hard truth of a growing aggressiveness in support of traditional interests is there for all to see.

The essentially uninterrupted history of Russian imperialism leads right back, through the communist era, to the czars. While totalitarian communism changed the rhetoric and reordered the political framework, the line of imperialist undertakings was unbroken.

Whether it was the Russo-Japanese War, the Russian role in the First World War, the Soviet-Nazi treaty before the Second World War, or the use of the end of the war in 1945 to establish a totalitarian empire throughout Eastern Europe — the Russian path was clear. Russia's relations with China show a similar pattern of early support for the communist regime followed by hostility over competing spheres of influence and border disputes. Russian support for North Vietnam during the Vietnam War, Russian assistance to India during her problems with China in the late 1960s and early 1970s, Russian troops crushing the democrats of Czechoslovakia in 1967 — all speak to a similar theme. Mother Russia's elites, whether of the czarist or politburo variety or of the more contemporary democratic variety, share a common view of where Russia's territorial and geopolitical interests take her.

In the past, this excess spawned an arms race, as well as an expansionist and adventuresome foreign policy that saw everything from client-state alliances with Egypt, Syria, Cuba to a host of insurgent terrorist groups throughout Africa and the Middle East. Under the communists, Soviet policy was based on aggression in support of the empire. Last year's thirty-fifth anniversary of the Cuban Missile Crisis reminded us all of that. In today's more democratic Russia, a Russia that still holds hostage neighbouring Baltic and CIS states by virtue of its self-declared hegemony in its self-defined sphere of influence, strains of the old tunes can still be heard.

In the Middle East, Russia acted to weaken UN support for swift action against Iraq, which remains in violation of international agreements on chemical weapons. And now, in defence of the Serbian interest in Kosovo, despite the intimidation and killing of ethnic Albanians, Russia stands not with those who want to use sanctions against the government in Belgrade, but with those who want to look the other way. Russia's position on the nations that once made up the old Yugoslavia remains intransigently partisan and disconnected from the larger humanitarian concerns. President Boris Yeltsin is either fermenting this policy or acquiescing to it in defence of his own nationalist flank.

In Russia, some of the old strains of anti-foreign, anti-U.S., and anti-minority politics are emerging. Much of this is no doubt a result of the collapse of the middle class, the end of the tyranny of authoritarian communism, and difficult economic times for millions. As nationalists like Vladimir Zhirnovsky and others appeal to the old militarist and expansionist biases, informed observers are quick to marginalize their impact and relevance, which may well be true for the short term. But in the medium three-to-five-year period, we must be wary of Russian elites choosing to preserve themselves by externalizing the "enemy" and rallying nationalist forces to the old Russian theme of an expansionist and imperialist world-view.

It would be a mistake to view Kosovo or Iraq as aberrations. They are the early warning signals of an old pattern. While all who care about peace will hope that economic progress and the prospect of enhanced social stability will dilute this pattern, history teaches us that Russian elites behave consistently in good times and bad.

Russia is the second-largest nuclear power in the world. It has a huge underpaid and proud conventional army, navy, and air force, along with an espionage network that has not been dismantled. Some names have changed, and the old nuclear tensions are reduced. But the expansionist risk has not passed. We take this reality for granted at our peril.

DISMAL TREATMENT OF MILITARY IS A NATIONAL EMBARRASSMENT

Financial Post, *May 2, 1998*

One of the benefits of travelling the country is that one hears views from various regions on similar issues. In the past few weeks, I have been truly overwhelmed by the numbers of Canadians who are genuinely angry about the dismal pay levels for enlisted and non-commissioned members of the military, and who have stopped me on streets, in the subway, in airports, and in coffee shops to talk about it. They are saying this is a national embarrassment.

Even a partisan like myself would not conclude that a Liberal finance or defence minister could wilfully want this. What we must be facing is the result of neglect. The armed forces have been allowed to atrophy; they are spread so thin that several tours of duty in a peacekeeping war zone is now commonplace and the stress for military families is at an all-time high. Although Ottawa has made late but welcome progress on helicopters and submarines, Canadians in the field are far from the best equipped.

When Canadians see members of our forces deployed to assist our countrymen and -women in distress, advance international humanitarian aid, keep the peace, stop the bloodshed, protect our national borders, or train with our allies for joint defence preparation, we expect them to be motivated by at least three understandings:

1. They are acting in the national interest, and Canadians truly appreciate the risks they face and the discipline they bring to the task.
2. Canadians will stand behind them and their families in their quest for fair compensation while they are in the service, fair pensions when they retire, and support should they fall ill or be wounded while in the forces.
3. They can count on the best equipment and material the nation can afford.

It is simply unreasonable to order a soldier into a dangerous military situation unless these basic beliefs are backed up by national policy. At least, it is to most Canadians.

There may be some who caution Ottawa against any broad corrective action because so few Canadians are involved in the military. This isolation of the military from the population as a whole is part of the price we pay for endless years of Liberal dilution of defence budgets and reduction of armed forces staffing levels.

Removing regular officer-training programs from the nation's campuses and closing military colleges are part of the same sad litany. All conspire to support the myth that a weakened military capacity is no concern because the end of the Cold War meant the end of any threat to national security. Media tendencies, largely reflective and not conspiratorial, to exaggerate any problems involving military personnel also contribute to weakened morale and isolation.

The men and women in our armed forces are not strangers or foreign mercenaries. They are our nation's sons and daughters. When they wear the maple leaf shoulder swatch of the forces, they are all of us, to be trusted and supported. Ask those whom they helped in the Saguenay, the Red River valley, or eastern Ontario, or southwestern Quebec. Ask the seniors who were afraid to leave their homes for shelters that were warm and safe until a young reservist or regular-force member came to escort them. Ask the folks who knew their evacuated homes were safe because the forces patrolled steadily. Ask anyone who saw Canadian forces convoys with generators, blankets, food, and supplies heading into those areas hit by national disasters. All this only adds to the tradition of sacrifice, courage, and determination that has always typified our air, sea, and land forces in time of war.

Canadians are slow to anger, but when we are hit by the raw injustice of something easily fixed, our outrage can strike like a whirlwind. The forces are part of our national psyche. The men and women who serve full time as members of the regular forces or as part-time reservists are husbands and mothers, neighbours and friends. They pledge to defend our national interests at home and abroad, and face personal danger and risk of serious proportions. There is no excuse for treating them as second-class citizens.

PART SEVEN

A New Approach
to Governing

I TRULY BELIEVE THAT CANADIANS ARE WELL SERVED BY THE FINEST public servants in the world. There are few countries that can match Canadian civil-service standards — including those at the provincial level — of competence, honesty, even-handedness, or professionalism.

My concern — which I've expressed in articles, columns, and speeches over the years — is about the system within which public servants must work. It is a system that has many strengths and some glaring weaknesses. These should be addressed so the civil service can attend to the public interest well. These weaknesses, which discourage risk and responsibility and sacrifice innovation and creativity to the pressures of a hierarchy that is accountable to form rather than results, can lead to the victimization of both the public and the public servants.

We need to be frank about these weaknesses. By confronting them, we will begin to turn government into an effective instrument for advancing legitimate collective local, provincial, and federal initiatives that protect freedom, enhance economic opportunities, and preserve social cohesion and civility.

These ideas are a contribution to the debate about how best to do that.

RE-INVENTING GOVERNMENT AND THE PUBLIC SERVICE

*Speech to the Queen's University School of Policy Studies, Kingston, Ontario,
April 30, 1994*

The notion that Parliament has time for question period and thespian histrionics but precious little time to examine the design, substance, and real-time reality of instrument choice and program operation speaks volumes. The histrionics of question period speak eloquently to the victory of entertainment over substance in large parts of partisan ritual. But our inability to make a change in how we govern will become, if it is not already, a serious competitive impediment to all Canadians. If we are lucky, this inability to change will simply marginalize government to the point where it will matter to the journalists who must cover it as the cheapest source of on-air programming next to the test pattern, but it will not be of great consequence to anyone else. The danger, of course, is that the complete marginalization of government unleashes what neo-conservatives call the invisible hand of the marketplace. As I do not know where that hand has been, changes that keep government relevant, reserved, and market- and reality-sensitive would be my first choice.

At the political level, we should deal with the inexorable make-work burden that the "full-time" elected politician imposes on democracy. People seeking office should be encouraged to hold another job in their riding as well. Parliament should never meet more than one or two weeks any month, and never in successive months. This alone would ensure real and rooted representatives who spend more time as part of their communities and families than they do being caught in Ottawa's isolated self-absorption.

A prime minister could reform the Senate, without constitutional change, by merely stating that he would not appoint anyone who had not been elected or chosen by a more non-partisan, citizen-participation formula. That renewed Senate would be given the task of examining governing and regulatory instruments. Question period could be held twice a week, with full cabinet participation on those two days.

All senior public servants should have tenure replaced with performance-specific, renewable contracts. Public servants above the director's level would be compensated for the lack of security in the new arrangement. In addition, we should have all government service departments subject to a competitive bidding process for every non-military and non-judicial practice — from running the airports to sending out cheques, policing the borders for contraband, and everything else in between.

We could then challenge the larger institutional world with notions that include: (i) reordering the CBC balance sheet to permit partial minority privatization, in order to have public broadcasting with fiscal discipline; (ii) offering incentive funding, including giving employees a percentage of savings for any department that reduces the costs of delivering its own services; (iii) replacing the auditor-general with a rolling private-sector audit that would report publicly every quarter, not just once a year; (iv) shrinking federal government departments to ten; (v) seeking to devolve service delivery with appropriate tax points and equalization, where appropriate, to provinces, municipalities, or community organizations.

Canada cannot afford a government structure that is overextended, overspent, and ineffective. Either we move to make the necessary changes, or some relatively proximate fiscal crisis will impose draconian measures willy-nilly when all illusion of sovereign choice around self-governance is gone. The issue is one of our own maturity and our will as a nation to fix what we know to be wrong. A less-than-dynamic approach to governance is a less-than-realistic approach. All around us the world is changing, and a failure of government to anticipate and implement appropriate change would be more than disastrous. It would be a clear and perpetual weakening of the instruments that a democracy has to advance its collective wisdom and judgement. When democracy is seen to be chronically inefficient or ineffective, or both, then you can count on certain elements to suggest options from the far right or the far left that exclude the democratic option. Let me share what a former clerk of the Privy Council had to say shortly after leaving that post:

> Rather than the survival of the individual corporation, what is at stake here is the credibility of the political process. Rather than the competitiveness of the corporation, what I see at stake in public-service re-engineering is the ability to make our nation competitive. The public service must re-engineer so it can de-regulate and lessen the burden of government. It must re-engineer in order to remove the obstacles to growth in the economy.

I have recognized, largely as a result of my experience in Ottawa, that you cannot expect to create change through tentative, half-hearted, and timid measures. The need for re-engineering is urgent. The measures must be bold.

I am sure many will tell me that such boldness is not appropriate for the public service. ... The problem with this cautious and evolutionary approach is threefold. First, the public sector is gradually losing its relevancy and credibility among Canadians. We must move quickly to reverse this trend. Second, if reform does not come from within, it will be imposed by the politicians, who will have no choice and will provide no options. And third, in that long, evolutionary period of transition, it will be more and more difficult to continue recruiting the best and the brightest from Canadian universities: careers in the public service will be too uncertain.

I gave twenty-five years of my life to the public service. I am still very proud of this institution. I will argue with anyone that this is the best public service in the world. But it has to change. And it has to change quickly if it is to remain the best in the world. These changes will not come about through timid, collegial compromises. They require leadership, boldness, and vision.

(Paul Tellier, senior deputy in the Trudeau government and clerk of the Privy Council in the Mulroney government, during a speech to the Canadian Institute in Ottawa, February 21, 1994)

I could not have said it any better myself.

IMAGINING A MORE EFFECTIVE PUBLIC SERVICE

Speech to the Canadian and Commonwealth Institutes of Public Administration, Charlottetown, Prince Edward Island, August 29, 1994

One cannot be associated with financial markets in any way without concluding that ever-larger chunks of monetary and fiscal policy are made by markets that operate in a fashion that is not necessarily at odds with democratic governments or publicly stated policy, but is substantially disconnected from those decision structures. Currency traders are driven by a series of factors, some of which relate to discrete monetary policy decisions made by central banking authorities, but most of which relate to a series of other elements that are simply not within the realm of the governing process. The mobility of capital, the ability for large sums to move across borders and hemispheres through digital pulses bounced off a satellite, makes the regulatory and policy processes, as defined by sovereign states, more and more irrelevant every day.

Fiscal policy — the setting of tax and spending policies — is very much in the purview of government, and the globalization of trade and capital flows means that governments that act outside a relatively narrow band will pay a relatively high price. Hence, on the fundamental levers of monetary and fiscal policy, many democratic decision processes have been marginalized in terms of their relevance.

It has long been my view that a realistic theory of government should no longer focus on government as the instrument of control, regulation, or even agenda-setting for a society. Rather, government should be seen as a "force for good," operating largely at the margins of social, economic, political, and community structures and within the broader economic reality. This force would operate at the national level, at the local or provincial or state level, or at the municipal and township levels. But in all these contexts, the government acts as a force for good, as opposed to a central controlling presence.

It is in this context of being a force for good that our debates and political battles over which party should govern, which philosophy should be dominant, and which group of leaders or intellectual leadership or policy purposes should be advanced define the essence of our political process. Overall, governments win a mandate either to change what was objectionable in the previous administration or to put into effect a specific program, such as a particular social or economic policy. Government, in this context, is an instrument of advocacy that is given a specific mandate for a specific time period to move in a specific direction. The mandate is restrained by constitutional and legal realities until an election, when the voters once again pass judgement.

Where, then, is the role of the public service? What is the role of the civil service? These are questions that are vital to a democracy. Having watched the evolution of the public service over the past twenty years, I have reached some conclusions.

First, most bureaucracies have a series of systemic internal exigencies — often created by statute and relative to accountability for hiring, procurement, management procedures, expense management, security, and hiring of the handicapped and the disadvantaged — that are more precise than any possible accountability for results. These exigencies apply alongside the need to administer one government's policies, and often in direct conflict with the policies of the previous government. A huge structural time delay emerges for a new government to begin to implement its mandate. Competent people will try to respond to the policies of a new government, but they too will face systemic exigencies, career forces, hiring freezes, and a lack of horizontal or upward mobility, all of which make it difficult to generate the intellectual capital and energy — amid what are often stagnant public-service structures — to meet the changing policies and requirements of execution of a new administration. Yet if a new administration brings in advisers as senior public servants in order to introduce more of the outside realities, there is often an immediate point of friction and dysfunction.

Second, it is impossible for a minister to know and be held responsible for every action within his or her department. The fundamental problem is that the private sector has started using horizontal structures of interdisciplinary teams for working on projects or design issues or the re-engineering of corporations or the restructuring of manufacturing and production. Yet governments within the Commonwealth and elsewhere are largely tied to top-down, vertical, discrete organizations that relate poorly to each other. Because of these lines of contrived, statutory but rigid, ministerial vertical structure, we have a built-in "turf protectionism." Administrations develop a culture that becomes risk-averse and loses the capability to tolerate mistakes in judgement and miscalculation in pursuit of real solutions to real problems. One must, after all, always protect the minister from embarrassment, if only to protect one's career. The conclusion, therefore, that the public often reaches about the mediocrity of a particular public service is not necessarily a reflection on the quality of people but rather a reflection on the systemic constraints.

The point is that when people vote in an election to bring about change, and when that change does not happen because the government is systemically and instrumentally incapable of embracing or leveraging change, we are not doing much overall for the democratic process.

I am not suggesting that it is always the answer to break out of these kinds of vertical structures. Such structures often do make sense in the military or the police, where expenditure control and sign-off must reflect graduated levels of responsibility. What I am suggesting, however, is that if government is to be an effective "force for good," even at the margins, it will have to be liberated from vertical, irrelevant, and outdated structures, along with anti-entrepreneurial and anti-innovative systems.

Third, we should conclude that the notion that one can build a permanent career in government is as relevant in today's economic realities as the notion of working for one company only and in perpetuity. If democracy is to keep up with the dynamics of the marketplace, and with massive demographic and social change, it will have to become part of the operative global culture, and not continue to be set apart from it.

We have in Canada a series of laws, the Charter of Rights and Freedoms, and a number of constitutional provisions that justifiably constrain the freedom with which program development, policy implementation, and problem solving can be approached. Our societies are, by and large, societies of the rule of law vital to the maintenance of order and stability, so giving all governments complete entrepreneurial freedom to operate without regard to those constraints is clearly not the answer. The marketplace also places explicit and implicit constraints — through accountability to investors, employees, customers, clients, or stakeholders — upon what can be done and how it might be done. But these constraints do not operate intrinsically to dilute efficiency, diminish productivity, or fudge real accountability for results.

In the public service, there are statutory rules and regulations that make the service accountable with respect to hiring policy and other issues that do, in fact, work against achieving measures of productivity and efficiency. This accountability issue relates not only to our fiscal and economic capacity, but also to the tolerance that citizens have of a governmental process that may be seen to be, at best, benign and irrelevant and, at worst, highly problematic. While those of us who have been active in partisan politics may argue on occasion that these arcane questions of public-sector restructuring are beyond the purview of the traditional political debate, the reality is that unless those of us who believe in the political process get a handle on these structural questions and fundamental problems, we will find that fewer and fewer people will believe in the process and in the parties that are part of the process, and that people will be less and less prepared to participate as volunteers, as citizens, as voters, and as contributors.

I believe that people are willing to restructure, re-engineer, and recreate the means of public-policy execution, even at the margins. There are a number of structural options that can be put into effect that would help immediately. Senior public-service tenure could be ended immediately, not just for deputy ministers, who are largely Order-in-Council appointees, but for all above the director's level. Tenure could be replaced with two- to five-year contracts that offer specific incentives for performance, problem-solving, cost-reducing, and efficiency improvements. All other public-service functions could be reviewed for appropriateness for privatization or devolution. Vertical ministry structures could be replaced wherever possible with task-oriented, single-purpose interdisciplinary groups. Traditional ministerial accountability could be rationally modified to include a more realistic framework that embraces reality as well as tradition. Universities, government departments, and Crown agencies should receive incentive funding to abolish tenure and replace it with more productive and economically sound operational realities.

In other words, we should get on with making the instruments that service democracy congruent with the real-time and real-life situations that the voters and taxpayers who fund democracy face. Compared with challenges all nations have faced over the past century on peace and war, on economic and social development, none of this is excessive or unmanageable. The challenge remains in actually doing something.

BUILDING WITHOUT GOVERNMENT

Speech to the Kingston Chamber of Commerce, Kingston, Ontario, October 24, 1994

Leadership comes from many places in our society, and healthy societies do not depend only on leadership from government. In fact, the more we depend on government for leadership, the more likely we are to find that leadership unaffordable or disappointing, or both. It really makes little difference which political party is in power for this rule to apply. Leadership in a pluralist society must come from different sources, different power centres, and different areas of influence if we are to have solutions that really work. Solutions must be economic, streetwise, timely, and efficient or they are not solutions at all, merely new problems or disasters in the making.

Government is about process, not results. It is about reconciling the different views of elected spokespersons or political parties with constant, competing interests. By definition, this process is not about adding or creating value, but about dividing up and redistributing existing assets or, even worse, leveraging assets yet to be financed. But the services we need in our communities — water, sewage, health care, policing, and helping the disadvantaged — should be provided in a framework that is about results, outcomes, efficiency, and quality, not process, entitlement, turf wars, and endless compromising debates.

We no longer have time to change government by tinkering or fidgeting at the edges. Reorganizing the chain of command on a grounded vessel is not likely to advance the cause. The only way is to adapt an agenda that simply removes government from the centre, and that establishes a completely new framework to build our society outside the confines of public finance and government control. There is no reason for municipal governments to control local services beyond police and fire. A creative program of privatizing services such as refuse collection, recycling, transit, utilities, water, sewage, and even planning could vastly reduce tax burdens and the seemingly endless processes that consume city councils, often to the point of complete paralysis. Time and money are spent needlessly over issues that could be handled by the private sector. Queen's University has started to make progress in its privatization of its business school. Universities financed by government are doomed to face a fiscally dictated mediocrity that will serve neither students nor faculty. Long-term program privatization is a sane and rational course.

Clearly there are some areas where only the government can do the job, such as in foreign policy, policing, defence, and monetary policy. But do the governments and taxpayers have to run prisons, airlines, television networks, schools, housing developments, and agricultural research labs? Do governments have to run transit services, ambulances, all hospitals, and lotteries for these instruments to operate well? Do government agencies have to sell liquor, run airports, own investment agencies, and provide student loans for the world to work right? Where in all of the above would private capital not afford a respite for the steady growth of the taxpayer's liability, an impetus towards efficiency, and ongoing modernization and systems upgrades?

However, government is still where democratic arguments can be held about the parameters for those who bid to provide services from the private sector and about what criteria of service and cost would define contract awards.

Universal access to medicare is not the result of the government running hospitals on an exclusive public-sector basis. It is the result of an insurance program that covers certain insured services for all of us. Only ideological blinders could keep the private sector out of competing to provide insured services more effectively and productively.

However well government-owned tourist facilities do in terms of income, attendance, or contribution to the local economy, their budgets are really determined by other government fiscal priorities. So, for example, if Canada or Ontario has to cut spending because of cumulative deficits elsewhere, then these facilities are cut back regardless of how well they are doing. Many would be better financed by private capital, using depreciation and lease-back arrangements to generate both liquidity for government and long-term operating and business plans.

I have great respect for the hard work, often thankless and underpaid, done by school-board trustees and trustees of hospitals and universities, but this often results in blurred lines of accountability when the stakeholders' list is actually larger than the student enrolment and faculty complement combined. Schools that are owned by parents, and to which one could redirect educational taxes, would be more than well financed. Resources and accountability would be direct. We should try some pilot projects in Ontario.

Similarly, if the only issue was the efficient, responsive, and high-quality provision of services, economies of scale would reduce the clutter of local councils, boards, and authorities that eat up time, tax dollars, and legitimacy. Surely the hundreds of school boards, town councils, regional governments, and related authorities do not reflect efficient democracy, but instead diminish it by making it appear futile, narrow, and small-minded. The world will not wait for local councils to sort out turf wars; the world will move on. Our challenge is not one of diminishing what government can do, but rather of defining more narrowly what government can do *well* with its available resources.

This is not just about ideology. This is about a more efficient approach to how we govern ourselves, how we administer public services, how we finance them, and how we finance government overall. The burdens and liabilities for the taxpayer can be reduced by allowing the private sector to manage and finance our assets. All the deficit cutting and transfer payments and social-policy review efforts launched by Ottawa will mean little if the fundamental structure of public-service delivery in this country does not change.

The vertical, top-down management structures of government, while made inevitable by the equally vertical line of parliamentary and ministerial accountability, will contribute only to endless bureaucratic and systemic dilution of genuine efficiency and results. If federal and provincial governments are unable or unwilling to address the restructuring that private-sector organizations have had to face over the past five years, then perhaps the municipalities, universities, and school boards should start the process.

BUILDING WITH COMMUNITY FOR TOMORROW

Speech to Ongwanada Resource Centre Annual Meeting, Kingston, Ontario, May 25, 1995

We now need to understand how the social-service structure in modern post-industrial society will and should differ from the way things have been done in the past and the way they are done now. These changes will have the capacity to liberate communities, governments, and target populations from structural and cost burdens that are unsustainable in the long run, and to divert scarce cash from the people in the greatest need in the short term.

My belief in community solutions is not a product of a bias on the left or the right, but is based on my experience in politics — both in government and in opposition, federal and provincial. It is not that government does not try, or that its larger policy solutions have not worked. Rather, it is that community realities, like global realities, are changing so fast that government is not structured to adapt or apprehend change as quickly as reality clearly requires. For example, the rapid internationalization of labour-cost inputs has produced global rates for low and unskilled labour that massively reduce the ability of much of our workforce to enjoy steady, adequate, and pensionable incomes. As well, the structure of our tax base is changing, causing a reduction in the capacity of governments to equalize as much as in the past.

This is not all bad. If you look at equalization efforts generally, they can sometimes be quite problematic in terms of labour mobility. Tom Courchene, in his book *Social Canada at the Millennium,* illustrates clearly that equalization equalizes not between rich and poor people, but between the per capita spending capacity of richer and poorer governments. This means that in many of the poorer parts of Canada, the mix of local expenditure and unmortgaged, freehold home ownership creates powerful financial disincentives to labour mobility. The real value to an unemployed Maritimer, who has had to leave his mortgage-free home, his local infrastructure and friends, and his local social-support payments to move West to take specialized training and find work, is not substantially more, on an after-tax basis, than his present base income.

It is therefore possible that when the government runs out of money to support program designs that are counterproductive, it may not be such a bad thing. What is bad is when the government pretends this is temporary and local advocates seek to turn back the clock. Time has run out for that.

There is time, however, and a wonderful opportunity, to take the matter into our own community hands. For all problems, community solutions hold immense promise. But for that to happen, the old obsessions with organizational turf, competing mandates, and transfer funding will have to be replaced with a new belief in local flexibility, a job definition that is oriented to output rather than process, entrepreneurial self-financing, and a new kind of local and community accountability.

One result that will emerge from all this is trust. In a world where social services have been defined by fiscal agreements, budgetary provisions, parliamentary votes, local corporate charters, and even collective agreements, the idea of moving to informal local consensus-building, a redefinition of commitment and community solutions, seems very foreign and even frightening. But is the present system generating the results we want or need? Do we not often put more into the helping institution than we do the individual we are trying to help? Are there not too many institutional and professional structures that mediate between the purposes of social policy and those who should be the beneficiaries? Do institutional needs sometimes replace community realities? How much longer can we afford for any of this to go on?

In today's structural reality, institutions in the same region compete for funding in the same areas of activity. The vertical relationship with the state often discourages co-operation. Within this decade, local community outreach organizations, from medical services to social services and education, will have to find at least 50 percent of their "ability to operate" from sources other than federal or provincial funds. I use the term "ability to operate" as opposed to cash. Many things operate without excess cash, including volunteers, a barter system, and sharing of resources and professionals. We must have the ingenuity to develop these options for those who provide services in the community. I am not suggesting that we throw those in need to the vagaries of philanthropy, but that we have community solutions that reflect local consensus, economic realities, and local values. This does not mean that every solution will fit every community, nor will execution be easy. Bureaucrats and politicians — on the right and on the left, in business and in unions — will reject this change from uniformity. Most in the media will focus on the projects that fail.

With a population less than California's and a landmass many times the size of Europe, Canada can no longer deliver community services from the centre out. The centre must be there for the macro-realities of foreign policy, monetary and defence policy, and broad resource allocation. But community needs can no longer be served by programs designed outside the community. Our politicians have been trying to say this, but they have been overwhelmed by the systematic pressures that large systems impose. The public's will to return decisions and authority to the community is equally inexhaustible.

THE FUTURE OF THE PUBLIC SERVICE

Speech to the Queen's University Business School Program for Public Executives, Ottawa, February 10, 1997

My anxieties about the federal public service in the past have never been directed towards the outstanding men and women who make it up, but rather towards a systemic inertia that was produced by needs that were often mandated by statute. These laws or regulations came from governments, parliaments, or undertakings that were well-intentioned and often designed to protect such issues as equity, linguistic balance, freedom of information, protection of privacy, Treasury Board guidelines, and public service commission rules. When you combine these with the rules about conflict of interest, jobholder guidelines, and post-career constraints, you will have a mesh of process that has the effect of sealing off some levels and functions in the public service from the realities of clients or the statutory mandate of the department.

The kind of transitions that we are going through in society — in the organization of work, in the rapid movements of capital and people, in the exigencies of a trading and exporting country, and in the imposition on companies of an immutable doctrine of economic value-added perform-ance — conspire to impose some severe tests and hurdles on government. The elected leadership faces these tests on one level, and public servants face them at a different level, as they try to anticipate and implement the policies of those who have been elected. This does not remove the burden on public servants to make sure that, as far as is possible in a democracy, one's political masters are well advised about the rightness or wrongness of their policies. It just makes the conditions under which this advice must be offered even more demanding than in the simpler and more vertical past.

Let me reference a parallel with the corporate sector. Twenty years ago, when I was with John Labatt Ltd., the financial markets maintained that companies like Labatt's should not have all their holdings in one product — beer. So Labatt became part of the food-and-beverage business. It added wine, chocolate, milk, cheese, ice cream, grain milling and baking, pasta sauces, industrial catering capacity, the Great Canadian Soup Company, carrot cake, pizza-topping wholesalers, magazines, baseball teams, and broadcasting. The market then reversed itself after about a decade and decided that multifaceted conglomerates were hard to measure. Companies were spun off, sold, taken public, or merged with competitors. Now Labatt's is again single-focused. And because of the economic value-added rule and the pressure on institutional investors to maximize short-term yields, it is foreign-owned.

The federal public service has gone through part of that same cycle. It expanded into a host of activities and programs to respond to the postwar political consensus around a pervasive government role to ensure high stan-dards in all aspects of quality of life in Canada. The oil-induced inflationary and fiscal pressures of the early 1970s precipitated a world where dependence on oil was replaced with miniaturization in order to facilitate the movement of services and information and the diffused capacity to manufacture in the most economically viable context worldwide. The pressure on governments to reduce scope, refocus, and diminish the fiscal burden has become quite intense. It is this pressure, aided by the central Canadian recession of the late 1980s and early 1990s, that we are all living though today. The challenge for the public service is not to try to predict tomorrow's pressures, or even to determine when yesterday's are to be replaced by new ones. To some extent, that is the role of those seeking election. The real challenge is to ensure that the state has a full range of options so that it can respond to the kind of changes and requirements that will come.

Part of this exciting period of transition involves making a clear distinction between government policy and service delivery. Policy, like the criminal code or the Canada Health Act or the goods and services tax, is set by the government, whose members are duly elected and well advised. There is no evidence that Canadians want corporations, magazine editors, unions, or pressure groups on the right or the left to set policy. There is, however, ample evidence that Canadians want flexibility, adaptability, and performance-based rewards in areas of service delivery. Building the kind of horizontal organizations that can contract out, devolve, or privatize service delivery in new ways is not easy. But it is what the flexibility requirements of the future will necessitate, and it is easier to create organizations than it is to decommission them. It is also easier to structure new agencies than it is to divide old ones into semi-autonomous, co-operative, community-based mechanisms.

The ability to maintain policy legitimacy may be tied to the capacity to facilitate delivery of services in the least vertical or hidebound way. While progress has been made in the past decade, the demands for more continue. Many of the issues surrounding service delivery include growth of the role and relevance of the non-profit sector, a sector that we know little about; opportunities and challenges of intercontinental trade flows; fiscal instruments and their relative effectiveness; the role of the media and public opinion in forming the framework to assess the new opportunities.

Public servants are leaders. They have the capacity, if encouraged, to change cultures and liberate creative forces within the system. Let me cite one specific analysis. In a centralized bureaucracy, "people get placed in these rigid categories, regulations bind them, procedures bind them, the organizational chart binds them to the old ways of the past. ... The message over time to employees becomes: 'Don't try to do something new. Don't try to change established procedures. Don't try to adapt to the new circumstances your office or agency confronts. Because you are going to get in trouble if you try to do things differently.' ... Our long-term goal is to change the very culture of the federal government ... a government that puts people first puts its employees first too. It empowers them, freeing them from mind-numbing rules and regulations. It delegates authority and responsibility. And it provides a clear sense of mission." These are the words of U.S. vice-president Al Gore.

The issue is one of mixing the courage to reward risk-taking and innovation with the need to ensure accountability and responsible public administration. I do not think that government would be better if it were just like the private sector. Government has an accountability that is beyond a group of shareholders, a level of profitability, or a level of earned market share. It is accountable to that mix of law, democracy, natural justice, and fairness that respects the rights of all citizens, whether they are able to pay tax or not.

The private sector's mission is to generate growth, revenue, profits, and sales, and to develop all the innovative and creative tools necessary to sustain that mission. Beyond its own precincts, its stakeholders and employees, its shareholders and customers and bankers, it does not have a broader mission in society. The fact that it will be rewarded with public approval and market share if it goes the extra mile in terms of corporate responsibility is great. If governments do things in a cost-efficient and flexible fashion, they too will be rewarded with legitimacy and popularity. But governments are there to govern and money-making enterprises in the private sector are there to make money. It is a serious mistake to confuse the two.

It is critical as well that we do not underestimate the role of the public service in protecting against a massive democratic deficiency. By deficiency, I mean a series of arrangements made in such a way as to remove the capacity of citizens to change those arrangements through the democratic system. Privatizing a service or program may, in many circumstances, make great sense. But the way in which that happens must not dilute the citizen's right to say every four years or so that she would like aspects of the service or program changed, or that she wants a review of the core policy under-pinning the service. There are enough threats to democracy from enough sources without government adding to them.

Reconciling the public's desire for more efficiency with the public's desire for more consultation — or the desire for more data-set efficiency with genuine public angst about violated privacy rights; the desire for more decentralization and power closer to the people with strong national standards; the desire for economic union that is stronger than ever with competing desires for sovereignty — will not be easy. But this is well within the realm of a creative and truly entrepreneurial mindset that respects the traditions of public service and the exigencies of legitimate economic and social transformation that define the world of the Canadian public servant.

IF COMMUNITY IS THE ANSWER ... WHAT'S THE QUESTION?

Speech to the Canadian Centre for Philanthropy National Symposium, Toronto, May 1, 1997

If we reflect on society's quest for answers that seem to have some transcendent appeal for how we organize and structure ourselves, then perspective and balance are very useful analytical tools. In the postwar liberal consensus that swept across Canada, the United States, and much of the industrialized world, the transcendent answer was public policy and public monies.

If we could unite and pool both human and fiscal resources to successfully repel the Nazi threat to civilization, surely, as an enlightened society, we could find common answers to universal problems of lack of adequate housing, education, or health care. As our fiscal capacity expanded, so did the political culture that embraced government as an instrument for solving serious social ills. We were all trying to build great societies where equality of opportunity would be subsidized into reality. The only real difference between Liberals, Conservatives, socialists, Republicans, or Labourites was one of degree.

As happens with all panaceas, this one began to lose its lustre as the fiscal capacity of Western governments began to erode because of energy shocks, demographic client pressures, and the liberating effect on capital that new technologies provided. Capital is no longer as captive within the sovereign tax system of any country as it was some decades ago. Its mobility, combined with the effect of that mobility on competitive tax regimes, has further limited the fiscal capacity that financed social-policy largesse in the past.

Not surprisingly, the pervasive cultural impact on the world of the U.S. historic mercantile fascination produced the private sector and business as the new panacea just as the ushering in of the 1980s saw the public weal diminish in popularity. The pervasive logic of the business school, the broad notion that "if you can't measure it, you can't treasure it," became widely popular. Churches, synagogues, and charities began to develop business plans and business adopted mission statements. The old totems of state intervention, munificent government, and publicly funded social innovation were replaced with nostrums against social engineering, expenditure politics, and grand political and economic plans. It was as if the failure of the famous five-year plans behind the old Iron Curtain meant no planning at all by government was now appropriate.

Throughout all this pendulum swinging, the charitable and not-for-profit sector continued along its path, involving more and more people in more diverse kinds of endeavours. Some elements, like the statutory structures around health care and education, broadened their employment levels, their professionalism, and their economic significance. Some, like those involved at street level with the homeless and disenfranchised, sought more vigorous and diversified support in cash and in kind. Some, like those structured as community agencies, saw support levels begin to plateau.

But throughout all this, the not-for-profit sector generally grew and expanded its reach and impact, and its relevance increased for a host of different reasons. It was seen as being closer to people and the reality of need than much of government. It was also viewed, rightly or wrongly, as being devoid of bureaucratic or careerist conflicts; as being emblematic of an ethical and spiritual commitment to the community as a whole; as being less remote and more efficient; and as being more realistic about street-level reality and more optimistic about the capacity to help. As with essentially all good things, especially if they have been taken for granted or simply ignored for some time, rediscovery can have good and bad implications.

The non-profit sector is truly the connective tissue that sustains the sinews of democracy and civility. It is where citizens can, outside the political process, address and identify issues and causes they care about, and do something about them. Nevertheless, we do not have any up-to-date data that pertains

to Canada. Our understanding of clear operational and longitudinal outcomes and inputs is very limited. Both the United States and Great Britain
have a better understanding of their non-profit sectors than does Canada.
This becomes especially problematic when the sector is portrayed as a
panacea. When Jeremy Rifkin sees it as a potential source of employment for
all those who lose their jobs to technological change, and when both the far
right and the far left embrace the sector as the area where they see immense
political opportunity, we have the beginnings of a very serious problem.

It is a problem when the volunteer social-service sector is invested with
skills, capacities, and breadth that it may not, in fact, have. It is a problem
when expectations are raised to levels well above what reality might sustain.
It is a problem when the sector itself is awash in issues of definition, scope,
and structure that are not easily resolved. We have enough problems with
a relationship with government that is based on a common set of facts upon
which one might disagree. But if all we have is anecdotal information, then
decisions will inherently be flawed, however well intentioned.

If the not-for-profit reality that underlines how we "do community" in
Canada is the answer in many people's minds, we had better be sure that
we understand the question. Recently, the Kahanoff Foundation undertook
to support a series of research initiatives to broaden the base of understanding in Canada about the non-profit sector and to develop the capacity in research organizations and universities across Canada to help us better
understand the issues. Work has begun on developing a means to track data
on non-profit activity in a comprehensive way. The work is being done in
co-operation with Statistics Canada.

There are other research initiatives that will be looking at the larger
question of the definition of a not-for-profit organization in terms of tax
and regulatory structures, the issues around a development of a comprehensive non-profit compendium for Canada with an ongoing updating system, and the implications for the non-profit sector of the need to earn
income from other than charitable or government sources. The purpose is
to create a new and relevant body of data over time and a new intellectual
architecture around which better decisions can be made by government,
the private sector, and the not-for-profit sector itself.

The vitality of the sector depends in some measure on how well it is
understood. We have immense resources of data and information on the

public and government sector, and the private sector produces huge amounts of aggregate data on all aspects of its activities. But we cannot make balanced progress as a society unless we know and understand the many strengths and weaknesses of the not-for-profit sector, and that will happen only with equal access to data and facts. As governments emerge from a long fiscal tunnel, probably not quite as quickly as some politicians who ignore the size of our debt might hope, it is important that community and voluntarism be understood.

If the answer is community, what, then, is the question? My own faith in community as a core Canadian value and a compelling local signpost to a more cohesive and fair society does not protect me from being unsure about the question. Are we asking what is the best way to balance values of caring and compassion with the exigencies of a technological society? Are we asking about the level at which social services must operate in order to combat remoteness or bureaucratic overkill? Is the question one of how we organize ourselves as a society, or is it about what the cornerstone of democracy and civility truly must be in Canada? We need more hard information about the sector and what is truly evolving within it so that we get the questions right. It is only by getting the questions right that we can make sure that the answers are meaningful, and that they play a constructive role in the development and expansion of the sector and of informed public and private policy about the sector.

What is clear to me is that Canada's non-profit sector is becoming the infrastructure of civility that an enlightened and caring society must have. While I do not diminish the economic, concrete, and technological infrastructures our nation must have to sustain productivity and growth, the infrastructure of civility is clearly the most important infrastructure of all.

OTTAWA SHOULD THROW OPEN FISCAL AND SOCIAL POLICY DEBATE

Financial Post, *November 5, 1997*

The debate over fiscal policy in the months and years ahead is too important to leave just to the politicians and civil servants. While in the end, duly elected governments must make the decisions and be held accountable, surely this is a wonderful opportunity to broaden the base of discussion to include Canadians at large. For reasons that elude me, we seem able to embark upon consultative activity only when issues like the constitution are involved. But on issues that can, and often do, have a more direct impact on people's day-to-day lives, such as fiscal and economic policy, governments have been content to let the process roll out in the typical parliamentary/think-tank/media loop that often excludes the taxpayers and citizens, who surely have the right to participate.

Alberta premier Ralph Klein seems to have tried a broader approach with a province-wide summit on fiscal policy; Quebec premier Lucien Bouchard has done the same thing, especially when attempting to build consensus around restraints that must be shared among government, business, and labour. It would truly be a broadening of citizenship if the government and Parliament of Canada actively engaged in a process that allowed Canadians to deliberate in public about what spending priorities, debt-repayment initiatives, and taxation premises might best be targeted in the coming decade. Imagine how much more effectively we would begin the millennium if an open discussion to which all Canadians had been invited resulted in an economic and social consensus.

Of course, the other option is to let the governor of the Bank of Canada decide and the rest of us will just sense his intent when we see changes in interest rates. It is not that he or the minister of finance or the prime minister aren't well-meaning people with ultimate responsibilities on this issue. It is just that their decisions could be far better informed, particularly in terms of the Canadian public's views and ideas. Polling and market research can assist them, but as measurement instruments they reflect existing biases, not a deliberative process wherein citizens actually learn from each other and there is some measure of cross-pollination and democratic persuasion going on.

How might this process be put into effect? Parliament could, on a proposal from the minister of finance, approve a series of questions that each member would be encouraged to take back to his or her constituency for open and broad discussion. Local service clubs, community groups, high schools, and universities might well be involved in the process. The local labour council and the chamber of commerce would be called upon to set up public forums. Our cablecasters might be gently invited to televise as many of these as possible, both locally and nationally. At the end of this, MPs would be invited to participate in a multi-day parliamentary debate in which each MP, without regard to party discipline, could reflect on the consultations and the views expressed in her or his riding, adding his or her own views. There could be an agreement that taxpayer-financed house-holder mailings from MPs would include those questions approved by Parliament and a schedule of the events in each riding where citizens might speak in the debate or listen to the views of others. The Canadian daily and weekly newspaper associations might be asked to help by preparing a fact sheet for broad public consumption.

Issues such as taxes, debt repayment, and social spending could be broadly discussed and broadly understood. Millions of Canadians would have their say, and all would be reported and noted in Parliament before the minister of finance rises in his place sometime the following spring to lay out not only a budget, but also a vision for the coming fiscal and economic priorities for Canada.

Social justice, economic competitiveness, and fiscal balance are all vital components of a growing, healthy, and productive economy and society. Decisions made in the next two years will establish key trends well into the future. It would not hurt any cause or weaken any priority to let Canadians participate in the deliberations that must precede the decisions that must be made. In fact, it would make Canada, as a community and a society, a whole lot stronger.

MINISTERIAL ACCOUNTABILITY: CONFRONTING THE MYTH

Crosscurrents: Contemporary Political Issues, *3rd Ed. (Toronto: ITP Nelson, 1998)*

The evolution from absolutist monarchical government to responsible democracy had a series of milestones beyond the Magna Carta itself. The notion of an elected assembly, popularly chosen, to which the treasury benches are responsible is one of the crowning achievements of the Westminster model. The notion of ministerial accountability emerges from that model and history in a way that is equally emblematic of the evolution from the rule of one to a parliament of people.

With many great ideas and important principles, their continued and constructive relevance requires a careful eye turned to the negative effects distortion can bring to the original principle. In Canada, the principle of ministerial accountability has produced some serious problems that work against the ability of the public sector in general, and departmental operations in particular, to adapt to and better serve the public interest as their statutory mandate directs. When a principle of ministerial accountability to Parliament can be deployed both aggressively and passively to frustrate the core mandate of serving the public, surely it is time to reflect carefully on the operation of the principle.

In my experience in both provincial and federal government, and in opposition legislative work, the inappropriately applied principle of ministerial accountability has produced a series of negative results. These impacts tend to subvert rather than enhance accountability; depress rather than encourage innovation and improvement in public service; dilute rather than enhance the clarity of information coming to the minister, his or her staff, or Parliament itself; promote the "gotcha" phenomenon of mindless media coverage of the legislative process; diminish rather than encourage the need for an opposition to be well prepared and studied on specific issues; depress rather than encourage media competence on specific issues; oppress rather than liberate creative and thoughtful capacities in the public service; and dilute rather than enhance other statutory responsibilities. (But aside from these, the effect is rather benign!)

Let us begin with the core hypocrisy and charade associated with the ultimate reality of ministerial accountability. It is revealing even in its simplest and most flatly stated form. The simple notion that a minister of a department is directly responsible for everything that happens in that department is a corrosive and unhelpful proposition. It implies that in some way, he or she must know or be advised of all that is transpiring in every detailed aspect of a ministry's operations.

Let's follow this through.

Let us assume that a corrupt junior sales-tax auditor seeks a bribe while auditing a retail business, a bar, in British Columbia. Initially no one complains. The auditor's supervisor has no idea of the corrupt practice. The regional director has no idea, because the local supervisor has no idea. Because the regional director does not know, she has not told her director general of audit services. Because the director general does not know, he has not informed the assistant deputy minister. The ADM does not tell the deputy minister, nor is the matter discussed at the executive management committee of the ministry, because no one knows about the corrupt practice. Consequently, the minister had not been informed of anything untoward by her deputy minister.

But the parliamentary assumption is that the minister ought to know. How do we know that this is the parliamentary assumption? Well, because after hearing the bar owner boast about how he was able to reduce his true tax bill though a small understanding with a local sales-tax auditor, one of the bar owner's suppliers, who was sitting in the bar with the owner, remembered that his sister-in-law was heavily fined recently for not paying retail sales tax. The supplier found the boasts of his customer quite troubling and made an anonymous call to the local RCMP detachment, which began an investigation. Within days of the beginning of this investigation, a newspaper got wind of the affair and began asking questions at the local level. An opposition MLA heard about the investigation, now several weeks old, and raised the question in the legislature.

Now in this context, we should be clear about a few things. The opposition MLA knows there is no way the minister can know about a single auditor who decides to take the wrong course in life. The media know that the minister could not possibly know. And it is highly unlikely that the public would expect that the minister would or could know about this level of detail. But the parliamentary assumption is the opposite!

Similarly, the minister of justice and the solicitor general should not know, because the RCMP should be conducting its investigation without informing the ministers, just in case there is a broad conspiracy that spreads beyond one single auditor acting alone. Premature disclosure of an investigation in the House of Commons or a legislature could imperil the investigation.

When the question is asked in the House, the minister of revenue can say that she is not aware of any specific investigation but will take the question under advisement. Her department checks frantically all the way down the line to try to find out what is happening. Essentially, no one knows. A question goes across to the law officers of the Crown in the justice department, who have been advised by the police that confirming or denying an investigation could assist in the tampering with evidence or even in its destruction. By the second day in the legislature, the opposition MLA is alleging cover-up. The head of the provincial RCMP detachment issues a non-statement saying that investigations of many kinds are discussed all the time and are not disclosed so as to protect both the rights of the Crown and the rights of the innocent, and to assist in gathering evidence.

If the deputy minister of revenue is able to find out through formal or informal sources what is going on, the doctrine of ministerial accountability says that the minister must be informed. If the minister is informed, she must do something about the situation. If the minister is not informed, she does not know. If the deputy minister of justice speaks to the deputy minister of revenue and says that the RCMP is close to laying charges, but that confirmation of the investigation could result in the evidence, for which the RCMP is seeking a seizure warrant, being destroyed in the Kamloops area — an area that may have several occurrences of similar crimes — then the deputy minister of revenue is torn between a duty to the administration of justice and a duty to inform ministerial accountability. If the minister is informed by the deputy, and then is asked questions the next day in the House, the minister's choices are to respond honestly to the questions, to obfuscate and wiggle-waggle, or to avoid the truth and lie. She will then face the risk of being in contempt of the legislature, of having lied to the opposition, and in the minds of the press, of having been part of some sort of cover-up.

Not one person in the department, except the allegedly corrupt low-level auditor, knows much or anything about this. The minister has yet to be informed. The deputy has been cautioned by a colleague of equal rank in the justice department not to do anything that could jeopardize the investigation.

The public interest here is quite clear. The police should be allowed to continue their investigation. If the evidence warrants it, the auditor should be charged. The due process of the law should determine guilt or innocence. The department of revenue should then conduct an investigation, which should perhaps be done by an outsider, to see if there is any systemic problem. Once charges have are laid, a full statement, which does not refer to the matter now directly before the courts, should be made to the legislature concerning what the revenue department knew, how it assisted with the investigation, and what it now intends to do about the problem.

Chances of any of this happening are slim. The doctrinal application of ministerial accountability would force a feeding frenzy in the legislature and in the legislative press gallery, which is tied to the fiction that the minister should know and that she should have acted with dispatch as soon as she knew. Questions about who knew what when, and what they did about what they knew, prove far more important than the substance of the matter. And however trivial all of this might be or however marginal the matter is, everything becomes even more removed from any focused pursuit of the public interest by a minister and her senior officials.

We should consider the culture this breeds in terms of the relationship between the bureaucracy at all its levels and Parliament. Does the doctrine of ministerial accountability mean that the minister must defend the activities of his or her department at all times because when she is unable to do so she must accept personal blame? Should, as some have argued relative to the Al Mashat case, ministers accept responsibility for things they did not know anything about or in which they were not involved? Purists on this issue would argue in the affirmative, saying that what the minister of immigration knew at the time is essentially irrelevant, and that the minister has to accept responsibility in order to sustain the principle of ministerial accountability. By definition, this is to diminish the concept of public-service accountability, which is surely an undesired outcome from the point of view of responsible ministerial and public-service conduct.

The culture of accountability, which is a desirable context for the able, competent, and focused public servant, is not advanced when all the accountability rests in practical terms in only one place. The political price will be paid by the elected politician at the political level, but that should not absolve other competent and responsible players from their own duty.

There is no path of innovation in public service that does not carry with it some meaningful risk. New approaches to contracting out, new relationships with public-sector unions, and new approaches to job sharing or ensuring a more representative public service all require senior managers to take risks and try new procedures. The notion that every mistake, misstep, or experiment gone awry may plunge the minister and/or the government into some hot water is surely less than a liberating framework for innovation and growth. The hard truth of the matter is that the doctrine of ministerial accountability, applied as it is in Canada today, serves only to suppress innovation and discourage any risk-taking within the public-service culture. Often it is the same opposition that decries less than up-to-date approaches to public affairs that are the first, with allies in the media, to seize on any chance to use ministerial responsibility to end a career rather than improve government. New governments, when faced with this reality, often use different approaches to both keep their electoral promises yet avoid the daily melodrama of feigned horror at marginal events a minister could not possibly know much about.

Whenever elected officials say they want to take politics out of an issue, it usually means that there is absolutely no way they can be reasonably held accountable for the details of how that particular issue is addressed. The Ontario Health Restructuring Commission is a classic example of a case where a government had to hand the actual implementation of its publicly and electorally mandated restructuring of the health-care system to an extra-parliamentary organization, as mandated by statute. No minister of health, however brilliant, well-informed, balanced, or thoughtful, could have dealt on a day-to-day basis with the detailed calculations about decisions relevant to health-care rationalization for more appropriate and efficient care. Often, therefore, the purpose of ministerial accountability — namely, having a minister held accountable by Parliament for the actions of his or her department — produces the opposite effect — the statutory mandating of non-parliamentary bodies to perform functions that might have otherwise been performed in a more direct legislative context. This will tend over time to diminish the role of Parliament rather than enhance it.

The effect of ministerial accountability on the media is equally perverse. The media assess issues in terms of their capacity to trip up a minister, show the government to be incompetent, or, the media hope, end a minister's career, which is all fair enough in a competitive political environment. But the media (and they too have competitive survival pressures) are reduced to focusing on ministerial foul-ups, parliamentary peccadilloes, and feeding frenzies rather than on any sustained consideration of the larger issues at play. The result is media coverage that stresses minutiae and personalities rather than substance, making all politics seem petty, small-minded, and ritualized. There are consequences to continued and sustained pettiness.

Beyond the politics of legislative competition, there is also the reality of the larger competitive framework within which governments must contribute to, rather that dilute, national productivity. This reality clearly implies that a wide range of service-delivery options be deployed to ensure both value for money and adequate resources for those services that truly matter.

The minute one moves towards alternate forms of service delivery — from special operating agencies to Crown Corporations and models of co-determination or commercialization — there is a change in the simple vertical-line function of ministerial responsibility. What impact should this have on governments seeking innovative ways to supply services in a more cost-efficient or "citizen-friendly" manner, since they may not facilitate direct vertical accountability through the minister to Parliament? Surely this is using ministerial accountability to diminish rather than advance the premise of effective service to citizens.

The nature of our parliamentary democracy requires that Parliament give approval for estimates, budget bills, and appropriate ways and means motions, and that members of the cabinet be generally responsible to the House of Commons for the conduct of their departments. But the narrow doctrine of an all-inclusive ministerial accountability is a constricting valve that will staunch the flow of information and legitimacy to and from the legislative chamber. Instead, we should be looking for a way of more carefully articulating the underlying themes of that accountability in a fashion that enables creative and capable ministers, empowers the legitimate supremacy of the parliamentary part of the governance process, and diminishes the mindless ritual that serves no purpose other than to promote mockery and contrived outrage in the House at question period. We should be looking for a compelling definition of accountability that allows a culture of market sensitivity, citizen-friendly program design, and risk-taking, and that leads to better ways of serving the public.

How might this broader and more articulated definition move forward, and on what basis? Well, we might begin with the truth, however unappetizing it may be to proponents of a more traditional view of ministerial accountability.

Truth number one: A minister can be responsible to Parliament for only the broad policies that govern his or her department's goals, purposes, and operations, and for how the act governing the department is put into practice. This must include specifically all those matters that fall, by virtue of any legislation, within the precise discretion of the minister or of those staff members the minister has hired at the political level.

Truth number two: The deputy minister is appointed by the cabinet as a whole through an Order-in-Council whose content is determined by the cabinet or Privy Council Office with the express approval of the first minister. Deputy ministerial conduct is the responsibility of the government as a whole. Direct reports to the minister are the responsibility of the deputy minister, for which he or she is accountable to the secretary of the cabinet and the first minister.

Truth number three: No public service that is asked to perform effectively in a fast-paced and competitive environment can do so unless there is a legitimate tolerance for mistakes made and risks taken within existing statutory mandates. Ministers must not be accountable for these mistakes unless they are the product of explicit policy direction given by them or members of their political staff, or explicitly approved by them.

A clear division must be maintained between the role of policy in the department, for which the minister is responsible to Parliament, and the operational side of the department. This division will encourage deputies and bureaucracies to be less risk-averse and more adventuresome within existing statutory mandates (which were, and are, approved by Parliament in the normal legislative way). This division will also promote a clear and liberating operational mandate for the department and its officials.

The constructive use of these truths, while not in any way limiting the range of questions that can be asked in Parliament or at committee, will provide some discipline around the more excessive misuses of parliamentary ritual that showboat and overdramatize rather than seek information and hold governments accountable. Holding a minister accountable for a deputy whom the minister did not appoint or who does not truly report to the minister only sustains a charade that dilutes the first minister's responsibility for those matters a prime minister or premier is genuinely able to control. Accepting the difference between operations and policy allows deputies and public servants to speak more frankly at committee and when questioned about matters clearly within their purview. This division would in fact promote more information flow to our elected parliamentarians and the media than is now the case. Today we need to protect the minister because the doctrine of ministerial accountability produces a "need to know" hierarchy in departments that were operating on the premise that a minister cannot be held accountable for that which he or she does not know. This fails both to assist Parliament in doing its job and to provide transparency for the public or the media. A ritualistic assumption about a mythological accountability based on a false capacity to know everything actually works to constrain information flow and diminish parliamentary accountability in any real sense.

Public information, more dialogue between Parliament and the bureaucracy, more freedom for the bureaucracy to innovate in serving the public, less of a culture of information management and control — these would be among the very first benefits of this more modern and realistic approach to ministerial accountability.

Over time there would be others. The role of central agencies, such as the Treasury Board, the finance department, and the cabinet office, would no longer be obscured by a focus on ministerial accountability that takes the legislative eye off these other seminal forces. Key decisions about staffing levels, levels of remuneration, extent of departmental field service, and administrative accountabilities are usually made outside the ministry involved. There are a host of statutory accountabilities around hiring practices, financial practices, expenses, facilities, and purchasing that are determined outside most line departments. The narrow focus of ministerial accountability often obscures the importance and impact of these accountabilities. An approach that allowed a clear distinction between policy issues within the minister's realm and administrative accountabilities quite outside that realm would facilitate a broader debate on and understanding of those other accountabilities. While it would end up being more substantive and less dramatic than simple "good cop, bad cop" rituals, it would also produce a far broader and more widespread understanding of the ways in which government actually works.

From the point of view of the serious parliamentarian and the opposition research offices, the separation of policy from operations and the more clear definition of ministers' responsibilities to Parliament would result in better use of research facilities, resources, and House time. Ministers could be questioned on policy matters in great detail. At estimates hearings, the long, time-wasting, and drawn-out ministerial statements about the full and detailed nature of their departments' operations could well be done away with. A closer and more detailed analysis of administrative and operational issues with the deputies would be far more revealing. The deputies' appointment by the first minister's office would make that discussion as politically salient as any. The accountability of the public service, as well as the understanding of its role and function, would increase. Government as a shared responsibility between Parliament, the cabinet as a whole, the prime minister or premier, and the minister would no longer exclude the public service from accountability.

A minister and government today do not decide to support a public servant who has made a controversial or understandable mistake in good faith. Today, what is decided is whether the doctrine of ministerial accountability can include supporting a public servant who has taken a risk or made an honest mistake. This forces the public servant and the parliamentarian into a Catch-22 circumstance. True oversight and questioning is dealt with only in the context of the minister's responsibility. The minister faces the task of standing by his department to the last point of minutiae, whatever the facts may suggest in terms of right and wrong. The parliamentarian's capacity to generate any change for the better is tied utterly to his or her capacity to embarrass or catch the minister. The public servants who share precisely the same interest in good government as do the other players are largely prevented from interacting with the system because of the almost coercive doctrine of ministerial accountability.

None of this conspires to produce any real opportunities for a broad national debate through Parliament about how government can be improved, or about how government can be used either sparingly or otherwise to strengthen our way of life, our society, our compassion, our effectiveness, or our competence in the way we govern ourselves. In a sense, ministerial accountability is a shield that protects any government from any real discussion of how it manages its internal affairs, while at the same time protecting the opposition parties from any real duty to deal with the issues at hand in a serious, researched, and informed way. Ministerial accountability acts, no doubt unwittingly from the perspective of those who fought for responsible government centuries ago, to diminish the real responsibility of many of the players in the system.

As is the case with so much of our parliamentary heritage, our challenge is to save the best. We should be speaking about an updating that would not only strengthen the role of minister and public servant, but also, and more important, increase the relevance, impact, and capacity of the people we elect to Parliament and the provincial legislatures.

This, in terms of democracy and genuine accountability, would make a very significant difference indeed. It is a difference that would revitalize the parliamentary process and expand its genuine reach. It would help the process of public understanding of our governing realities and processes. And it would represent the setting aside of mythology for reality, which is often a step in the right direction.

System Would Work Better If Politicians Kept Their Day Jobs

Financial Post, *February 11, 1998*

The negative comments about the recent proposals to increase pay for members of Parliament, proposals that seem altogether reasonable, relate to a problem that is larger than the pay-packet question itself. Voters are not just critical about MP's salaries — they are cynical about the whole political process. At the root of this cynicism is the professionalization of politicians, which began in earnest in the 1970s with representation, press gallery, and political theatre all going full time.

There are myriad reasons why MPs became full-time employees of the taxpayer as opposed to your neighbours who travel to Ottawa a few months a year. Some members, including Conservatives perpetually in opposition, called for more committee work and more and longer sittings of the House so elected MPs could oversee the spending by a growing bureaucracy and cabinet — which only proves that one should be careful what one asks for!

As MPs spent more and more time in Ottawa, requests came for more staff, pay, and research support so they could do their jobs most effectively. As the media have a huge fixed-cost concentration in Ottawa, the more action in the hothouse of question period, the better and easier for them. Over time, most people seeking federal office had to do so on a full-time basis.

I have always believed and written that the Ottawa-centred reality of the political theatre is what turns the bright local personality who runs for office into one of "them," often but a few short months after being elected.

The man or woman who was elected from "here," who is one of "us," quickly becomes from "there" and no longer understands "us." This turn of events is every hardworking MP's nightmare, but it is part of the reason for such a large turnover in the House of Commons every election.

We would be immensely better off if MPs were encouraged to keep their day jobs in the ridings from which they came, and if the parliamentary schedule was tailored to the needs of local representation, as opposed to the interests of the press and bureaucracy.

If the House of Commons did not sit for more than two weeks at a time, and never in two consecutive months, many MPs could keep some measure of work activity, income, and employment in their own ridings. When they arrived in Ottawa, they would not be returning to an all-absorbing world that separates them from the real-life experiences of their fellow constituents, but would be bringing with them fresh views on the realities of life in their ridings. Rushing home on weekends to try to find some family time and meet with constituents is about as artificial as a whirl-wind trip to a foreign capital to understand the country in three days. It isn't real, balanced, or representative. It can produce huge distortions.

How would this change Ottawa? Well, the bureaucracy and cabinet would be on notice that if budgets or other bills can't be explained or dealt with in these more limited parliamentary periods, they would not be dealt with at all. This would mean simpler legislation and a lot less of it. Which in turn would mean less government, in and of itself a modest victory on the road to less public cynicism.

And at home on main street, the local MP would actually be just that. He or she would be involved in the community, and would hopefully still be doing some farming or teaching or being an entrepreneur or whatever his or her pre-election work was. He or she would be a local MP in all the true and noble meaning of that term, and in the framework of parliamentary democracy and no taxation without representation.

The need for full-time actors in Ottawa on the parliamentary broadcast stage is overdone. It is premised on the need for government and all the media attention it requires to just keep on growing. Increasing pay packets for full-time MPs makes sense within this premise. But in the long-term interests of the relevance of democracy, it is this premise that should and must change.

Towards a New Health-Care Model

Speech to the Little Orthopaedic Society Annual Conference, Kingston, Ontario, September 17, 1999

It is sad but often true that some in public life choose to focus on and exaggerate differences as opposed to areas of common challenge and opportunity. In no area is this more apparent or illogical than in the portrayal of the Canadian and American health-care systems. The simplistic view, often advanced in Canada, is that Canadians have an exemplary system that serves everyone according to medical need, not financial ability. In Canada, everyone is covered. In contrast, Americans — this same view holds — have a system that is great for the rich but inaccessible to the poor, and that allows as many as 30 to 40 million Americans to remain uninsured.

The truth is that we in Canada have an excellent health-care system that has been successful in most respects, but that is today seriously overtaxed by a triaged and inflexible hospital-based model, creating serious shortages of high-end diagnostic equipment, qualified personnel, and available beds. This already difficult situation has been exacerbated in recent years by cuts in the rate of health-care spending. The fiscal predicament in which provincial and federal governments found themselves during the early 1990s dramatically reduced the capacity of Canadian governments to sustain the level of increased funding upon which the functioning of the health-care system had been based. As a result, rather than face the waiting lists in Canadian hospitals, many wealthier Canadians simply go to the Mayo or Cleveland clinics to meet their health-care needs while less wealthy Canadians join the queue and are triaged based on urgency. Waiting lists for elective procedures and cancer treatment have become unacceptably long. The single-payer, state-funded model may be popular, but it — along with the Canada Health Act — has proven to be a formidable barrier to change. And these days, the single-payer systems in our provinces are sending many patients — every day — to adjacent U.S. treatment centres as a way of managing the pressures here!

Certainly, we cannot ignore the fact that at any one time, 30 million Americans may lack proper health insurance and therefore have limited access to the system. But it would be disingenuous to suggest that the Canadian system is not plagued by similar difficulties. In many cases, excessive waiting lists or queues also limit access to care. To pretend otherwise is to engage in the kind of ostrich-like behaviour our health-care system cannot sustain.

The truth is that the Canadian and American health-care systems have some glaring similarities. In both systems, anxiety on the part of doctors and patients runs high. In the U.S., this anxiety is the result of the attempts of some HMOs to discourage utilization and control costs and choices. In Canada, the anxiety is a result of ever-growing waiting lists, themselves at least in part the product of single-payer government health plans that seek to discourage utilization and control costs. On a macro level, the differences in the funding formulae of the two systems tend to be emphasized. But for the individual consumer of health-care services, the result is often quite similar: dealing with the health-care system, in whichever country, is all too often a needlessly complex and frustrating experience, no matter the source of funding.

If there is one weakness that typifies the postwar response of governments in Canada, the United States, and Western Europe to legitimate social-policy challenges, it has been the tendency to seek large, systemic solutions. In some cases, such as the U.S. social security system or Canada's Old Age Security and Canada Pension Plan, these may very well have been the right points of departure at the time.

But in an area as complex and intimate as the relationship between an individual and his or her physician, it is not at all clear that heavy systemic responses — by either government or private-sector actors — make any real sense. In fact, if we can draw any conclusion at all from our experience thus far, it is that the variations between rural and urban North America, the differing needs of various demographic groups, and the mix of therapies now available — as well as the range of choices and costs relating to models of care, diagnosis, treatment, and preventive activity — do not argue for the constraints of a single, heavy-handed government or HMO-dominated system. Rather, our experience suggests that we ought to embrace models of health-care delivery that accommodate and encourage diversity, not ones that suppress it. There is no relationship more personal than that between a doctor and his or her client. Health-care models should respect rather than frustrate that reality.

In *Who Is the Master?* — a blueprint for Canadian health-care reform published by the Institute for Research on Public Policy (IRPP) in 1998 — the authors called for the creation of a series of targeted medical agencies (TMAs), local or regional organizations with flexibility, accountability, and much more intimate community, patient, and provider relationships. Rather than recommending the rigid fee-for-service system for physicians and the global funding scheme for hospitals, the report advocates per patient capitation and locally negotiated service purchase from hospitals by the local TMA. This would encourage the efficient provider while reducing the pressures sometimes produced from "piecework" medicine.

The co-authors, a former Quebec minister of health, Claude Forget, and my predecessor at the IRPP, Monique Jerome Forget, herself a former assistant deputy minister of health at the federal level, introduced the issue of health-care reform by pointing out that Pope John Paul II rehabilitated Galileo in November 1992, some 350 years after he was condemned for agreeing with Copernicus that the earth was not at the centre of the universe. Some myths die hard. A fitting preamble for a careful look at health care.

We must find the courage to ask some of the tough questions that established interests on both sides of the border seem unwilling to address.

- Why can we not have competing models of health care within the same system? Why do we assume that greater choice within either HMOs or single-payer systems, or new organizational approaches will produce inequality, inefficiency, or waste?
- As the IRPP report asked, who is the master of the system — the sponsor, the provider, or the consumer? What price do we pay in terms of quality of medical care and patient rights if any of the constituents are disenfranchised by big-system rules?
- Are we sure that single-payer public funding or HMO arrangements, both of which necessitate a "big daddy" paymaster, are preferable in terms of outcomes to a voucher system where the government relates not to the provider but directly to the consumer, who chooses and pays?
- Are there built-in biases for certain kinds of therapy and treatment in the very structure of big, systemic approaches? And are these biases truly constructive in terms of health outcomes?
- Do consumers have the right to know more about the success rate of doctors, treatment protocols, procedures, hospitals, and clinics? If so, who should take the lead in providing some momentum on these rights, both in the U.S. and in Canada?

As a Canadian, I retain a fundamental belief that everyone in society has a right to basic medical care without regard to issues of affordability. But to be fair to the American system, it would simply be inaccurate to suggest that with all the hospitals that treat the uninsured and all the physicians who give free clinic time, there was not a similar sentiment among a majority of Americans.

The goals of universal access, excellence, improved outcomes, and more flexibility are real in Canada and attainable in the U.S. But they require not the certainty of the ideologue but the open-mindedness and creativity of a genuine search for new models. I believe we need to be adaptable as to means and approaches. Rigidity in defence of established approaches is no virtue. Creativity in search of better ways of achieving appropriate policy outcomes is no vice.

In fact, if we have learned anything during this period of enhanced mobility for both capital and people and the intense use of information technology to reduce the limits of space and time, it is that the old instruments of public policy that were conceived in the eighteenth or nineteenth centuries, or even in the 1940s, 1950s, and 1960s of the twentieth, may not be the best instruments for the age in which we now find ourselves. This does not mean that the goals of public policy are or were wrong. It may simply mean that the instruments by which we achieve them have to change.

It is precisely the wrong time to retreat behind national borders to look for new answers. It is precisely the right time for Canadians and Americans to pool expertise and experience to shape a constructive set of new options that each country could consider within the context of its own politics and culture. While our institutions, approaches, and visions for the future of health care may well differ, we should not be afraid to undertake research and fact-finding together.

A joint Canada-U.S. commission of inquiry into the health-care requirements of both societies could produce a gathering of expertise, intellect, experience, and policy breadth unparalleled in the history of both our countries. Each sovereign country would make its own decisions on the findings, but we would benefit by searching out options together. If there was ever a time for inspired peacetime collaboration, it is now. If there was ever a compelling issue on which to collaborate, it is health care.

Led by distinguished policy leaders from both countries and staffed by experts in clinical, financial, preventative, epidemiological, and medical-education areas, such a commission could pave the way for a new millennium of courageous policy and organizational choices for each country. If appointed in 1999 or 2000, this commission could report to both federal governments before the mid-term of the next administration — to be elected in the year 2000 in the U.S. and in 2001 here in Canada.

By inquiring with both vision and foresight, we could take a collaborative look at:

- the best practices in health promotion;
- new options for system organizations that enhance access, choice, and flexibility;
- a specific strategy to address the significant challenges of delivering quality health-care services to an ageing population;
- core planning issues in provider education;
- enhanced links between different parts of the system; and
- ways of increasing informed system use and the availability of diverse health-care models.

At a time when many provinces send their patients to U.S. centres for treatment because it is cheaper than building increased capacity here in Canada, and at a time when more and more Americans are choosing Canada for certain elective procedures because of cost, both systems would be terribly naive to believe that they are hermetically sealed from one another. They clearly are not. And it strikes me that we would be well served to move beyond the rhetoric of those in Canada who portray our system as more pure or altruistic, as well as beyond that of those in the U.S. who portray the American system as more patient-sensitive and technologically advanced. We have a tremendous amount to learn from each other, and we can learn a great deal more and achieve great things if we work together.

Getting health care right is about as vital a concern for Americans and Canadians as one could imagine. It is high time political leadership in all parties on both sides of the border embraced and engaged in a genuine effort to make the progress on this issue that Americans and Canadians deserve.

PART EIGHT

Policies for
the Future

THERE ARE HUGE DIFFERENCES IN WRITING A COLUMN OF OPINION, writing an essay for a journal of international affairs, and communicating policy during a leadership campaign. The policy papers in this chapter, which were distributed as part of my bid for the leadership of the Progressive Conservative Party in 1998, represent not just my own beliefs, but also those of a policy committee with deep roots in the party. But in the end, the final version is the candidate's responsibility, as it should be. It represents his or her best judgement at the time in the context of what was right for the country, and the policies that best fit with Conservative Party principles and traditions. Today, events and circumstances have overtaken the ideas of spring 1998. But the importance of ideas is never eclipsed.

Implicit in this approach is the belief that policy substance and detail actually matter. While, at the time, many in the media called me an organizer, the truth of my political involvement is that it has been almost exclusively on the policy side. The importance of policy may have been a view not shared elsewhere. Joe Clark's background, in fact, is largely as an organizer, and the results on October 24, 1998, seem to underscore the greater relevance of this skill set — to his credit. In any case, policy was a vital part of our campaign, and I owe a great debt to the many people who gave both quiet and public help.

The purpose of politics is policy — as well as the choice afforded voters in a democracy by the different policies and visions brought to the table by parties, their members at large, and their leaders. While partisan politics is the present preoccupation of others, I will continue to believe that thoughtful policy debate is the hallmark of a civilized democracy.

These papers were "discussion papers" simply because *no* leader of any party should impose policy. But I believe that candidates for leader have a duty at any time to tell party members and the public what their priorities would be if elected. (Leaders elected without a clear policy framework risk being held hostage to "events du jour" or, worse, the ideas of their partisan opponent.) Then, when the party meets to decide on a platform, the leader would be a participant on substance as well as form. It is not clear how important this concern was in the leadership process of 1998. In the end, our campaign members did what they thought was right and, on policy, I believe they did it well.

These ideas now belong to the larger debate about choices for the millennium, a debate that should involve all political parties and interested Canadians.

PUBLIC POLICY AND TOLERANCE

Canadian Council for Christians and Jews, Annual Meeting, Toronto, October 1, 1999

My purpose this morning is to make the case for one simple idea: that sustaining understanding between Canadians is directly related to continuing the search for understanding on the critical issues that affect us all. It follows as surely as we are sitting here today that if we ever stop looking for new ideas to address the issues that affect us, that surrender of will, that complacency, would quickly become a serious breeding ground for insensitivity, anger, racism, and bigotry.

Václav Havel made the point, after the success of the velvet revolution in Czechoslovakia, that in picking his staff and advisers, he would rather surround himself with people looking for the truth than with those who are sure they have already found it. What he understood, from having been jailed for his opposition to the totalitarian communist regime, is that those who are sure they have all the answers — because of either an all-encompassing ideology or a world-view that ignores dissent — are more likely to move a society away from the truth than closer to it.

And when we face real problems — such as lower and lower voter turnout; a distorted mix of tax policies, child poverty, homelessness, health-care congestion, and resource mismatch; and an outdated social infrastructure — a failure both to look for new options and to seek improvement would be a serious abdication. It would be an abdication not only of the benefits of public-policy research, but also of our collective responsibility to a society whose balance and fairness is in no small measure associated with how we manage and update our community's responses to its economic and social challenges.

As we go forward, let me suggest that the separate agendas of understanding between people and understanding the challenges facing people, while different, are not only complementary, but also absolutely mutually dependent.

There is a doctrine we see out there these days — one no less troubling than the orthodoxy of old-style Marxism — that is referred to by policy wonks as TINA and says that "there is no alternative" to most public-policy challenges. We are told that because of the nature of the financial world, because of productivity and competitive pressures, we have no choice on many policy issues. Some suggest that democratic choices are diminished because of the importance of international organizations such as the World Trade Organization, the UN, NAFTA, and the rest. This view is taken by people such as Pat Buchanan on the nativist, xenophobic American far right and, ironically, by some on the far left in parts of our own trade union movement. Both are defeatist analyses — however they may be differently inspired or intended — and they are advanced by two different extremes on the spectrum.

It is precisely that defeatism that can breed despair on the part of those who are encouraged to see their own disadvantage or problem as a product of either systemic paralysis or, worse, systemic conspiracy. It is that defeatism that can breed the kind of nativist isolationism we see too often in American politics, as well as the resultant xenophobia, racism, and bigotry that so often explode when people feel trapped. It is that defeatism that leaves some people without hope for new or better ideas to address our common challenges.

The commitment to search out new choices and better solutions must go beyond those of us in this room. This understanding must be the kind of society-wide commitment that is real and palpable in the lives of our fellow citizens.

Having served in government, I understand the need to imply, through sure-footed public policy and competent administration, that someone is in control, that there is a plan, that there are standards. But it is wrong and harmful for any government, at any level, to confuse that stance with a public or official notion that we are no longer looking for better ways to strengthen our society, to enhance our freedom or economic prospects.

As a society, we have some real choices to make:

- How do we maximize both economic growth and social progress? What are the specifics of economic policy and social infrastructure that are essential to that success?
- How do we organize governments in our federation to maximize the capacity to compete at home and abroad, and to benefit from the accommodations that uniquely shape our historical development?
- How do we ensure the legitimacy of our political and democratic

system, so that in the face of seriously reduced voter turnout and a persistent denigration of the importance of government, we can strengthen Canadian democracy and our real-time ability to make decisions as Canadians and do so together?

• How do we maximize the range of choices Canadians have in defending our own domestic and international interests?

There is no contradiction between a belief in the creativity and effectiveness of private markets and the will not to leave people behind, through sins of either omission or commission. And clearly, as we interact as a society with other societies that are geographically far removed — both in economic and trade domains and through the broadband linkage of the Internet and satellite networks — our benchmarks for economic and social progress cannot only be domestic. But our values, our standards, and our ideas here in Canada are never a bad place to start.

The family we call Canada, from its oldest members to the newest arrival, is never any stronger than the weakest among us. It is never wrong to worry about the most vulnerable — and a society as broad as ours need not hold back the best and brightest because we extend both hands and hope to the least advantaged.

At Queen's Park, I learned that working with people is better than imposing things upon people. In Ottawa, I learned that this country of ours, while strong and resilient, can be fragile and insecure. In the private sector, I learned that making a profit fuels job creation, economic growth, and the ability to finance the infrastructure of civility. At Queen's University, I have learned that teaching is just another form of learning, that there are very few students who do not teach as they learn, and that the challenge for the professor is to be able to learn from the students as one attempts to teach and instruct.

The country we have built is truly multinational, in a way that makes us more flexible and adaptable than the average unitary nation-state. We do not define our country by ethnicity, by religion, or even by common ancestral origin. We define it by geography, shared values, and a democratic process by which we articulate our values in each city and province and linguistic community.

If the Industrial Revolution, despite the immense progress it spawned, was achieved in some measure by exploitation — an exploitation that produced socialism, communism, and all the costs for so many that resulted from excesses in both — then we must be mindful that our new information technology revolution is being achieved not by exploitation, but with some exclusion of those unable to be in the digital loop. The Canadian tradition is to reach out to maximize both the size of our economic mainstream and the number of people at home and abroad who can participate. It has been a postwar, free-market Canadian priority.

At the end of this century, we should be asking how best to do that. Understanding the issues, challenges, and options underlying that priority will define not only our success as a country of competence and humanity, but also — and just as importantly — the kind of influence Canada exerts as a free and economically robust society in an ever more challenging, complex, yet promising world.

FACING THE POVERTY ISSUE

Jonquière, Quebec, August 1998

Parents have the primary responsibility for the care and nurture of their children. However, all families — poor and wealthy alike — at some point have needs and encounter difficulties that they cannot handle entirely on their own. We must enhance parents' ability to give their children the best possible start in life.

It is in everyone's interest to ensure that all Canadian children grow up secure, healthy, and well educated. We all reap the benefits of a nation of strong and healthy children. We all benefit from the hard work that parents perform in raising tomorrow's workers, taxpayers, and citizens. We all pay for the social and economic damage wrought by poverty, and so we all have a responsibility to Canada's parents and children.

In 1989, the House of Commons unanimously passed a resolution to "seek to achieve the goal of eliminating poverty among Canadian children by the year 2000." That ambitious commitment was a watershed because the government formally acknowledged what children's advocates and specialists had been arguing convincingly for decades: *Child poverty is intolerable in a country as rich and resourceful as Canada.*

Poverty exerts a heavy toll not only on many children and their parents, but also on government, the economy, and society. Poverty places obstacles in the way of equal opportunity for all our children, and in the end all Canadians pay a heavy price. The economic costs of poverty include increased expenditures for welfare, employment insurance, social services, health care, the courts, and the penal system; lost tax revenues; and wasted productivity.

Contrary to popular perception, poverty is not an affliction inherited by a small, hard-core group and passed down from one generation to another. The majority of low-income Canadians escape poverty, never to return; some cycle in and out of poverty; only a minority tend to remain poor year after year. Close to one-third of Canadians have a low income at least once in their lives, though half of those who fall below the poverty line in a given year rise above it the next. About the same number of people leave poverty as enter each year, indicating that there are massive flows in and out of the low-income population (though the people flowing in and out are usually not the same families and individuals).

New research has provided some important insights into the relative risks of short- and long-term poverty. The conclusion is clear: The longer a person remains below the poverty line, the less likely he or she will be able to rise above it. As well, the longer a person remains above the poverty line, the lower the risk of falling back.

Researchers in Canada and other countries have amassed a comprehensive body of evidence over many years documenting the consequences of life below the poverty line. The struggle to live on an inadequate income has been shown to increase the range, frequency, and severity of stress for families, thereby increasing parents' and children's susceptibility to a wide range of physical, psychological, and social problems. Compared with children from middle-income and well-off families, low-income children run a greater risk of developing these problems.

Although most low-income children manage to grow up and out of poverty, the harmful effects of poverty in childhood can linger long into their adult years, especially for those who do not complete their education. Not every adult who is poor is poorly educated, but there is a strong and consistent link between poverty and educational attainment: the lower the level of education, the greater the likelihood of ending up poor.

Unfortunately, research indicates that low-income children are more likely to have a lower education, thus increasing their risk of poverty when they grow up.

Child poverty has attracted a good deal of media, public, and political attention in recent years, but it is by no means a new phenomenon. Child poverty — or more accurately, family poverty, since children are poor because their parents are poor — is a persistent problem that is deeply embedded in Canada's economy and society. But family poverty shows no signs of abating as the twentieth century draws to a close. The profound changes sweeping over the workplace, the family, and the community are sustaining, if not intensifying, the powerful forces that keep one-fifth of the nation's children below the poverty line.

Supports to families have been shaken in recent years by cuts to human services that were made as part of the war the Liberals chose to fight on the deficit. The federal government's anti-deficit campaign involved significant reductions in federal transfer payments to the provinces for health, welfare, social services, and post-secondary education. There is fear that with the new Canada Health and Social Transfer (CHST), which will reduce federal funding for provincial social programs, there will be even wider differences in social standards across the country than in the past.

We cannot build strong families by tearing down the network of community resources that provides support and respite for parents and children. The corporate sector can, however, make an important contribution by helping families balance their work and family responsibilities. This contribution can include parental leave, flexible hours, child sick leave, and time off work for child-related school and health appointments. More and more companies are becoming aware of the need to introduce these kinds of "family-friendly" policies to their workplaces.

But there is a long way to go yet. And here again, corporations cannot, and should not, work alone. Fortunately, we have seen in recent years an exciting development across Canada: non-profit groups and business increasingly are collaborating in creative ways to promote economic and social well-being in their communities. Workplace volunteerism is another example of how corporations can contribute to communities — not through money necessarily, but through the time and expertise of their employees.

I suggest that governments work together with business and the non-profit sector, as well as with parents themselves, to develop a five-step commitment to eradicating poverty and improving the lives of all of Canada's children. This commitment would involve the following:

1. *A national parents' and children's agenda.* Canada is fortunate to possess an invaluable asset in the fight against poverty — a solid and growing stock of knowledge and experience built up over the years by researchers, children's advocates, and policy-makers. There is no dearth of ideas about what to do to tackle child poverty. What is still lacking, however, is a national consensus about how to move from promise to reality, from rhetoric to action.

   A national parents' and children's agenda must be created and pursued without creating further jurisdictional conflicts. It must provide a comprehensive and detailed framework for strengthening the Canadian family. Such an initiative must involve not just all levels of government, but also employers, children's advocates, communities, and citizens, including low-income families themselves. It should be based on the strategies of building caring communities and ensuring economic security, while also recognizing provincial sovereignty in this domain.

   The federal and provincial governments must work out a new partnership — and what better way to begin than by co-operatively constructing and putting in place a national parents' and children's agenda? The objective should not be to restore the old federally driven "co-operative federalism" of the past, which was conceived in a very different time, has become increasingly dysfunctional in recent years, and has undermined the fundamental principles of federalism. Canada needs a new kind of social union in which governments, while respecting each other's jurisdictions, work as equal partners in devising and applying workable principles, objectives, standards, and conditions for our social programs. For example, Quebec, through its various governments, has been pursuing a progressive and innovative family policy. It has a great deal to offer to the development of such a national parents' and children's agenda, as do all Canadian provinces.

2. *Indexation of the National Child Benefit.* Inflation is both eroding improvements in child benefits for low-income families and steadily reducing payments to non-poor families, which have experienced a sizeable loss in child benefits since the mid-1980s. The federal government should fully index the Canada Child Tax Benefit and gradually increase payments to not only the poor but also modest-income and middle-income families.

Diane St. Jacques, Progressive Conservative MP from Shefford, Quebec, moved a private member's motion in the House of Commons in November 1997 requesting that the government fully index the Child Tax Benefit. Such a change would protect the value of the benefit from the corrosive effects of inflation and would be "an important safeguard against the devastating effects of child poverty." The Liberals' response was that restoring full indexation of the Child Tax Benefit would cost too much. The question to ask, then, is how committed is the Liberal government to preventing and reducing child poverty?

The Canada Child Tax Benefit is Ottawa's contribution to the new National Child Benefit, a new kind of social partnership between the federal and provincial governments. It will replace the current uncoordinated, inefficient, and inequitable collection of federal child benefits and provincial/territorial social-assistance payments on behalf of children with a geared-to-income system providing equal benefits to all low-income families with children.

When fully in place, the National Child Benefit will provide equal child benefits to all low-income families, whatever their major source of income (welfare, employment, employment insurance, or some combination thereof). Increases in federal child benefits will enable the provinces and territories to re-invest savings from welfare payments to children in constructive programs and services for low-income families, such as income and wage supplements, childcare, early childhood development, and supplementary health-care benefits. The National Child Benefit will begin the long-overdue job of replacing the outmoded, incentive-destroying welfare system with modern and effective income supports that enhance opportunities and treat people with dignity and respect.

But the National Child Benefit only lays the foundation for a better system of child benefits. As well as fully indexing the Child Tax Benefit, Ottawa should eventually raise the maximum benefit, so that all low-income parents, including those on social assistance, will have a more secure and adequate income to provide for their families.

3. *Expand the caregiver tax credit to include stay-at-home parents.* The 1998 federal budget announced a caregiver tax credit, which will provide federal tax savings for Canadians who live with and provide in-home care for a parent or grandparent over sixty-five or an infirm, dependent relative, including a child. The new tax credit will reduce provincial income tax. This caregiver credit should be expanded to provide assistance to parents who work in the home caring for pre-school children. Such assistance should be geared to income, to target it to low- and middle-income parents.

4. *Greater support to private-sector organizations involved in public/private partnerships.* Support for our more vulnerable citizens must be a priority of any government. However, I firmly believe that business and community groups also have a role to play in providing support to Canadians in need, and that investment by one sector should not be an excuse for another sector to reduce its support. If anything, each investment should be seen as a way of leveraging even more resources.

Government's role should be to provide funds on a matching basis to groups (community and private sector) that become part of public/private partnerships. With matching funds from the government, small- and medium-sized companies will have more opportunity to support their communities. But of course, though such partnerships can supplement some of the social services available for society's most vulnerable people, they *cannot* replace the publicly funded services and programs that provide these supports.

Some companies, such as Chevron Canada Resources, have developed corporate policies that allow employees a certain number of hours of paid time to volunteer in community activities of their choice. Chevron is a founding member of the Calgary-based Workplace Volunteer Council, which is composed of representatives from business, community organizations, and the Volunteer Centre of Calgary.

The Body Shop is another company that encourages its employees to volunteer in the community. A Body Shop in the Ottawa area, for example, has placed volunteers with a Military Family Resource Centre. Two employees participate once a week for two hours in the centre's Parents and Tots Program, which is designed to help parents develop support networks while their children learn to socialize and play in groups.

The Dufferin Mall in Toronto is an example of a partnership that has helped build a caring community. Situated within the catchment area of six schools, the mall is a meeting place for teens. Over the years, there were more frequent disturbances involving attacks on customers and store break-ins. The manager of the company that ran the mall was faced with a difficult choice. Either he could turn the mall into a fortress with multiple security systems or he could address the problem in a more constructive way. He chose the latter route.

The mall management met with the schools in the area, as well as with a group of twelve youth-serving agencies. After having discussions about the problem and some possible solutions, this committee decided to set up a one-stop social-services centre for youth. Today, the centre provides individual and family counselling, information and referral, job training, and community outreach. In addition to the youth centre, the mall merchants are involved in various programs that teach work skills to students and provide co-op placements. The mall has also become the base for a theatre group, sports groups, and other activities for teens.

5. *Establish a national forum on income security.* A fundamental question that underlies our ability to address child poverty and provide support for the less advantaged in our society is this: Should our government seek to replace a myriad of existing and expensive social programs with a basic income floor for all citizens? This is not a new question. Academics and researchers have discussed it for many years, and the answer to it is not straightforward or obvious. There are cost implications in both policy and dollar terms.

I would establish a national forum on income security that would give Ottawa, the provinces, and frontline agencies an opportunity to build some genuine cohesion and momentum.

The best way to fight poverty is to promote the well-being of all citizens. This can be accomplished only by an inclusive approach that draws upon the rich resources of a civil society. This means that all citizens and sectors — government, corporate, and community — must contribute to building a caring and mutually responsible society. These three sectors together offer a wealth of resources, skills, and expertise. These assets should be used to a much greater extent to build caring communities and ensure economic security.

RENEWING MEDICARE FOR THE MILLENNIUM

Saskatoon, August 1998

There is a difference between good health and health care and medical services. Medicare is a program that pays for health care and medical services; good health is the product of a lot of other factors. For years, we have focused on building excellent modern health-care services in Canada. We have undertaken a series of royal commissions, task forces, studies, and reports, most of which have concluded that the formal health-care system — doctors, nurses, hospitals, technicians — is only one factor affecting the health of people and their communities.

In fact, much of the credit for our improved longevity belongs to improvements in income, diet, housing, education, sanitation, and other public policy and social factors. Yet there can be no question that we still need high-quality health services as we work to improve our performance on the other, broader determinants of health. Canadians must know that the health-care services they have come to count on will be there when they, their families, and their friends need them most.

As a society, we have chosen to pay collectively, through our taxes, for health services. As a society, we have chosen to provide health care to those who are ill and need it, rather than only to those who can individually afford it. There is nothing wrong with the basic principles of medicare. In fact, our commitment to our health-care system is largely a measure of who we are and how we see ourselves. There is, however, something wrong with the rigidities that have crept into the delivery of health services. We need to show imagination and creativity if our health-care system is to continue. We, as citizens, need to accept responsibility and accountability for its survival.

From 1975 until 1991, Canadian health expenditures grew at an average of 11.2 percent per year — far faster than inflation, population growth, or any reasonable measure of need. As a country with a young population, we spent heavily on health services. In the early 1990s, faced with insupportable deficits and cuts to federal transfers, provincial governments initiated a long-overdue but painful renovation of health-care delivery. Through closure of redundant hospital beds, as well as entire hospitals, the provinces have done part of the needed job. As a result, throughout the 1990s, total health spending has grown much more slowly. From 1991–95, for example, it increased by 2.9 percent per annum. In the past two years, it grew by only 1.4 percent. Now it is time to reinvest in health services, though carefully and strategically, not at the unsustainable growth rates of the 1970s and 1980s. The provinces have carried out these difficult changes with no assistance from the federal government. Despite the advice of the National Forum on Health, the federal government appears to be uncertain of its role.

Without federal investment and leadership, those who cling to an unsustainable status quo and demand vastly increased sums to prop up the existing system will ultimately succeed only in dooming it. We will slowly but inevitably lose the system that serves all, not just those who can afford special treatment. Only then will we learn that all Canadians are required to carry the financial responsibility for health-care services.

Medicare must meet the needs of all Canadians, and to do that it must be reformed. Reforming the system for the next millennium involves recognizing and adapting to the challenges the system is already facing. These challenges include:

- better-informed patients who are taking a more pro-active role in evaluating different treatment options and demanding accountability from the health-care system;
- the differing demands of Canada's changing demographic structure;
- the ongoing impact of the information and technology revolutions on both treatment and service delivery;

- the shift towards integrated delivery systems and alternative delivery methods, such as community care, home care, and long-term care;
- the dissatisfaction of our health-care providers;
- the abuse of the system by inappropriate use; and
- the need to strike the right balances between health promotion, prevention, and "sickness care."

If our health-care system is going to provide comprehensive and quality services to all Canadians, then all Canadians must understand that in addition to having rights within the system, we have responsibilities to it. Governments, health organizations, providers, and consumers need to work co-operatively to reshape our health system. A code of rights and responsibilities will allow this to happen. Among other things, the code will protect the right to information, the right to respect and dignity, the right to timely diagnosis and treatment, the right to be consulted on treatment options, the right to full disclosure of quality and outcomes data, the right to expect effective and efficient care, and responsibility for system use.

When Prime Minister Margaret Thatcher turned her attention to the troubled National Health Service in England, one of her most successful reforms was the Patient Charter, which clearly established legitimate rights and expectations to which the system had to respond. Our Canadian code will help make those who are delivering health services accountable to the consumer for performance, outcomes, and waits for service. It will also help make consumers more responsible for the way in which they use the system.

A code of rights and responsibilities will be an important element of a reformed Canada Health Act. The benefits of enhanced accountability — for both providers and users — will lead to improved quality and speed in the delivery of care services.

Of course, many Canadians need health care not in hospitals but in their communities and their homes. Investing in home care is a sensible and urgently needed priority for the future of medicare. This would be a re-investment not only in community care, but also in long-term care. Modern medications and therapies render this a cost-effective and wise alternative. It is a solid strategic investment that meets the needs of an ageing population facing many chronic diseases. It is time for the federal and provincial governments, along with those in the front line of delivery, to plan a national initiative to bring home care fully under the auspices of medicare. The National Forum on Health urged this more than a year ago. To date, however, no action has been taken by the federal Liberal government.

Once in office, a Conservative government should pursue the forum's recommendation for a federal government investment of $1 billion to be phased in over five years. When this new money is added to the existing $2 billion of provincial home-care spending and matched by continuing provincial spending growth, the result would be a doubling of the total home-care effort.

We have provided in our tax system for the creation of Registered Retirement Savings Plans (RRSPs) to encourage Canadians to save for their retirement. More recently, Registered Education Savings Plans (RESPs) have been enhanced to support our children in attaining a university education. Both of these plans have complemented and supplemented existing public programs — the Canada Pension Plan for retirement and the public funding of universities. Both RRSPs and RESPs enjoy wide support.

Germany, with a more aged population than Canada's, views long-term care insurance as a separate requirement from sickness insurance. Canada, by contrast, is relying entirely on medicare for its support to the frail elderly. With our ageing population, the cost of care for those over the age of eighty-five will increase rapidly. Now is the time to implement a mechanism to encourage savings to offset the risk of long-term care.

A Conservative government would seek to create a tax-favoured savings plan for long-term care. A form of Registered Long-Term Care Plan (RLTP) would allow Canadians to save against the possibility of their need for a lengthy period of care. Our medicare system should continue to provide the medical treatment component of long-term care, but Canadians should also be allowed a tax exemption for any funds placed in a savings vehicle with an insurance element to cover the staggering potential cost of other care.

The private sector also has much to contribute to a reformed medicare system — information technology, new drugs, new forms of home-care delivery, new imaging technologies, and an ability to provide efficiencies. Without altering the fundamental principle of a single universal health-care system based on need, it is possible to gain the benefits of private-sector efficiencies.

Already many health organizations have contracted with expert private-sector companies. In areas such as the management of laboratories, food services, and information technology, these partnerships are benefiting the Canadian health-care system. There is room for more partnerships like these. The Canadian government should fund the necessary pilot projects to explore new and innovative partnerships while developing rules that will ensure that their benefits accrue to both the Canadian health-care system and to stakeholders.

There is also important work to be done to renew a productive partnership between the government of Canada and the provincial governments. Without a viable partnership, it will prove impossible to achieve the necessary changes. For example, to meet the growing shortages of doctors in rural Canada, there is a clear need to reorganize our primary-care system. Rural and northern fee-for-service family practitioners, often in solo practices, are being crushed by the two-pronged burden of long hours and no support. The federal government should work co-operatively with the provinces to develop innovative approaches to the delivery of health care in rural and northern areas; such approaches should involve physicians, nurses, and multi-disciplinary staff. These changes will need federal-provincial partnerships as well as partnerships with communities and health-care professionals.

Finally, the heart of this new co-operation in health care must be a new financial relationship between the federal government and the provinces. We need to create a fresh approach to financing health care that will secure its future by providing predictability and stability. The federal role in health care should no longer be based solely on fiscal force. The federal government should once and for all provide the provinces and territories with the fiscal capacity to finance health care themselves. I propose a fixed five-year funding formula based on a mix of transfers and tax points; the base level would be $13 billion, adjusted annually for demographic change.

Giving the provinces and territories the fiscal capacity to finance health care would end the circular route currently taken by health-care dollars. It makes no sense that, simply to protect federal government visibility, tax dollars go from taxpayers to the federal government then back to the provinces and territories, where they are spent on the very individuals who paid the taxes in the first place. In addition to ending this circuitousness, transferring tax points will eliminate forever the risk that the federal government will "take its cut" before passing the money along.

This approach will also enable the federal and provincial/territorial governments to agree on common standards for health care, commit to achieving those standards, measure progress towards their attainment, and establish a binding enforcement mechanism beyond the Canada Health Act. It is a way to recognize the maturity of the Canadian federation while still displaying uncompromising respect for the principles of medicare.

These are but three examples of the greater requirement for a renewal of partnership in the health field. Only strong federal leadership that understands the primary role of the provinces can accomplish a renewed partnership. Only a renewed partnership can accomplish the changes that Canadians need and want.

Taken together, these initiatives represent a viable and positive plan to reform Canadian medicare. Rebuilding the partnership among governments is a key first step. Forging a new partnership with Canadian consumers to reshape the health-services system to meet individual needs while still protecting its universality is a critical second step.

Our health-care system can meet our needs in the twenty-first century, but only if we have the courage and leadership to manage change rather than settling for less of the same. By taking a constructive approach, we will be rewarded with a more efficient system that balances the twin goals of creating health and treating illness. Medicare is what we make it. It can be as dynamic and modern as we, through our governments, choose. It can also be allowed to decay. Medicare will be maintained not by putting it in a museum, but by reforming it. Federal leadership that focuses on the need to protect the well-being of all Canadians is essential to preparing our health-care system for the next millennium.

REBUILDING CANADA'S NATIONAL DEFENCE

Halifax, August 1998

Canada's fighting forces have developed an enviable and honourable legacy through two world wars, the Korean conflict, the Gulf War, and countless overseas peacekeeping missions and domestic assignments to aid Canadians in distress.

The current challenges facing the Canadian armed forces are the result of three distinct crises: (i) a crisis in command, as detailed in the *Inquiry into the Deployment of the Canadian Forces to Somalia;* (ii) a crisis in policy, in both defence procurement and force deployment, that is a result of the government's failure to establish a coherent defence policy and to blend our defence policy with our foreign policy effectively; and (iii) a most unfortunate crisis in morale that results from the federal government's lack of attention to the needs of men and women who have chosen to serve their country. Collectively, these crises clearly indicate that Canada's defence policy is aimless, and that our country's ability to contribute to national defence and to international efforts to improve global security has been reduced as a result.

In Canada, we have an armed forces that is not being given the resources to meet all tasks and that does not have a focus that is sufficiently refined to ensure the effectiveness of our military men and women. Canada continues to need a professional military to uphold and defend the country's national interests in the world and to ensure the protection of Canadian sovereignty. We need a military that will support civil authorities, contribute to collective security and world peace operations, and defend international obligations and allies.

The new Canadian military must focus on four primary areas of responsibility: (i) an assurance of Canadian sovereignty; (ii) a commitment to contractual treaties with our NATO and NORAD allies; (iii) a continuing responsibility to international peace operations wherever and whenever required and appropriate; and (iv) a mobile capacity to protect Canadian interests in an ever more unpredictable world environment.

The defence of Canada will not improve simply by increasing budgets or making random acquisitions of new equipment. Building a national defence system for Canada in the twenty-first century means finding a strategy to join ends and means under the active direction of the government. Canadians traditionally expect the armed forces to defend Canada, to defend North America in co-operation with the United States, and to undertake commitments abroad with like-minded states in support of collective defence and security. However, the essence of Canada's defence policy resides in the military capabilities Canadians choose for their forces. A national defence strategy relating these traditional tasks to military means would require the Canadian forces to have the capabilities:

- to demonstrate Canada's sovereignty in and over Canadian territory;
- to operate on a technically compatible basis with the armed forces of the United States in the defence of North America; and
- to deploy and sustain a joint Canadian military force consisting of a brigade group with air and sea augmentation.

To build an effective armed force for the new millennium, it is important that we first restore command integrity. Officers, and especially senior officers, must be selected, promoted, and appointed to positions of command based solely on demonstrated professional merit. No officer should command Canadians if he or she fails this minimal test. In future, every officer nominated for promotion to general or flag rank, and for appointment to command a significant Canadian forces contingent outside Canada, should first be interviewed by a committee of the House of Commons. That committee should then offer to the government its opinion on the appropriateness of the appointment.

Senior officers, in the normal course of their careers, can expect to work with officials in the federal public service, but they are not and must not be part of that service. Nor is any public servant a member of the Canadian forces. Civil control of the armed forces means control by civilians elected to Parliament, and this is a duty that cannot be delegated to anyone. These fundamental principles must be plainly evident in the structure of the Canadian forces and the Department of National Defence, and in the relationship of officers and officials to cabinet ministers. The chief of the defence staff is charged under the National Defence Act with the control and administration of the Canadian forces, and he should have an appropriate military staff and a Canadian forces headquarters apart from his ministry office. The separation of a Canadian forces headquarters from the Department of National Defence must be an absolute priority.

The next important step is to restore policy coherence. The crises of capabilities and of policy cannot be separated completely, but different processes are needed to address them adequately. The selection of capabilities for the Canadian forces and the allocation of funds to buy and sustain them are complex policy matters. The usual — and unfortunately incorrect — way to proceed is to allocate funds and hope the capabilities the government desires somehow appear in the future. The smart way to proceed is to agree on precise capabilities and allocate appropriate funds to acquire and maintain them. This more effective process requires a consensus between the government and its technical advisers at the beginning of the policy process. A consensus-building system, led in every respect by cabinet ministers, would clarify defence objectives, expose the true costs of acquiring capabilities, and provide a spending program that ministers could more easily audit.

A defence policy built on a wide consensus would facilitate the day-to-day management of the armed forces and close the dangerous expectations/capability gap that separates the foreign policies of the Liberal government from the realities of the Canadian forces today. Once capabilities are agreed upon and produced, future missions for the armed forces could be selected rationally and, as a result, the chief negative characteristics of current operations (i.e., the command vacuum and the morale problems) might be brought under control.

It is obvious that the restoration of Canada's military capabilities demands some increased strategic spending. The Liberal government freeze on defence allocations cannot be sustained without doing more harm to Canada's national defence and its international stature. Members of the Canadian forces and the Department of National Defence have realized considerable economies under a so-called re-engineering program that has been in effect for more than four years. Unfortunately, these savings in overhead were not reinvested in the future Canadian forces. Rebuilding the armed forces calls for the gradual return to pre-freeze funding levels of about $12 billion annually. The majority of this money should be spent to acquire new, agreed-upon capabilities; to reinforce personnel in combat-related occupations; and to improve the conditions for serving members of the Canadian forces and their families.

An agreement between the chief of the defence staff for the armed forces and the government about the capabilities necessary for national defence and international operations would solve one aspect of the crisis in policy. A reliable mechanism for policy coordination is needed to solve the other critical aspect of this crisis. Officers who tried to arrange a Canadian-led multinational force in Zaire complained that the only result of their meetings with members of the Department of Foreign Affairs and International Trade prior to the deployment to Africa was frustration. A revitalized defence policy is of little use if there is no credible mechanism to coordinate it. Canada urgently requires an agency of government — a Cabinet Council on National Security, for example — where intelligence, research, national policy planning, and the operational coordination of anticipated and ongoing missions can be managed by ministers.

The final important step is to revitalize the reserve force. The reserve component of the Canadian forces provides an important military capability to Canada. Reservists prove their worth every day in the former Yugoslavia, in operations in other distant lands, and in domestic emergencies. Yet the reserves struggle under policies and procedures that hamper and discourage even the most stalwart volunteer. Canada must enact legislation that facilitates the employment of members of the reserve force while compensating fairly their civilian employers. Tax incentives for both parties are a way to serve this end.

Canada also needs a more efficient system of military recruitment for both the regular and the reserve components of the Canadian forces. The present practice of long-term enrolment in the regular force is costly, inefficient, and absorbs almost half of the annual defence budget. The reserve force, on the other hand, suffers from limited training opportunities and low retention rates, especially among junior members. These problems can be redressed partly through a new recruitment system based on contracted, short-service engagements of young Canadians. Under a contract process, individuals would be enrolled in the regular force for a period of three to five years, and would then serve with the reserve force part time for a similar period. A percentage of specially selected recruits who prove themselves in service could be offered full-time employment in the regular forces and would form the basis of a permanent cadre for the armed forces. This program would help to control personnel costs by reducing the expensive "in for a day, in for life" policies of the Canadian forces. The result would be a greatly improved reserve force and a more viable and flexible armed force for Canada.

∼

The crisis in the forces and in defence policy calls for immediate action by Canadians. I suggest a ten-point program for rebuilding our national defence. At a minimum, such a program of defence renewal should aim to:

1. ensure that officers of the Canadian forces enter into a thoroughly professional cadre based on merit and uncoupled completely from the public service;
2. clarify command responsibility and accountability by establishing a Canadian forces headquarters that is separate and distinct from the Department of National Defence;
3. revitalize the reserves and regular forces with a new pay system, more intense reserve training, and a tax-incentive system that compensates employers of reservists who take time for training and service;
4. develop a more rational, modern, and flexible recruiting system that is based in part on contracted, three- to five-year engagements for young Canadians, and that sees those recruits who excel offered long-term, full-time employment;
5. commence a program of strategic re-investment to bring the forces, over a five-year period, back to a $12-billion budgetary base;
6. commit to a program of enhanced base quality, facilities, and salaries for members of the Canadian forces and their families, beginning with the non-commissioned ranks;
7. provide ongoing education to all members of the forces, at all ranks (every member of the forces should have a personal development plan that aims to expand his or her abilities in the combat, technology, and analytical disciplines);
8. establish a Cabinet Council on National Security, which would include the heads of CSIS and the RCMP, as well as the solicitor general and the ministers of foreign affairs, national defence, and immigration, and be able to second staff as necessary;
9. establish a brigade group with appropriate air/sea augmentation to enable rapid deployment of Canadian forces to meet international and security emergencies;
10. broaden the base of the present veterans' policy to include support for those who served in the merchant marine, which supplied our allies during the darkest days of the Second World War, and a strong government-wide commitment to gain a specific apology and precise compensation plan from Japan for the veterans of Canada's Hong Kong garrison, who were treated with utter inhumanity and cruelty during the Second World War.

Canada's armed forces have faced competing demands, political uncertainty, severe budget cuts, and rapidly changing social and ethical expectations over the past five years. While there have been setbacks, gross failures of leadership, and serious mistakes, we must also remember that in a host of foreign theatres — from Cyprus to the Golan, Central America to Eastern Europe, the Middle East to our NATO allies — Canadian troops are respected for competence, dependability, and courage in difficult circumstances.

At home — from Oka to the Saguenay, from the Red River Valley to eastern Ontario and western Quebec — our forces, both regular and reserve, reflect the desire of Canadians to reach out to help each other in the face of natural disasters and personal calamity. This tradition of service — on land, sea, and in the air; in military, security, peace, and search-and-rescue operations — reflects a pride and patriotism that speaks to the best of the Canadian way of life. It also builds on a tradition of courage, sacrifice, and effectiveness that saw the battlefields of Europe and Asia, in two world wars, give birth to the independence of Canada as a country and the values of freedom and security that Canadians still share.

The blemishes on the face of our armed forces are real and must be addressed. The changes required in leadership and accountability must be implemented. The underlying will of the men and women of our armed forces to serve with distinction, valour, and courage must be protected, enhanced, and supported by a coherent public policy that serves the national interest.

RESTORING THE CONFEDERAL UNION

Montreal, September 1998

Canada is the greatest country in the world in which to live — the United Nations says so, and few Canadians would disagree. Thousands of people every year immigrate to our country, knowing they will find a place and a people dedicated to equality of opportunity, fairness, and justice. Yet for more than two decades, Canadians have been struggling with the fundamental issues of nationhood — the core of what makes this country Canada. Other than the recent Supreme Court decision, the news on the issue of Quebec sovereignty has been relatively quiet for the past year. We must, however, realize that just because we aren't hearing about them day after day, the issues that divide Quebec from the rest of the country — and many Québécois among themselves — have not gone away, and they won't. Unfortunately, this sleepwalking approach was the one taken by the present prime minister during the last referendum.

I believe that the time has come to adopt a new point of view and to speak plainly and clearly. We should get beyond arguing constitutional fine points and get back to the essential truths that got us to this juncture in the first place. By doing this, by acknowledging what Quebecers have the right to hear, we can move forward — away from constitutional debate and on to the business of building a country, a new confederal union that no province would want to leave.

Originally, Canada was built on the concept of two founding nations and two founding peoples — the French and the English. While there have been important changes since the founding of the country, it is vital that we remember and emphasize this key fact of history. For decades prior to 1982, Canada existed under the dual premises that the two founding peoples each had a *de facto* "veto" over any proposed changes to the existing order of things, and that both sides respected each other and respected the right to have different, as well as similar, needs. It was part of the core compromise that bound the country together.

Rhetorical flourishes around the events of 1981-82 (however overdramatic they were about the impact of patriation and the Charter of Rights), the failure of the Meech Lake and Charlottetown accords, and the near-death experience of 1995 all give rise to the need for a new approach.

An appropriate approach to federalism should be built on two fundamental principles: (i) we can govern Canada well only as a working and dynamic partnership between federal and provincial governments; and (ii) this partnership must exist only to serve the interests of citizens. It is not about the partisan or bureaucratic concerns of governments; we need a citizens' federalism. These principles mean that we must create the tools for a more effective partnership, and that we must provide all Canadians with opportunities to ensure that the partnership is more responsive and accountable.

Why a partnership? Canadians are an inherently confederal people. We identify with and celebrate not only the country but also our provinces, regions, and neighbourhoods. We want our provinces to be free to respond to our regional needs and concerns, but we are equally committed to having the freedom to live and work anywhere in the country and to the principle of sharing our resources and opportunities. We want our national government to respond to regional interests and our provincial governments to recognize the national implications their activities may have.

The powers necessary to meet major challenges — whether in economic development, social policy, or the environment — are inevitably exercised by both levels of government. That means that few issues can be effectively addressed by one government alone. It also means that there is enormous potential for frustration — for contradictory programs, for costly duplication and overlap, for wrangling over who should be doing what — while problems go unsolved and citizens carry the burdens of uncoordinated taxation. Much as we may wish it, it is simply not possible in a country like Canada to place all governmental responsibilities into two watertight compartments, one labelled provincial and the other federal. Partnership provides a far more creative way to adapt our system to new needs and concerns than does the cumbersome, conflicting, and time-consuming process of constitutional change.

Many of the success stories of Canadian public life were products of effective partnerships: the Trans-Canada Highway, medicare, support for higher education, old-age pensions, the Canada Assistance Plan, equalization, and others. Many of the failures, such as the National Energy Program and FIRA, were the direct result of Ottawa's abandonment of partnership by acting unilaterally.

An effective partnership would demonstrate to all Canadians the value and benefits of participating in the Canadian federation. This could be as valid for Quebecers as it would be for Westerners, British Columbians, Maritimers, or Ontarians. There is only one taxpayer. He or she has the right to governments that co-operate without regard to partisanship. Downloading responsibilities might help the budget of one government, but it may not do anything to help the average citizen, who just has to pay somewhere else.

The Liberal government has recently, once again, placed the federal-provincial partnership in jeopardy. First it slashed billions of dollars in support of health, education, and social welfare without consultation or discussion, then it left the provinces to take the political heat for cuts they had to make as a direct result. At the same time as its support for these services was plummeting, Ottawa continued to insist on acting as judge and jury on provincial actions. If the federal government was no longer paying the piper, what right, provinces could reasonably ask, did it have to continue to call the tune? Now, as it begins to enjoy surpluses, Ottawa again threatens the partnership by introducing new programs, again without consultation, in areas where the provinces have the major responsibility and spending obligation. Whether it's cutting or spending, the same federal attitude persists: We know best; we don't trust the provinces.

Canadians both want and need a healthy partnership between federal and provincial governments. How do we build it? Almost unnoticed, the provinces have been putting some of the essential elements in place. The annual premiers' conference has become a vital forum for co-operation and collaboration. Ministerial councils and task forces have been created to promote co-operation, sort out responsibilities, and debate national standards in many policy areas. A Progressive Conservative government should create a new, more positive context for agreement by its own actions. It should:

- remove some of the last vestiges of undue federal dominance inherited from the nineteenth century by declaring that the powers of "disallowance" and "reservation," by which Ottawa could unilaterally overturn provincial legislation, will be set aside permanently;
- not use unilateral power to take over major projects unless it has majority provincial consent;
- eliminate the federal mindset that sees provinces as "junior partners" subject to federal guidance and monitoring;
- seek provincial nominations to the boards of the Bank of Canada and other major national regulatory bodies, such as the CRTC, whose rulings have major impacts on provinces and regions; and
- restrict the spending power that enables the federal government to intrude unilaterally in provincial jurisdictions.

A Progressive Conservative government would work with provinces to establish the mechanisms that will allow an effective partnership to flourish.

These mechanisms will include an annual First Ministers' Conference, held on a fixed timetable rather than on an ad hoc, crisis-driven basis, as is the case today, and a network of Councils of Ministers (federal, provincial, and territorial) that will be consulted in each major policy field.

The intergovernmental partnership Conservatives envision is designed to serve citizens, not to exclude or frustrate them; it must promote, not undermine, the principles of parliamentary democracy. Hence, as we develop more effective intergovernmental mechanisms, we must ensure that they are responsive, transparent, and open to citizen influence, and we must strengthen the role of legislatures in debating and monitoring the work of their executive in the conduct of intergovernmental relations.

In the institutions of partnership, democracy means that federal-provincial deliberations will no longer be hidden by the current exemption in the Freedom of Information Act (FOI); that at least part of all First Ministers' conferences will be in open, public sessions; that ministerial councils will be directed to include consultation with interested groups as a normal part of their deliberations; and that all citizens will have direct access to any dispute-resolution mechanisms adopted by intergovernmental agreement. Strengthening legislative involvement in the federal-provincial partnership requires at a minimum that the federal House of Commons establish a permanent standing committee on federal-provincial co-operation; that ministers will consult with the committee prior to major meetings and report back on results; that all intergovernmental agreements will be tabled in the House of Commons; that agreements that involve substantial commitment by the federal government must be passed by resolution before they can take effect; and that representatives of the official opposition will be invited to participate on federal delegations to major intergovernmental meetings.

The next step to strengthening the confederal union will be to break down internal trade barriers. The abolition of many international trade barriers, through the FTA and NAFTA — as brought in by the Conservative government — has been a success and contributed to the creation of wealth and jobs. Yet interprovincial barriers still exist in Canada's internal market, and these constitute an impediment to the development of new economic opportunities for Canadians.

Every province and every Canadian should gain with a new confederal union and with new policies that celebrate this relationship. The first steps could be taken in the area of interprovincial trade. It has long been thought ridiculous that it is easier for Vancouver to trade with Seattle than with Saskatoon, or that pharmacists cannot move from Winnipeg to Thunder Bay and practise without taking a licensing examination. The limitations on the movements of goods and services within our country are more restrictive than those outside our borders, and this is what we must work to change. To start, we should:

- establish an Inter-Provincial Trade Commission (IPTC), which would regulate and enforce the rules of interprovincial trade and replace all other internal trade-governance structures;
- give the provinces a one-year deadline to reach an agreement on the IPTC (if an agreement is not reached, the federal government can use its authority to take the initiative in establishing the IPTC);
- establish an enforceable dispute-settlement mechanism that will allow governments, businesses, and eventually individuals to take action against barriers; and
- work co-operatively with governments and organizations to remove restrictions that prevent individuals from living and working where they choose within the country.

These measures are just a start, but they are intended to signal a clear new direction. New interprovincial guidelines arrived at co-operatively with input from the Prime Minister's Office will provide another strong link between the provinces and will also increase the economic benefits of belonging to the federation.

CREATING GROWTH AND OPPORTUNITY

Toronto, September 1998

I have travelled across this country and throughout other parts of the world in various capacities — business person, politician, educator, and tourist. Throughout my travels, I have never ceased to be impressed by the straightforward and logical manner in which individual members of society make choices about their own, their family's, and their communities' financial well-being. At the same time, I am disheartened, as are many of the citizens with whom I have met, by how quickly unfocused governments can nullify the positive economic contributions most individuals make to society from day to day. This discussion paper is about how we can change this situation to one in which government works towards a transfer of economic power to Canadians so that they can take charge of meeting their daily challenges without the burden of excessive taxation. It is only through this transfer that we can strengthen communities and their values.

Fairness and economic success are best achieved by the open interaction of individuals in a market economy. That is virtually impossible to achieve if government intervention and taxation skew or create disincentives that unduly inhibit those interactions. In Canada, we have a long history of wanting to ensure that people are treated decently, and that the disenfranchised and disadvantaged are included in our country's economic success. It is this adherence to the idea of equality of opportunity that actually sets us apart from our neighbours to the south. It is this quality of Canada that people from all walks of life worry is heavily under attack. In a rapidly changing global order, Canadians need to know that as we make significant changes in other areas, our governments remain committed to these aspects that so clearly contribute to a Canadian community of opportunity.

This paper begins with a fundamental belief that government's basic goals must be to provide opportunity for all and to encourage individual responsibility. These are goals that can be achieved only by small steps. Whether I'm discussing tax cuts or the promotion of long-term savings, my message and intent is the same: If we free up individuals to make decisions about the economic well-being of their families and communities, Canada will succeed dramatically in the twenty-first century.

The United Nations calls Canada the most liveable country on the planet. This is a fact we already knew, but one that we can all take some credit for achieving. In recent years, Canadian governments of all political stripes have required their electorate to make sacrifices to clean up the messes created by the free-spending ways of the past. Canadians responded to this challenge admirably. Canadian businesses also understood what was necessary, and they acted by embracing the new global economy; responding to more open and competitive markets; and investing in new technology, plants, and equipment. And yet, despite our gains, which show up in economic statistics reporting gross domestic product (GDP), something is not right in the eyes of many individual Canadians. The fruits of their labour are not being realized. Canadians are working harder and harder and keeping less and less. They are paying more and more taxes and getting less and less service. People are fearful of the future, and we must replace that fear with hope. After six years of economic growth, Canadians are still facing some disturbing realities about their individual well-being and their lack of power to change these realities.

Consider the situation of the average Canadian today. Despite the fact that the federal government will run a large government surplus this year, the percentage of personal income transferred to government is at a record high. The gap between what Canadians pay and what our U.S. neighbours pay is at or near a historical high. Such a gap weighs heavily on the incentive to work and on the ability of Canadians to save and invest. Sales tax rates are nearly double what consumers face in the United States. This is stifling consumer and retail spending — a key engine of employment growth. Capital gains taxes are double those in the U.S., creating a disincentive for Canadians to invest and thereby limiting the creation of wealth in the economy. When compared with the OECD average, Canadian personal income taxes, as a percentage of GDP, are too high.

Regretfully, "bracket creep" in the tax system has left Canada with a tax threshold that is the lowest among our trading partners. The impact has been devastating to poorer individuals in our society. As a result, more than a million of those individuals have been absorbed into the tax system since the late 1980s.

Federal and provincial corporate tax rates in Canada continue to exceed those in the U.S. and are restricting companies from making job-creating investments in the country. Again, this is killing the opportunity to reduce the chronic underemployment that is evident in so many of our communities. What is most disturbing about these high tax inequities is the fact that it means that the best and brightest Canadians are leaving the country to find opportunities elsewhere. The outflow of doctors, engineers, computer scientists, professors, and teachers is many times greater than the inflow. This is a national disaster that must be addressed. Equally frightening for those of us who decide to stay in the country should be the fact that the typical American is now 25 percent richer than the typical Canadian! There is no logical explanation for this, other than the impact of high taxation on Canadians and the companies they work for.

There is no doubt that Canadian workers and businesses have made many of the same adjustments to compete in the global environment that American workers and businesses have, and yet our unemployment rate remains almost twice as high as that in the United States.

Beyond the unhealthy tax burden that we Canadians must endure, we also face a mountain of debt that is sustainable only as long as interest rates continue to hold at their current historic lows. But hoping for a continued low interest rate is not a strategy. Canadians must demand that their governments set out a plan to pay down the national debt and to outlaw the type of deficit spending that has created our current debt dilemma.

With all this, it is little wonder that Canadians are doubtful about the prime minister's claims of economic bliss throughout our country. Those claims are simply unfounded. For most Canadians, their families, and their communities, the reality has been that while they may have the skills and human capital to prosper in an increasingly competitive domestic and global environment, government continues to erode that capacity. It has delayed the transfer of power that people must have to move ahead economically, to assist their families and communities, and to maintain the Canadian values of fairness and compassion for those less fortunate.

A new Conservative government should reflect those distinctly Canadian values of fairness and compassion in its day-to-day activities and its proposals to the Canadian people. When in office, it must make decisions that are guided by those values and that are true to the traditions of the party, including the promotion of free enterprise, open markets, fiscal restraint, low taxation, smaller government, a strong national economy that creates wealth, and a commitment to social justice.

Below are a number of proposed policies and ideas. They do not constitute a definitive or seamless package, but rather they illustrate the policy directions I think Conservatives should explore. Our enquiry will, of necessity, have to take into account the evolving economic environment and the impact it may have on these proposals. Paramount to any dialogue is a continued commitment to tax cuts, no deficit financing, and debt reduction.

The following proposals for tax reductions are put forward as an illustration of my suggested economic policy stance. I have assumed 2.5 percent GDP growth and savings from a 10 percent cut to direct operating expenses of "other programs." The cost of any proposals we implement, including the impact of economic and revenue growth, will be in the context of balanced or surplus budgets. Obviously, not all the proposals listed below can be fully implemented in one mandate, nor are they all the policy options open for debate. But they indicate our suggested direction. While full economic and fiscal modelling may change the specific mix of tax cuts to be implemented, the message to Canadians should be clear: Under this proposal, the excessive tax burden Canadians now shoulder will be reduced by between 20 and 25 percent. There are numerous examples in jurisdictions across North America where such a concerted effort to reduce taxes has been accomplished while maintaining fiscal balance, boosting economic growth, and creating jobs.

Proposal 1: Eliminate "bracket creep." Canadians made significant sacrifices to achieve the low-inflation environment they now enjoy, and yet the tax system continues to penalize taxpayers for winning this important battle. Today, the tax brackets in Canada do not move with inflation under a 3 percent level. The result of this partial de-indexation is that those Canadian workers who receive only cost-of-living increases in their wages (i.e., no real increase in wages) are being bumped into higher tax brackets for simply keeping pace with the inflation rate. To increase their taxes for this reason is unfair and punitive and undermines the basic value of just treatment. It devalues and ignores the efforts that Canadians and Canadian businesses have taken to bring inflation under control and achieve price stability. To ask Canadian families to pay higher taxes solely as a result of the federal government's refusal to advance the tax brackets with inflation is an inexcusable abuse of taxing power.

All Canadians will benefit from this change, but Canadians whose wage and salary increases are tied to inflation will benefit most. These workers, who are the engine of growth, will be able to maintain their standard of living through this change.

Proposal 2: Drop employment insurance (EI) premiums from 2.7 to 1.7 percent. There is no need for a cumulative $20-billion surplus in the EI account (the forecasted surplus for 1998–99). During the last recession, the cumulative deficit never reached more than $6.2 billion. The current surplus is, therefore, totally unwarranted. The goal in managing the EI account should be to have, over a business cycle, a reasonably stable balance, which would be sufficient to pay for the administrative cost of the program. It is a widely accepted economic fact that payroll taxes such as EI have a significant downward effect on employment. Lower EI premiums will lead to a lower effective wage rate for the employer and therefore promote hiring. For the employee, the premium cut implies an increase in wages, which can lead to an increase in consumer spending. Initial analysis would suggest that if there were a one percent drop in the EI premiums paid, GDP would rise by almost 2 percent within the first two years. Employment would also be impacted positively, with approximately 175,000 new jobs being created in the first two years.

All employees and employers will benefit. The impact will likely be greatest for employees and employers in small businesses, where the payroll taxes can have a dramatic effect on the decision to hire new employees.

Proposal 3: (a) Raise the tax-paying threshold for lower incomes from $7,000 to $9,000 over five years. This will recognize the reality that those who are at the lowest end of the scale should be given a chance to work their way up before being asked to pay into the system. All Canadians will benefit from an increased basic credit, and more than 1.5 million lower-income workers will have to pay no federal personal tax at all.

(b) Raise the middle-income threshold from $30,000 to $37,000. We should begin cutting the marginal tax rate for middle-income Canadians by changing the definition of middle income. Currently middle-income earners are those who have a net income between $30,000 and $55,000, and the federal tax rate for this income level is 26 percent. When one includes payroll taxes and provincial taxes, the marginal tax rate for someone earning roughly $30,000 is about 50 percent. This is a rate that rivals the highest in the world, and it acts as a massive disincentive to work, innovation, and the creation of wealth and investment in the economy. Conservatives propose defining middle-income earners as those whose income falls into the $37,000 to $68,000 range.

(c) Work with the provinces to reduce the marginal tax rate at the highest

end of the spectrum from 51 to 45 percent over five years. While it is imperative that those at the highest end of the spectrum pay their fair share, paying a marginal tax rate of 51 to 53 percent is a huge disincentive to work, stay in Canada, and contribute to our economic growth.

(d) Cut capital gains taxes by 10 percent. To encourage Canadians to invest, we must cut our capital gains taxes, which are double those in the U.S. Although even further cuts would be welcomed, I believe that this would be a prudent step towards stimulating international and domestic investment in this country, and thus increasing our level of economic activity.

Middle-income Canadians act as the engine for our economy. Lowering the tax rate they now face will have the greatest impact on the growth of the economy. Such a change will also allow families who are at the low end of the current range (i.e., $30,000) to achieve an effective tax cut (because they would be moved into the 17 percent tax bracket). The change will also make staying in Canada a more attractive option for young, educated, and skilled workers looking to friendlier tax climates (particularly those south of the border). In a knowledge-intensive era, we cannot afford to lose educated workers because of tax rates that punish them for remaining in Canada.

All Canadians will benefit from this tax reduction. The entire economy will benefit from improvements in the tax situation. The increased economic activity as a result of this change will benefit workers, businesses, and governments across the country.

Proposal 4: Reduce the GST from 7 to 6 percent, with the ultimate goal, when fiscally appropriate, of reducing it to 5 percent. Keeping more money in the hands of Canadians is one of the best ways to stimulate consumer confidence. There would be immediate economic benefits for all Canadians through increased spending by consumers, which would then lead to more employment and income growth. A 10 percent reduction is the first step, but the ultimate goal should be, when fiscally responsible, to reduce the GST to 5 percent. Our analysis of this 30 percent reduction suggests that it would stimulate around 200,000 new jobs in the first three to four years alone. At the same time, the economy would improve, with real GDP growth of 1.7 percent. In addition to having an effect on consumers, this growth would also affect entrepreneurs and retailers. There are few things more encouraging to entrepreneurs than consumers with money in their pockets.

All Canadians pay the GST, and so all will benefit from its reduction. Once again, those with lower incomes will realize the greatest benefits. That said, all consumers, and therefore all businesses, will benefit.

Proposal 5: Maintain balanced budgets and reduce our debt. To avoid repeating the pain that has been incurred over the past decade in our battle to balance the budget, we need to establish a serious balanced-budget law. At the same time, we must lower Canada's debt burden by setting targets for debt reduction until the federal government achieves a GDP ratio of about 35 percent. We must commit to making these payments over the next twenty years, as we would with a mortgage, to put our house in order.

Canadians understand the pain of deficits and debt, but governments often lose sight of this. The only way to truly protect our citizens from government largesse is to put in place tough yet manageable balanced-budget legislation and debt-reduction targets. Everyone — families, workers, business, investors — will benefit.

Proposal 6: Establish a binding covenant with the provinces to ensure that the health-care and education systems will be underpinned by a growing federal cash-transfer system. The ad hoc nature of recent cuts, caps, and freezes of federal/provincial transfers has threatened the very fabric of the pan-Canadian socio-economic union. This is not a sustainable path to follow. Canadians understand the value of our health-care system and the importance of a vibrant, well-funded education infrastructure. But such systems can be maintained only through a covenant between the provinces and the federal government involving the transfer of tax points.

Clearly, Canadians who rely on the health-care and education systems will greatly benefit. But so, too, will the federal and provincial governments, which, with a covenant in place, will be able to manage those systems within an agreed-upon framework. The possibility that the system will be changed at the whim of the federal finance minister will no longer exist. This in turn will protect individual taxpayers and businesses from getting stuck at the last minute with special levies or taxes to keep the various programs funded.

Lowering federal personal income taxes by 20 to 25 percent, reducing debt to about 35 percent of the GDP within twenty years, and maintaining the ability of our federation to finance our provincial health-care and post-secondary education systems are the essential pillars of a Conservative commitment to community and enterprise. Taken together, these proposals will strengthen Canada, encourage economic growth and opportunity, and lead to the creation of more than one million new jobs by year five of the plan.

Still, we must not stop with the proposals listed above. There are other areas of the economy for which new ideas are needed. We should, for example, design measures to improve productivity, eliminate interprovincial trade barriers, regulate reform, expand R&D opportunities, increase access to global markets, and reduce corporate taxes. I would like to see the Progressive Conservative Party engage in a vigorous debate with Canadians about the many issues that are important to our economic well-being.

THE PEOPLE'S GOVERNMENT

Ottawa, September 1998

What are the challenges that Canadians rank as among the most important faced by the nation? Declining confidence in our health-care system; uncertain employment prospects, particularly for young Canadians; an education system that needs reform; and constitutional tensions within our country.

How do we address these important issues? One step that must be taken is to have a close look at the way we, as a country, make decisions. If we are to move forward together, there must be confidence not only in the individuals making decisions, but also in our national institutions and the process of selecting decision-makers. It is *our* government. And as it is our government, we, as voters and taxpayers, must be a part of it.

In short, institutional change and a revamped electoral system are necessary ingredients in any plan to address the challenges that lie ahead for Canada. We must make the way government is run and decisions are made more responsive to the kind of future Canadians want for themselves and for their children. Nothing is as fundamental, or as fragile, as the consensus among Canadians about our system of government. If consensus and confidence continue to erode, our ability to address the pressing issues of the country also erodes. For this reason, it is important for those who seek positions of leadership in Canada to be open to new, progressive ideas for improving government.

Let's face it, a sense of disconnection from government exists today, and it is growing worse. Voter participation rates continue to decline. It is becoming increasingly difficult for all parties to attract good candidates. And worst of all, every day another Canadian becomes convinced that what goes on in our national government is irrelevant to his or her daily life. Since the very founding of Canada, the Progressive Conservative Party has been involved in defining and refining our national institutions. We have been inspired by many, including Sir John A. Macdonald and George-Étienne Cartier, who led us into Confederation, and John Diefenbaker, who gave us our first bill of rights. Now, as we approach the twenty-first century, it is time once again for us to take a serious look at the way Canada is governed. We must reach a new consensus with Canadians on our system of government. This is the true millennium project for Canada.

If we are to adequately address the challenges and opportunities that the new millennium will bring, then we must have modern, effective institutions that allow all Canadians to participate in the process of making decisions. This also requires a concentrated effort to reduce the arbitrary power of the prime minister by introducing an enhanced role for the parliamentary part of Canada's democratic system. I offer the following initial suggestions for institutional and electoral reform:

Political parties. Many Canadians feel disassociated from our political parties — they feel that they are secretive, are run by insiders, and have no insight into the lives of everyday Canadians. Many Canadians have no idea where the dollars come from to run them. But political parties are public institutions. They are run on taxpayer-financed dollars and must be more accountable to the voter. Therefore, all registered political parties should have to report on donations and expenditures on a quarterly basis; no donation in excess of $50,000 should be allowed from any one source in any one calendar year. These changes would improve public perception about the way our parties operate.

Transparency and openness. The government should operate in a transparent and open manner. Why couldn't the federal government be bound to transparency rules similar to those of a publicly traded company in Canada? Specifically, the federal government should be subject to the following scrutiny: (i) the auditor-general should report quarterly; (ii) every Canadian taxpayer should receive an annual report covering all aspects of government activity, including financial activity; (iii) all Crown corporations, agencies, boards, and commissions should have similar reporting requirements; (iv) an external board of auditors should be appointed to advise Parliament on the operations of the auditor-general, including his or her competence, methodology, and value for money; (v) the Standing Committee on Public Accounts should have an independent and enhanced research staff; and (vi) there should be quarterly reviews by Parliament of all Orders-in-Council and regulatory decisions.

Parliament and democracy. Many people argue that we cannot make substantive changes to our system of government because to do so would require formal constitutional ratification, which is extremely difficult to achieve. But can we make improvements to our system of government that do not require formal constitutional ratification? Why could we not try? In order to modernize and strengthen our democracy, the following specific actions should be taken:

1. *The Senate.* Many changes to the Senate have been discussed and one has even been enacted in Alberta. I believe that the time has come for change, and that we must act decisively to create an elected and effective Senate. In order to democratize the Senate without constitutional change, the prime minister should announce that, effective immediately, no appointment will be made to the Senate unless a proposed individual has been elected in his or her home province by rules established by that province. This will have the effect of making the Senate an elected body. Next, to make the Senate more effective, each newly elected senator should be required to file a letter of resignation dated ten years from his or her moment of election. This would establish a fixed term of office. Until such time as constitutional agreement can be reached on Senate reform, this

practice of electing senators and fixing their term should stand.

2. *The House of Commons.* Under the present system, MPs spend more time in Ottawa than in their home ridings. Canadians often believe that, once elected, their representatives forget about the problems at home. The following are suggestions to address this all-too-common perception.

  a) Better representatives. Sittings of the House of Commons should be limited to no more than two weeks in each month. This would allow MPs to spend more time in their ridings. In addition, they could be encouraged to maintain local employment and volunteer commitments. In this way, MPs will avoid becoming hostages to Ottawa processes and, as a result, will be better local representatives. In other words, MPs will represent their constituents to Ottawa, not the other way around.

  b) Appointments. Prime ministerial appointments and Orders-in-Council should be subject to parliamentary review and oversight.

  c) Free votes. Confidence votes should be limited and decided upon early in every new Parliament. In this way, any issue not specified as a confidence issue would be open for free votes by MPs. This maintains the flexibility of the government of the day to face a confidence vote over a major initiative, such as one it may have campaigned on, while at the same time creating pressure on all parties to limit confidence items.

  d) Better debate. Research budgets for opposition parties should be increased to promote better-informed debate in the House of Commons, the Senate, and in committees. These funds should be reallocated from existing House of Commons budgets — no new dollars should be spent.

3. *Modern institutions.* In order to justify and sustain our national institutions, we must establish stronger links between the institutions and the people. These can be accomplished in a number of ways. First, we should have a referendum on electing the governor general! The important responsibility of dissolving Parliament and signing legislation into law (or refusing to sign) should not reside in a patronage appointment. Second, Supreme Court judges should be appointed by the prime minister only from lists recommended by

the provinces. Third, all Supreme Court nominees, before appointment, should be required to appear before a joint House/Senate committee on judicial affairs to respond to questions from members.

4. *Electoral reform.* Our existing first-past-the-post, single-member constituency system has a tendency to produce majority governments for parties that have attracted far less than 50 percent of voter support. In addition, members of Parliament are often elected by fewer than 40 percent of the voters in their riding. This leaves 60 percent plus of local voters feeling that their ballots did not count, and that their viewpoint is not represented in the House of Commons.

5. An all-party committee should be established to review the way we elect public officials, and to recommend changes to the Elections Act. Issues referred to that committee should include the following items: (i) When no one candidate in a riding attracts 50 percent or more of voter support on election day, why not have a run-off election one week later featuring the top two candidates? In this way, no MP would be elected without the support of 50 percent of the voters in the riding. (ii) Should some form of proportional representation, which would cover up to one-third of the available seats in the House of Commons, be put into effect? In this way, more voters will see their choices reflected in the makeup of Parliament. (iii) Should the voting age be lowered to 17? This initiative could widen the voting pool, bring a new and important perspective to national debates, and involve a group of Canadians who already carry many adult responsibilities.

It is time to review our institutions, the way we are governed, and the way we reach decisions together. As we enter the twenty-first century, government must not be afraid to take a hard look at itself, to applaud what has sustained Canadians through more than a hundred years of democracy, and to identify what does not work and fix it. Good government is a basic right, but with rights come responsibilities. And the responsibility for Canadians is to take the time to participate in a national discussion on how we want to be governed in the twenty-first century.

Epilogue

MANY EVENTS IN LIFE TEACH US THE VALUE OF HUMILITY. REVIEW-ing and editing a series of columns, speeches, and papers that spans sixteen years is very much one of those events. I was so sure of so much, and was so easily partisan. Goodness, the clarity of correct policies, and the risks of lesser policies were never hard to pick out, identify, or articulate.

I did not attain prominence in my party by being compulsively uncertain. In partisan organizations — political or policy — one's loyalty to, and identification with, the "cause" is an important anchor. Other abilities may count or be counted by others, but they do not even get to be assessed if the core identification is less than real.

This premium on certainty is also a likely condition of entry because many of the jobs I held within the party are very much for the younger among us — people young enough to have no serious family or financial ties, young enough to be certain of more things than they could possibly understand. That certainty does dilute with maturity — and the more seasoned judgement that dilution implies may be, for the fortunate, the beginnings of wisdom. But none of that diminishes the essential role of young people in supplying both the motivation and the energy that free economies, governments, and parties need. It was young people who, in the 1960s and 1970s, democratized the Conservative Party; young people who built, sustained, and advanced the Quiet Revolution in Quebec; young people who worked with Peter Lougheed to take Alberta from the grip of the Social Credit; young people who voted with their feet in cities right across Canada to build entrepreneurial and business cultures in the 1980s and 1990s.

This is not a new pattern. Young people throughout North America marched for civil rights. Young people in Ottawa marched against the anti-French-Canadian condescension of Donald Gordon and the Canadian National Railway. It is their very certainty that often lets them lead or challenge when others are unwilling, conflicted, or disengaged.

Young Canadians were the heart of my campaign for the Tory leadership. Their certainty about me — and the imperative for a policy-based leadership for the country and the party — was both the key motivating force in the campaign and an important part of the successes we had in cities like Toronto, Montreal, Quebec, Corner Brook, Barrie, Prince George, Mantane, Kingston, and a very few small towns elsewhere. That idealism — along with my key opponent's brand name and one or two other insurmountable obstacles —might well have cost us along the way, but in a sense there was both logic and symmetry to the result.

A policy-based leadership is not without risk; however much taking that risk may have seemed appropriate in face of a fifth-place standing in Parliament, the fact that a clear plurality on the first ballot would have preferred the familiarity of prominence is not, on reflection, surprising. For all those who believed risk and innovation were appropriate, there were twice as many who thought it precisely the wrong choice.

Still, I learned a great deal from my run for the leadership, and what I now know about the certainties of partisanship and policy stands out in stark relief. There were many places, speeches, and community visits that had so much to do with Canadians' desire for a new beginning in the public life of the country and so little to do with partisan preference. I saw it in the eyes of farmers in Saskatchewan, small business people in Corner Brook, high-school students in Prince Edward Island. Even the self-assured and dynamic business leaders at myriad receptions at the Calgary Stampede wanted a new balance that spoke more to the requirements of tomorrow than to the trade-offs of yesterday.

I learned, perhaps the hard way, that in public life — as in private life — people do not care how much you know until they know how much you care. Even after thirty years in a party, one's own passion can never be taken for granted. Choosing to moderate that passion — either out of respect for one's opponent or to avoid offending — may well be the ultimate disservice to one's supporters, principles, and cause.

But the good fortune I have had serving in various government and party roles, along with the joy I have had in my many corporate activities, have convinced me that the similarities between different spheres of activity far outweigh the differences. There are high priests in politics, government, industry, and academe who work tirelessly at increasing the sense of compelling differences and unnecessary complexity. This often creates the fog of disconnect that is used to keep accountability at a distance. It is a practice and approach that reality cannot sustain.

Partisanship is not the source of all truth, but it can adapt to and reflect the real truth of economic and social necessities. Its ability to project that truth is tied to its ability to receive real signals from real people on policies and conditions of life that truly matter. Excessive partisanship (of which, in the past, I have certainly been guilty) or intense ideology block the successful reception of real-life and real-time signals, as does a leadership focused more on form and less on substance. This is equally true in business, where the lack of a plan, the lack of a responsive and sensitive link to day-to-day market realities, will imperil any product or service.

If anything, the non-partisan nature of my present research and academic activities allows me the great privilege of working with the best minds in the country to look for the right policy answers without the burden of partisan precondition. I consider it a rare privilege to look for non-partisan insights and empirical conclusions to add to the choices all governments and political parties have to consider.

Still, my respect for the partisan process, and my affection for those who sacrifice and exert to participate in it, is undiminished. That I know first hand what participation in the partisan process can cost — in personal, financial, and social terms — only deepens my admiration for those who continue the struggle.

My personal partisan struggle was suspended in October 1998. My ongoing commitment to encourage new policy research and the politics of new ideas and new beginnings is now expressed through the venerable and non-partisan Institute for Research on Public Policy.

I believe more resolutely than ever that the choices we now face in a rapidly changing world will increase and not diminish. Developing new insights into how economic and social imperatives relate to each other has never mattered more. Political parties and voters will benefit from having a genuine range of choices that defies the notion, on any issue, that there is no alternative. The fragility of democracy and the public legitimacy it requires to stay strong relate to the sense that there are real choices to be made and that our democratic system actually lets people make those choices.

When my grandparents chose Canada — on my mother's side in the 1880s and on my father's after the communist revolution — they chose the mix of economic opportunity, religious tolerance, and social conditions that was among the best the world could offer. That promise still attracts thousands to our shores — and manufactures a framework of growth, freedom, and stability we must never take for granted.

Complacency has many forms. Imposing an ideological filter on the truth is one that is especially pernicious. And in any form, complacency is not something the continued hypothesis that is Canada can afford. Canada is many things — not the least of which is a compelling idea. It is an idea that still needs renewal, an idea that still matters.

Index

Department of National Defence, 187, 254, 255, 257
deputy ministers, 223
Diana, Princess of Wales, 46–47
Diefenbaker, John, 18, 21, 25–26, 37, 104, 147, 272
Dion, Stéphane, 57, 127, 129, 155
disarmament groups, 169
disclosure rules, 136, 137
dispute resolution, 262, 263
Dufferin Mall, 246
Dumont, Mario, 123
Duplessis, Maurice, 35

Eastern Europe, 258
economic competitiveness, 216
economic freedom, 14, 123
economic growth, 8, 14, 29, 71, 92–93, 132, 148, 160, 265, 267
  and deficits/debts, 80, 87, 95
  and social justice, 7, 15, 16, 25, 238, 239
economic literacy, 5
economic policy, 15, 107–8, 109, 215, 238. *See also* fiscal policy; monetary policy
economic union, 109, 211
education, 19, 43, 148, 211, 212, 241–42, 244
  cuts to, 16, 242, 260–61
  funding for, 270, 271
  post-secondary, 91, 109, 242, 260
  reform of, 39, 271
Eggleton, Art, 187–88
Egypt, 186, 189
Eisenhower, Dwight D., 2
elections. *See* federal elections; media; *specific provinces*
Elections Act, 275
electoral reform, 149–51, 271, 272, 275
electoral system, first-past-the-post, 153, 275
Elizabeth II, Queen of Great Britain, 117
emigration
  from Canada, 6, 265, 269
  from Quebec, 114
employment insurance (EI). *See* unemployment insurance
energy crisis, 211

equality of opportunity, 6, 21, 85, 86, 93, 148, 158, 211, 258, 264
  conditions for, 9, 15–16, 20
  vs. equality of outcome, 14, 39, 148
equalization, 86, 129, 149, 151, 197, 206
  as federal power, 104, 109, 148, 260
Europe, 51, 207, 229

fairness, 15–16, 258
family allowance, 69, 72–73
family policy, in Quebec, 243
family poverty, 242
federal elections
  1968, 135
  1972, 19, 59, 135, 149
  1974, 135
  1979, 19, 66, 135
  1984, 19, 139, 144–45
  1988, 19, 44, 135
  1993, 19, 41, 58, 80–81, 82, 135, 139, 159
  1997, 42, 101, 125, 151, 153–54, 159
federal government. *See also* government
  and British Columbia, 129, 130
  and separatism, 102, 103, 106, 107, 108, 119, 120–21, 124, 125, 127, 130–32 (*see also under* Supreme Court of Canada)
federalism, 29, 35, 36, 58, 110–12, 154, 238, 243. *See also* centralization; confederal union; decentralization
  in United States, 121
Fenian raids, 123
Filmon, Gary, 111
Financial Post, 28, 53, 54, 159
First Ministers' Conference, 262
First World War, 170, 174, 175, 189, 252, 258
fiscal dividend, 78, 79, 80–81, 85–86, 87, 92
fiscal policy, 198, 199, 214, 215
fiscal responsibility, 80, 81, 108, 122, 157, 266, 267
  and social justice, 14, 67, 148, 216
fisheries, 129–30
Florida, 168
food banks, 187
foreign aid, 163, 168

Foreign Investment Review Agency (FIRA), 59, 104, 260
foreign policy, 34, 46, 93, 109, 129, 148, 154, 163–64, 169, 185, 203
and defence policy, 253, 255
prime minister and, 167, 168
Forget, Claude, 230
Forget, Monique Jerome, 230
Fort Garry Horse, 175
founding nations, 259
France, 101, 119, 139, 172, 181–82, 185, 186
and Quebec, 115, 122
la Francophonie, 163
Freedom of Information Act (FOI), 262
freedom-of-information laws, 146
free enterprise, 8, 14, 15, 22, 25, 26–27, 30, 266
free trade, 27, 29, 66, 89, 93, 129, 135, 152, 155. *See also* interprovincial trade barriers
effect of, 20, 23, 44, 76
and MacDonald Commission, 69, 74
Free Trade Agreement (FTA), 20, 104, 262
French language, 110, 116, 118
French Revolution, 137
From Protest to Power, 39
Frum, David, 159

G7. *See* Group of Seven (G7)
Galileo, 230
General Motors, 5
George III, King of Great Britain, 23
Germany, 66, 168, 170, 186, 189, 250
Getty, Don, 36
Ghiz, Joe, 37–38
Gillies, James, 66
globalization, 72, 199, 264
Globe and Mail, 54
Golan, 258
Goldenberg, 41
Goodman, E.A. (Eddie), Col., 175
goods and services tax (GST), 78, 80, 89, 152, 155, 209
reduction of, 83, 269–70
Gordon, Donald, 278
Gore, Al, 210
government. *See also* federal government
accountability of, 210, 214

municipal, 203, 204, 205
powers, 103–5, 109–10, 148, 260, 261
role of, 7, 8–9, 16, 28, 29, 30, 85, 199, 245, 247
service delivery by, 203–4, 209, 245
size of, 21, 22, 41, 85, 147, 197, 227, 266
government spending, 80–81, 90, 92, 108, 109, 149, 215, 216, 261. *See also* spending powers, federal
excessive, 28–29, 78, 83–84, 85, 88, 89, 110, 264
governor general, 274
Grady, Patrick, 74
Great Canadian Soup Company, 208
Great Depression, 21
Greece, 101
gross domestic product (GDP), 265, 267, 269
Grossman, Allan, 43
Grossman, Carol, 43
Grossman, Jamie, 43
Grossman, Larry, 42–44
Grossman, Melissa, 43
Grossman, Robby, 43
Group of Seven (G7), 94, 163, 167
The Group of 22, 99
GST. *See* goods and services tax (GST)
guaranteed annual income, 68–69, 71, 73, 74, 75, 76–79, 148, 246
Guaranteed Annual Income (GAI) supplement (Ont.), 68
Guaranteed Income Supplement, 68, 73
Gulf States, 186
Gulf War, 166, 177, 182, 185, 252
gun control, 148
Gwyn, Richard, 110

Hamilton, Alvin, 21
harmonized sales tax, 80
Harper, Stephen, 156, 159
Harris, Mike, 107, 109, 175
Harter, John, 70
Hatfield, Richard, 36
Havel, Václav, 237
health, factors in, 247
health care, 10, 24, 43, 67, 79, 99, 158, 211, 212, 237, 241, 244. *See also* medicare; patient rights and responsibilities

health care *(continued)*
  accountability in, 229, 248, 249
  cuts to, 16, 86, 121, 228, 242, 248,
    260–61
  federal role in, 93, 148, 248, 250, 251,
    270
  financing of, 151, 247, 248, 251, 270,
    271
  and government powers, 93, 109, 203
  home care, 249–50
  long-term care, 249–50
  primary care, 251
  private sector in, 250–51
  reform, 6, 229–30, 231–32, 248–52
  right to, 231
  standards for, 252
  in United Kingdom, 249
  in United States, 91, 228–29, 230,
    231–32
Heath, Ted, 115
Hees, George, 21
helicopters, 29, 179–81, 187, 188,
    190
Hellyer, Paul, 41, 156
Helms-Burton bill (U.S.), 184
Henry, Prince Harry of Wales, 47
Hibernia, 152
Hitler, Adolf, 27
HMOs, 229, 230
Holland, 175
homelessness, 212, 237
Hong Kong, 44–46, 173
Hong Kong garrison, 257
hopelessness, culture of, 15
hospitals, 203, 204
housing, 9, 211
human nature, 23–24
Human Resources Canada, 77
human rights, 25, 35, 154
Hungary, 13
Hurricane Andrew, 168
Hussein, Saddam, 181, 182, 186

ice storm, 53–55, 187, 191, 258
IDEA Corp., 43
ideology, 158
immigration, 93, 119, 148, 258
Imperial Finance, 66–67, 173
Inco, 61
income, 9, 84, 85, 91, 244, 267, 269

income-security programs, 69–71, 72,
    73–74, 86, 93, 246–47
  eligibility for, 75, 76, 78, 244
income taxes, 86, 265, 271
  increases, 67, 81, 84, 121, 265
  individual, supremacy of, 14
Industrial Revolution, 239–40
industry, 43
inflation, 28, 67, 80, 92, 244, 248, 267
information technology, 231, 240, 248,
    250, 251
infrastructure, 87
*Inquiry into the Deployment of the
  Canadian Forces in Somalia.
  See* Somalia inquiry
Institute for Research on Public Policy
    (IRPP), 229, 230, 279
institutional reform, 272–75
interest groups, 139, 140, 143, 215
interest rates, 90, 92, 108
  and debt/deficits, 66, 80, 84, 87, 95,
    266
internationalism, 169
International Labour Office, 70
international law, 120
interprovincial agreements, 109
interprovincial trade barriers, 43, 44, 99,
    262, 263, 271
intifada, 178
Inuit Tapirisat, 40
investment, 7, 83, 84, 109, 148, 264
investment tax credit, 79
Iran, 179, 182, 185
Iraq, 51, 177, 179, 181–83, 185–86,
    189, 190
Ireland, 103, 119
Israel, 178–79
Italy, 27, 101, 175, 176

Japan, 27, 66, 101, 257
Jerusalem Post, 178
job creation, 16, 73, 93, 160, 239, 265
  private sector, 81, 84
  and tax cuts, 83, 267, 268, 269, 271
job training, 69, 73, 93
John Labatt Ltd., 208
John Paul II, Pope, 183, 184, 185,
    230
Johnson, Daniel, Jr., 55–57, 101,
    107

Johnson, Daniel, Sr., 19, 35, 56, 111
Johnson, Pierre-Marc, 56, 113
Jordan, 186
Joseph, Sir Keith, 24
justice, 29, 148, 258

Kahanoff Foundation, 213
Kent, Tom, 85–86
King, William Lyon Mackenzie, 152
Kingston (Ont.), 40, 54, 181
Kingston Whig-Standard, 54
Klein, Ralph, 107, 109, 175, 215
Korean War, 34, 175, 252
Kosovo, 189, 190
Kuptana, Rosemary, 40
Kurds, 186
Kuwait, 182, 186

labour, 27, 205, 206
Labour Party (U.K.), 26, 211
land mines, 163
language rights, 19, 116, 124
Laurier, Sir Wilfrid, 110, 115
law and order, 14, 15, 29, 148, 160
leadership, 202–3, 278
Lebanon, 34, 179
Lesage, Jean, 35, 111
Lessard, Daniel, 125
Lévesque, René, 79, 111, 116, 131
Lewis, David, 59
Lewis, Stephen, 34–35
Liberal Party (Canada), 5, 19, 41, 90, 139, 145, 152, 153, 169, 211
economic/fiscal policy, 67, 81
and Progressive Conservative Party, 28–29, 30, 159
and Quebec, 55, 125
and Reform Party, 155–56
Liberal Party (Nfld.), 49
Liberal Party (Que.), 36, 57, 101
Liberal Party (U.K.), 27
libertarianism, 24–25
Libya, 182
"life, liberty, and the pursuit of happiness," 23
Lougheed, Peter, 19, 36, 111, 114, 157, 277
Louisiana, 118

Lower Canada, 18, 35, 123
Loyalists, 23

MacDonald, David, 22
Macdonald, Sir John A., 18, 22, 105, 110, 123, 152, 272
MacDonald Royal Commission on Canada's Economic Union and Development Prospects, 69, 70, 73–74
Magna Carta, 216
Maine, 118
Mallorytown (Ont.), 53, 54
Mandela, Nelson, 26
Manitoba, 187
Manning, Ernest C., 117, 157
Manning, Preston, 2, 58, 151, 154, 156–57, 158
and Quebec, 107, 122, 125, 155
Marchand, Jean, 53
Maritime Command, 165
Maritime provinces, 18, 22
market research, 215
married exemption, 69
Martin, Paul, Jr., 36, 108, 156
economic/fiscal policy, 40–42, 66, 80, 81, 83–84, 91, 92, 107, 121, 158
1998 budget, 88–89, 89–90
Martin, Paul, Sr., 42
Massachusetts, 118
Masse, Marcel, 57
Maxwell, Judith, 7, 112
Mayo Clinic, 228
McDonagh, Alexa, 80, 121, 149, 151–52
McDougall, Barbara, 44
McKenna, Frank, 109, 127
McMurtry, Roy, 61
Mead, Laurence M., 75
media, 139, 142, 143, 207, 209, 215–16, 221, 223, 224. *See also* political-media complex; press gallery
coverage of defence, 169, 176, 177, 191
coverage of elections, 145, 147, 149, 150, 151, 153
coverage of Parliament, 140, 217, 226, 227
and Ice Storm, 54
local, 146

medicare, 86, 111–12, 204, 247, 252,
  260. *See also* health care
single-payer system, 228, 229, 230
Meech Lake Accord, 36, 37, 41, 107,
  113, 122, 152
  collapse of, 73, 105–6, 259
  provisions of, 99–100, 109
merchant marine, 257
Mercredi, Ovide, 40
Middle East, 13, 34, 87, 167, 174, 177,
  178–79, 182, 189, 258
military colleges, 191
Military Family Resource Centre, 246
military-industrial complex, 2
Millennium Fund, 89
ministerial accountability. *See* accountability, ministerial
minority rights, 19, 124, 132
Mississauga (Ont.), 61
Mitterand, François, 182
monarchy, 23, 26, 47, 137, 216
Mondale, Walter, 136–37
monetary policy, 41, 66, 103, 109, 198,
  199, 203
monopolies, 27
Monte Cassino (Italy), 175
Montreal (Que.), 52
mortgage-interest deductions, 66–67,
  90, 92
mothers' allowances, 73
Mulroney, Brian, 2, 19, 33, 36, 73, 83,
  135, 145, 147, 152–53, 157
  federalism of, 111, 132, 175
  foreign policy, 21, 34
  and free trade, 23, 44, 104
  municipal services, 203
Murray, Lowell, 117

NAFTA. *See* North American Free Trade
  Agreement (NAFTA)
Namibia, 167
"The National," 4
National Child Benefit, 244
National Defence Act, 173, 254
National Defence Headquarters
  (NDHQ), 167, 254, 257
National Defence Sub-Committee, 165
National Energy Program (NEP), 23,
  59, 104, 260
National Forum on Health, 248

National Health Service, 249
national unity, 99, 130–31, 148, 155
NATO, 115, 163, 165, 167, 170, 174,
  176, 188, 253, 258
naval forces, 165–66, 177. *See also*
  defence procurement
neo-conservatism, 20, 23–24, 85, 140
Netanyahu, Benjamin, 178, 179
New Brunswick, 37, 116, 123
New Deal, 21
New Democratic Party (NDP), 42, 59,
  67, 83, 151–52, 153, 169
New England, 115, 128
Newfoundland, 36, 37, 48, 49, 73, 105,
  130
New Hampshire, 118
newspapers, 142
Nobel Prize, 163
No Holds Barred, 48
non-profit sector, 207, 209, 212–14,
  242, 243, 245, 247
NORAD, 163, 253
Normandy (France), 175
North American Free Trade Agreement
  (NAFTA), 113, 118, 128, 152, 163,
  238, 262
Northern Ireland, 103, 119, 179
North Vietnam, 189
notwithstanding clause, 116
Nova Scotia, 123, 130
nuclear weapons, 165, 166, 167, 169,
  170

O'Brien, Conor Cruise, 141
OECD, 265
oil prices, 87
Oka crisis, 35, 177, 258
old-age security, 69, 73, 74, 229
Ontario, 35, 41, 43, 44, 106, 116, 123
  after Quebec secession, 127, 128
  provincial elections, 43–44, 149
Ontario Health Restructuring
  Commission, 221
Ontario Hydro, 53, 55
Ontario Natural Resources, 54
open markets, 266
Organization of American States,
  163
Oslo agreement, 178
Ottawa (Ont.), 278

public service *(continued)*
  role of, 199, 210
  structure of, 200–201, 202, 205
*The Pursuit of Virtue and Other Tory
  Notions*, 24

Quebec, 22, 35, 41, 80, 119, 123, 243
  economy, 56, 57–58, 102, 113–14
  partition, 110, 126–27, 128, 131
  provincial elections, 35, 101
  uniqueness of, 37, 115, 118
Quebec Act, 35, 115
Quebec nationalism, 36, 122
Quebec referendums, 42, 122
  1980, 102, 114, 116, 125
  1995, 52, 55–56, 58, 105–7, 113–14,
    123, 152, 259
  thresholds, 110, 125–26
Quebec secession, 112, 118, 120, 127.
  See also Canada, without Quebec
Quebec separatism, 5, 41–42, 53, 56,
  119, 120–21, 122, 125–26, 128,
  258–59. *See also under* federal
  government; Supreme Court of
  Canada
  and the economy, 102, 107–8
  mythologies of, 115–17
  polls on, 124
Queen's University, 203
question period, 196
Quiet Revolution, 277

Rae, Bob, 36, 39–40, 111
RCMP, 59, 257
Reagan, Ronald, 19
recession, 101, 114, 209, 268
Red River valley (Man.), 176–77, 181,
  191, 258
Reform Party, 12, 42, 57, 67, 81, 101,
  109, 151, 153, 169
  and Liberal Party, 155–56
  and Progressive Conservative Party,
    153–54, 158–60
  and Quebec, 103, 122, 125, 131, 154
regional development, 109
regionalism, 37
Registered Education Savings Plans
  (RESPs), 250
Registered Long-Term Care Plan
  (RLTP), 250

Registered Retirement Savings Plans
  (RRSPs), 250
Remeni (Italy), 175
Republican Guard, 186
Republican Party (U.S.), 21, 41, 211
research and development, 88, 271
retirement, 6
Richler, Mordecai, 114
Rifkin, Jeremy, 213
Riley, Jack, 28
Robarts, John, 43, 110
Rock, Allan, 92
Roman Catholic Church, 183
Romanow, Roy, 107, 109, 111
Roosevelt, Franklin D., 21
Royal Bank of Canada, 155
Royal Commission on Aboriginal
  Peoples, 82
Rubin, Jeff, 67, 89
rural vs. urban divide, 6
Russia, 45, 51, 168, 170, 173, 175
  foreign policy, 181–82, 185, 186,
    188–90
Russo-Japanese War, 189
Ryan, Claude, 71

Saguenay (Que.), 176, 181, 191, 258
sales taxes, 265
Saskatchewan, 127
Saudi Arabia, 186
school boards, 204, 205
Second World War, 27, 28, 164, 189,
  211
  Canadian troops in, 117–18, 167,
    175, 252, 257, 258
Senate, 106, 146, 196, 273–74
separatism. *See* Quebec separatism
Serbia, 127, 170, 188, 189
Sharp, Mitchell, 41
Shultz, George, 136–37
Simpson, Jeffrey, 138, 154
Smallwood, Joey, 48
SNC Lavalin, 119
social assistance. *See* welfare
Social Assistance Review Committee,
  70
Social Canada at the Millennium, 206
Social Conservative Party, 157
Social Contract, 39
Social Credit Party, 67, 101, 157, 277